# Travel Wild Wisconsin

# Travel Wild Wisconsin

*A Seasonal Guide to*
*Wildlife Encounters in Natural Places*

CANDICE GAUKEL ANDREWS

THE UNIVERSITY OF WISCONSIN PRESS

The University of Wisconsin Press
1930 Monroe Street, 3rd Floor
Madison, Wisconsin 53711-2059
uwpress.wisc.edu

3 Henrietta Street
London WC2E 8LU, England
eurospanbookstore.com

Printed in the United States of America

Library of Congress Cataloging-in-Publication Data

Andrews, Candice Gaukel.
Travel wild Wisconsin : a seasonal guide to wildlife encounters in natural places /
Candice Gaukel Andrews.
p.   cm.
Includes bibliographical references and index.
ISBN 978-0-299-29164-8 (pbk. : alk. paper)
ISBN 978-0-299-29163-1 (e-book)
1. Wildlife watching—Wisconsin. 2. Wildlife viewing sites—Wisconsin.
3. Wisconsin—Guidebooks. I. Title.
QL214.A53   2013
590.72'34775—dc23
2012035300

Maps by John T. Andrews

It is not down in any map; true places never are.

—HERMAN MELVILLE, *Moby-Dick* (1851)

For all of you who seek
the true places.

Travel Wild Wisconsin Locations

# Contents

# Preface

*It's Discovery—Not Distance—That Matters*

My father never had the "urge for going," as songwriter-singer Joni Mitchell calls it—the desire to travel. I place the blame for that fact squarely on the shoulders of World War II. As a young man, my dad was sent—compliments of the U.S. Army—to France in the bottom of a transport ship to take part in the D-day invasion. It was the first time he'd ever been abroad. From then on, traveling just didn't have a positive association for him. Besides, he'd ask me, why should he want to leave home when what was dearest to him—his family—was here?

And so, when I was growing up, my family never went "away on vacation" as my friends' families did. Perhaps that's why as a child I was drawn to reading books set in wild, far-off places I assumed I'd never see, books such as Benedict and Nancy Freedman's *Mrs. Mike*, published in 1947, which takes place in the blizzard and grizzly bear regions of northwest Canada, and tales from authors who made location as powerful as any protagonist in their stories—such as Jack London in his Klondike adventures, John Steinbeck in his California novels, and Robert Louis Stevenson in his South Seas fiction.

Since I've become an adult, however, my work as a nature-travel writer has taken me all over the world: from the sub-Arctic down to the Galapagos at the equator and Patagonia and New Zealand in the Southern Hemisphere. But in the last two years, I've concentrated my travels a little closer to home, within Wisconsin's borders, to see some of our most beautiful, natural places and to seek genuine encounters with the wildlife there.

The spots I traveled to were varied, from a preserve situated in the environs of a city to a remote barrens you won't be able to find on any highway map. It occurred to me that many of you—like me before writing this book—aren't aware of the opportunities there are in the state to get close to the birds, fish, mammals, and even insects that reside or regularly pass through. So, I decided to write this book and take you along with me.

As you see by the chapter titles, the emphasis is on verbs. These are things you can *do* to see wildlife in Wisconsin. For example, it's possible to sit in a blind at dawn on the largest grassland east of the Mississippi River and watch greater prairie chickens do a dance they've been doing since time immemorial. And did you know that here you can witness the waters of one of the largest inland lakes in the United States roil with ancient, monster fish?

Within the pages of this book, you'll go to a distinctive landscape filled with even more fancy footsteps by a bird that inhabits neither grassland nor forest, but the singular land in between. You'll count loons on a renowned flowage—one of the most undeveloped and quiet "lakes" in northwest Wisconsin today—and look for elk in an enormous national forest. You'll search for one of the rarest cranes in the world in a national wildlife refuge, and then watch as common ones come in by the thousands to a huge, state-owned wildlife area. You'll try to spot bald eagles as they spend a season near the Wisconsin River, and then be awed by the tundra swans that move through the country's mightiest waterway and flyway in a matter of weeks.

You'll tag tiny monarchs in the state's oldest private nature preserve and track a large carnivore—the gray wolf—in the expansive wilds of northern Wisconsin. You'll glimpse a time that once was by visiting a group of American bison whose ancestors had flowed across the state's grasslands in massive herds, and then seek what streams across the terrain today: white-tailed deer. You'll go to a festival and touch a tiny, wild saw-whet owl, and then confront in the largest wetland in the Upper Midwest the very large Canada goose and face your feelings about this bird: migration phenomenon or nuisance?

In these searches for Wisconsin wildlife, we can't forget that people are part of the nature-travel experience, too. We are inextricably entwined with the animals, fish, reptiles, birds, and insects we live with. So, you'll also hear from wildlife technicians, biologists, educators, researchers, and festival organizers; environmental center property managers and naturalists; and citizen scientists, counters, and trackers.

Today, I think I can appreciate my dad's sentiments about long-distance travel more than I could when I was young. He was right: If what you love—wild places and wildlife—are nearby, you don't need to travel all over the world to be with what's dear to you. There's a lot right at home, within our state. And it seems Wisconsin Public Television host of the series *In Wisconsin*, Patty

Loew, would agree. She once said, "Hiding in the wilds of Wisconsin are a vast array of amazing animals most of us will never see."

But *you* can. Reading this book is the first step. After you do, I hope you'll get the urge to pull out your calendar and make seasonal dates with yourself—just see the table of contents—to go "out there" and find them.

C. G. A.
*Sun Prairie, Wisconsin*

# Acknowledgments

As much as *writing* a book is a solitary pursuit, *producing* a book is a team effort—one that takes years to complete. It's never accomplished without the understanding and support of family, friends, and publishing experts.

I'd like to thank John T. Andrews, my husband, who not only indulges my wanderlust but comes along—for the most part, with much enthusiasm—to take the majority of the photos.

My deepest appreciation goes to Shane Ryan Andrews, who kept the home fires burning while I was away and watched my "wildlife" at home—both dogs and cats. His scientist's sensibility and perspective helped bring clarity to many of these passages.

I'm sincerely grateful for Travis John Andrews's encouragement and love. His musician's timing and poetry were inspirational. This project would have been far less meaningful for me if he were not there to share the experience.

I'd also like to say a special thank-you to the University of Wisconsin Press senior acquisitions editor, Raphael Kadushin, who encouraged me to write the book I wanted to write, despite the forces that, occasionally, bumped up against it. He somehow manages to navigate two worlds with equal proficiency, those of editor and writer.

And, I'd like to thank the staff at the University of Wisconsin Press for helping all along the way to make this book the best it can possibly be.

# SPRING

(Photo: John T. Andrews)

# Greater Prairie Chickens:
# Sitting Out the Dance

*Buena Vista Wildlife Area in Bancroft*

CENTRAL WISCONSIN
PRAIRIE CHICKEN FESTIVAL AND BLINDS

What looks like a sliver of an orange peel—only so out of place—is hanging very low on the black backdrop of the early morning sky. *What the heck is that fruity bit doing there?* I wonder. Still sleepy from getting up at 2:00 a.m. and then driving north for two hours in the dark, I slowly realize that what I'm looking at through my car's front windshield is an unaccustomed, unobstructed view of the moon. I'm parked at the kiosk on Highway W in central Wisconsin, on the edge of the Buena Vista Wildlife Area in southwestern Portage County near Bancroft.

It happens that today is my birthday, April 8. In recent memory, I don't recall ever having to wear fleece in preparation for thirty-degree temperatures on the anniversary of my birth. Then again, I don't believe I've ever before been up and dressed for an outdoor adventure this early on my birthday. But this year is different. This year, I'm hoping to secretly spy on some dancing chickens.

## FIND THE BLIND

Right on schedule, at 4:45 a.m., Sharon Schwab, coordinator for the Central Wisconsin Grassland Conservation Area (CWGCA) Partnership and an organizer of the annual Central Wisconsin Prairie Chicken Festival, pulls up in her car alongside my vehicle. She throws a cheery "Follow me!" outside her rolled-down window, and we make our way to Highway F. After a couple of passes up and down a stretch of road, she finally pulls over to the shoulder and parks.

"Sorry," she says as she jumps out of her car and walks back to my driver's-side. "The path was kind of hard to find in the dark."

With that, she points me to a faint trail in the grass and bids me good luck as she returns to her car and pulls away. I pull well off the road and park. I grab my camera equipment, gloves, a blanket, my spiral notebook, a pen, and a digital recorder. I stretch my headlamp on over my wool hat, switch it on, and begin the half-mile hike in.

The frosty grass makes a loud crunch under every one of my footsteps, and where my headlamp spotlights the ground in front of me, the gray-green stalks sparkle. With my concentration centered on my feet, I almost run into the two wooden, upright posts that mark the location of my destination: a low, four-foot-by-eight-foot, plywood box where I'll hide for the next few hours.

I duck into my "blind," latch the door behind me, and quietly open the wooden panels placed over the windows on the front, sides, and back of my box. I set up the tripod and camera in front of one of the windows and position myself on the sparse, wooden bench, the kind that would make a Pilgrim proud.

Then, I wait for the coming of *Tympanuchus cupido pinnatus*, or the "drummer of love."

## SPRING DANCE

Every day in April in central Wisconsin, male greater prairie chickens gather on grassy knobs, their preferred breeding sites, known as *leks* or *booming grounds*. Here, they "dance" by stutter-stomping their feet, fanning their tails, and holding their long neck feathers (or pinnae) erect, all in an attempt to attract a female. These looking-for-love males inflate their bright orange neck sacks and sound a low, resonating, booming call in an effort to make themselves desirable to hens.

And every spring, people sign up for the privilege of having a ringside seat—in a blind—for the show.

Lesa Kardash, the CWGCA biologist, who has held that position for the past five years, tells me about her first prairie-chicken-booming viewing experience.

"In the first spring after I started my job, I helped set up blinds," says Lesa. "This was even before I had an opportunity to sit in one and see what the viewing experience was all about. So, one morning, I went out by myself to a blind in the Paul J. Olson Wildlife Area. I really didn't know what to expect. As it got lighter and lighter, I started to see little, dark silhouettes racing back and forth. Most of the blinds used on Buena Vista are plywood. But the one I was in was portable, more like a tent or a tarp. One of the subordinate males, on the edge of the grounds, then jumped on top of the tent and started drumming. I lightly put my hand up on the inside of the tent, and he drummed right on my hand!" she says, excitedly.

Males raise their pinnae feathers to look like horns during their mating dance. (Photo: John T. Andrews)

According to Lesa, 90 percent of all of the prairie chickens in the state can be found in four wildlife areas in central Wisconsin: the Buena Vista Wildlife Area, the Paul J. Olson Wildlife Area, the George W. Mead Wildlife Area, and the Leola Wildlife Area. The other 10 percent of the population is scattered in the outskirts. The place where I've chosen to have my first viewing experience, the Buena Vista Wildlife Area, holds the majority of the chickens in our state and is currently the largest grassland east of the Mississippi River.

## CUTTING CROP CIRCLES

Today, Wisconsin's greater prairie chickens are found *only* in the central portion of the state. But presettlement, the birds were located solely in the southern third of Wisconsin, which was covered by native prairies. Across the country, the story is a familiar one: When European settlers came to farm in the nineteenth century, they made several changes to the landscape. They drained wetlands, burned acres to make way for crops, and—particularly in northern Wisconsin— cut down trees. A lot of land was opened up, and by 1900 there were prairie chickens in every Wisconsin county. One early estimate put the state's greater prairie chicken population at about fifty-four thousand birds. In the early twentieth century, however, succession began—trees grew back in the north, larger cities sprouted up in the south, and fire controls were put in place in both areas— and prairie chickens got pinched into the center section of the state, where a lot of farming was still going on.

Says Lesa, "Central Wisconsin is really a surrogate for our greater prairie chickens. They originally resided in the native grasslands in the southern part of the state, but today they live entirely on grasslands such as Buena Vista, with its cool-season grasses, such as orchardgrass, smooth brome, and timothy. That's the enigma of Buena Vista: prairie chickens are now found in Wisconsin *only* on a habitat that they hadn't adapted to originally but that now they thrive on."

The Buena Vista Wildlife Area has few native, warm-season grasses, such as little and big bluestem or Indiangrass. The reason that prairie chickens do so well in such a habitat is that what they really depend on is the structure of grasslands, not the composition. In other words, what is most important for them is that they have cover, which is grass—not what kind of grass it is. For breeding prairie chickens, vegetation height, density, patchiness, and canopy are all more important factors than the species of plants themselves.

In spring, however, when a male is dancing his heart out to attract a mate, cover is not one of the features he looks for in a lek. Says Lesa, "In general, preferred booming grounds tend to be flat with short vegetation so that the chickens can see each other doing their displays. They also need an elevated area so that they can more easily spot approaching predators while they're preoccupied with their steps. In the fall, we help prairie chickens out by mowing the traditional booming grounds they go to. We use a tractor to cut a one-acre circle so that in the spring, it's better for the prairie chickens—and better for us to watch them."

## GRASSLANDS GOING;
## GREEN POWER GROWING

From annual surveys taken on booming grounds and in other areas frequented by greater prairie chickens, it's estimated that there are fewer than a thousand of the birds in the state today. While they are not on Wisconsin's Endangered Species List, they have been considered "threatened" here since 1979.

What may be even more at risk, however, is their habitat. Grasslands are one of the most endangered places in the United States today. The National Geographic Society estimates that only 5 percent of America's original grasslands remain today.

That statistic is so low probably in part because grasslands tend to suffer from an image problem. Like a movie star handicapped with the same affliction, I'm sure they'd benefit from hiring a publicist. Unlike many others of our esteemed natural landscapes, they are bereft of the cascading waterfalls, stunning mountain peaks, or other spectacular visuals that usually command our attention—and, often, our protection. Perhaps it's because for many people the term *grass* sounds so common and conjures up images of monotonous city lawns or boring vistas, places made up of only one uniform plant.

For much of our nation's history, then, grasslands (or prairies) have been plowed under or paved over. Their ecological significance as a provider of a variety of crucial habitats for dozens of species of ground-nesting birds and other wildlife has been largely overlooked or simply ignored.

When those first European settlers began rolling across the country in wagons, approximately 360 million acres of short-grass, tall-grass, and mixed-grass prairie carpeted the continent from Canada to Mexico. Waving strands of green and gold stretched from the foot of the Rockies to the deciduous forests of the East Coast. But today, only about 70 million acres are left.

Three out of four grassland bird species have suffered population declines over the last thirty years—the steepest decreases of any group of North American birds. A full 40 percent of the country's diminishing bird species are those that depend on grasslands. Nationwide, greater prairie chicken numbers plummeted by some 60 percent between 1966 and 2007.

Birds such as greater prairie chickens (and sharp-tailed grouse; see chapter 3, "Sharp-Tailed Grouse: Liking the Land Between") are reluctant to nest near roads or tall structures, such as power lines. And with wind-power-generating plants gaining more acceptance and ground, there's another new threat for the birds. Studies at a southwest Minnesota wind generator site found that species richness among grassland birds was four times less within 590 feet of each turbine. It didn't make any difference whether the blades were spinning or not.

This extreme sensitivity to human activity and any kind of grassland degradation—whether it is a physical change or just *next* to an intrusion—makes prairie chickens a good indicator of a healthy or an imperiled grassland ecosystem. Says Lesa, "The prairie chicken is an 'umbrella species.' They require the largest area of grasslands of any other grassland species. That means that any kind of animal that lives in the same area as a prairie chicken does is going to benefit if the prairie chicken benefits. So when we do things for prairie chickens, we are, in effect, doing well by numerous species that depend on grasslands."

But to date, the conversion of grasslands to croplands has probably been the biggest blow to prairie chickens. From 2006 to 2007 alone, corn production in the United States increased 19 percent. Unfortunately, corn is one of the worst crops for grassland birds. Most won't nest in corn, and corn production requires high inputs of chemical herbicides and fertilizers—both of which are bad for natural ecosystems in general.

Explains Lesa, "While you might think farming would help the chickens because it clears the land, it's actually a detriment. The *type* of farming is what affects chickens. High-intensity farming, such as what's required with corn, potatoes, or cranberries, doesn't allow the chickens to nest or give them enough freedom to move through or bring the chicks in to search for insects and seeds. It takes away habitat for most of their life cycle. Low-intensity farming, however, such as grazing, might actually help prairie chickens," she states. "At least, it doesn't take away the grassland habitat."

In fact, on the Buena Vista Wildlife Area, grazing has been a valuable tool and has been an important component of the prairie chicken management program since the mid-1980s. Carefully regulated grazing keeps away the unwanted woody vegetation and stimulates the growth of desirable grassland plants. Says Lesa, "There is one key landowner who has a couple of thousand acres adjacent to the Buena Vista Wildlife Area. A good portion of it he puts into grazing. That's very conducive for the chickens. While it doesn't make the greatest nesting habitat, it does make a great range for taking the chicks out to forage and for booming grounds. Basically, it keeps the land in grass."

High-intensity crops on farmlands take another toll on prairie chickens: they fragment the landscape, creating the kind of edges that predators prefer. Animals such as foxes and raccoons thrive on those edges; you can often see them working along the fringes of crop fields or woodlots. Not only does fragmentation favor the prairie chickens' predators, it also prevents the birds from dispersing to breed with other populations to augment their gene pool.

"The prairie chickens in the Buena Vista Wildlife Area and Leola Wildlife Area to the south don't mix and breed with birds that are north of Wisconsin Rapids—in the Paul J. Olson Wildlife Area and George W. Mead Wildlife Area—anymore," explains Lesa. "The landscape has been fragmented with high-intensity croplands, development, cities, and trees. What happens then, obviously, is that the chickens keep breeding in the same area with the same birds. Their genetic diversity has gone down greatly as a result. When that happens, there are many other negative impacts. If you're a prairie chicken, it means that you're not going to be able to breed as well, that your egg laying will be affected, that your chance of successfully hatching those eggs is negatively impacted, and your ability to deal with diseases is impaired."

The concern in central Wisconsin was so great that, in 2004, a conservation genetics committee was formed that consisted of genetics and prairie chicken experts from Wisconsin and across the country. The committee concluded that birds needed to be brought in from another state to increase genetic diversity. Hens from northwestern Minnesota, in the Crookston area, were trapped and released on the Buena Vista Wildlife Area in the fall of 2006. The process was repeated in 2007, 2008, and 2009. "We monitored the birds by radio collars," says Lesa. "We were able to show that the Minnesota hens that were brought in *did* breed and were able to produce offspring, and that those offspring produced offspring, and so on."

Currently, biological studies by blood sampling are being conducted to determine if the relocation of the birds from Minnesota to Wisconsin increased genetic fitness.

## Old Yellowlegs Is in the House

Scientifically speaking, greater prairie chickens belong to the *Phasianidae* family, a group of birds that includes partridges, grouse, and turkeys. Other names for the greater prairie chicken include *pinneated grouse, prairie hen,* and *old yellowlegs.*

Not only are the greater prairie chicken's legs yellow, but males of the species have fleshy, yellow-orange eye combs. Their feathers are colored dark brown, cinnamon, and pale buff above and below, and they are heavily barred. Greater prairie chickens may be from seventeen to eighteen inches long and have a wingspan of twenty-eight inches. They have short, rounded tails.

But their most famous aspect, of course, is their mating ritual, called *booming*. Courting males make a deep *ooo-loo-woo* sound, which can be heard up to a mile away. The boom is made by forcing air past the syrinx (or vocal box). It is made louder by their version of a "speaker system": esophageal air sacs that manifest themselves as two round, orange, featherless neck patches. When booming for a female's attention, these neck patches inflate, increasing the volume. Males will also raise their orange eye combs (or "eyebrows") and pinnae feathers to look like horns during their mating dance.

Diurnal birds, greater prairie chickens feed during the day and rest at night. They do not migrate; most will remain in their home area during the winter. To survive the cold Wisconsin nights, they tunnel under the snow or group up in grass or shrub shelters. A group of prairie chickens is known as a *pack* or a *little house*.

In Wisconsin, prairie chickens nest during May and June. The female will find a bowl-shaped, slight depression in the ground and line it with feathers and dry vegetation left over from the previous year. She will incubate the ten to fourteen eggs she lays for twenty-three to twenty-six days, taking a break only in the early morning and late evening to feed.

The chicks have some feathers when they hatch, but the hen will brood them for the first two weeks—the time it takes for their feathers to grow all the way in. Juveniles have brown, patterned feathers that disguise them among the plants around them, for they soon leave the nest to feed on insects and seeds.

But even with such camouflage, less than half of the young will make it to their second year. Predators, such as foxes, hawks, raccoons, and coyotes, find them to be a tasty meal. In their first winter, prairie chicken juveniles may flock together to move to a wintering area. They can breed after their first year.

A greater prairie chicken's pattern of flight is fast wing beats, followed by a glide. Once they get to a sailing glide, they can fly forty to fifty miles per hour. When males fight each other, they will lower their pinnae feathers, let the air out of their orange neck sacs, leap in the air, and attack with their beaks, wings, and feet in full force. It can be a fight to the death.

Hopefully, however, greater prairie chickens will continue to live—and thrive—in central Wisconsin long into the future. Says Lesa, "In the 1950s, we had what we call a *bottleneck* in the greater prairie chicken population. That's when a population goes from an adequate number down to a very, very small count in a short amount of time. Then, genetic diversity gets greatly reduced. That's happened to other populations and species where they *didn't* recover. An example would be the heath hen [*Tympanuchus cupido cupido*]."

Heath hens once lived in the barrens of coastal North America, from southern New Hampshire to northern Virginia. Due to intense hunting, however, the heath hen population declined rapidly, and by 1870, the birds had been extirpated on the mainland.

"When you're in a bottleneck situation," continues Lesa, "you're very vulnerable to natural disasters and diseases. So the Department of Natural Resources made the decision to close the prairie chicken hunting season for good, and the last legal hunt in Wisconsin was in 1955."

With the help of that management tactic—and other than the hens that were brought in from Minnesota in 2006, 2007, 2008, and 2009—greater prairie chickens did not have to be reintroduced in the state. Says Lesa, "Several things happened that helped the prairie chickens recover here. Not only was hunting banned, but from the 1950s on, the Wisconsin Department of Natural Resources started purchasing land—a *lot* of land, thousands of acres—and converting it into grassland. The department also instituted a more intensive management regime, especially at the Buena Vista Wildlife Area. The DNR cut down trees, conducted burns, and used herbicides. And that disturbance immensely improved the habitat. The chickens responded; their numbers started to go back up."

## DANCE LIKE NO ONE'S WATCHING

I've been sitting in the dark in my little box of a blind for about forty minutes now, and my fingertips and toes are starting to freeze. Gazing out one of the small windows, I keep straining to find that first glimmer of light that will shine on a patch of that twelve-thousand-acre expanse that I know stretches out and away from me in every direction, that great grassland called Buena Vista. Vast, open spaces that never seem to end and that touch the horizon all around have always appealed to me. They make me believe that there are still giant tracts of undeveloped land in our country that we can escape to, that we can be alone in, that we can find some quiet and peace in.

Lesa knows what I'm talking about. "The Buena Vista Wildlife Area really has a landscape you can't find anywhere else in the state," she says. "Even where there are other grasslands in Wisconsin, they're not flat. A lot of people will drive through here, thinking, 'This is a wasteland. There's nothing to see.' But if

you spend any amount of time here—especially with someone who's a birder—
Buena Vista is just a plethora of amazing things. Not only does it hold the
majority of our prairie chickens, it has the most reliable nesting population of
short-eared owls in the state. There are amazing grassland-nesting, migratory
bird species here, too: grasshopper sparrows, upland sandpipers, bobolinks, and
meadowlarks.

"I live near the Leola Wildlife Area, which is just a few miles from the Buena
Vista Wildlife Area," continues Lesa. "It almost feels like I'm living out West
on the Great Plains. We have some of the best sunrises and sunsets out there.
I'll get up early in the mornings on weekends and go running just for that
reason."

Just as the sun starts to rise on my morning in the grasslands, at about 5:50
a.m., I faintly hear a low cooing sound coming from somewhere in the grass
in front of my blind. The male prairie chickens have arrived! In the slowly increasing light, quick, fleeting shadows soon become the forms of birds. One . . .
two . . . three . . . four . . . there are now nine males preparing to perform.

The booming gets louder as yellow legs and feet begin stomping furiously
on the ground. Neon orange cheeks blow out into bright bulbs. Heads dip, and
little horns appear. When two males get face to face, their eyes lock and they

Tussles between males sometimes break out, but they are short lived and the birds
quickly get back to the business of dancing. (Photo: John T. Andrews)

wait, motionless. Then one inevitably hops up in the air over the other one. Sometimes a tussle between two males breaks out and they fly at each other, but it is always short lived. I soon count three females—where did they come from?—but they seemed unimpressed.

Eventually, one female disappears. About ten minutes later, the second female flies off into the far trees. The third female lingers for a long time. But at 7:30 a.m., she calls it quits, too. Although I strongly disagree with the hens' opinion, apparently none of the males have danced well enough today to deserve more than a few unimpassioned looks.

The nine males stay on the lek for a few minutes longer. Then, they, too, begin to disperse through the grass.

I fill out the survey sheet on the clipboard left in the blind, drop the panels over the windows, and latch them down. I unfold my legs, duck out, and secure the door behind me.

I take my time walking out of the grasslands, where an ancient, huge, glacial lake, Lake Wisconsin, once lay, sparkling in the sun. I stop to do a slow, IMAX-like turn, to get one last, long, 360-degree view of the horizon. As I rotate, I think to myself that this is a rare place, a place where a bird with yellow legs stomps quick, little feet and blows his neck up like a ripe, round orange.

And here is a place where the sliver of a moon can hang low, like that orange's peel.

## HOW TO HAVE A GENUINE GREATER PRAIRIE CHICKEN ENCOUNTER OF YOUR OWN

The Becoming an Outdoors-Woman program at the University of Wisconsin–Stevens Point makes arrangements for **renting viewing blinds** at the Buena Vista Wildlife Area for a small fee during the month of April (except during the weekend of the annual Central Wisconsin Prairie Chicken Festival). Visit their website at www.uwsp.edu/wildlife/pchicken. Remember to make your reservations early (starting in November), as spots in the blinds fill up fast.

During the Central Wisconsin Prairie Chicken Festival weekend (which occurs on a Friday, Saturday, and Sunday in mid-April), you can make blind reservations at several wildlife areas by contacting the Golden Sands Resource Conservation and Development Council, Inc. Go to www.prairiechickenfestival.org.

A portion of your blind rental fee will be used to help fund a graduate student's research and to help build new blinds and repair old ones.

**HOW TO BECOME INVOLVED WITH
GREATER PRAIRIE CHICKEN CONSERVATION EFFORTS**

To support greater prairie chickens and their habitat, you can make a donation to the Buena Vista Wildlife Area Gift Fund. Contact staff at the Wisconsin Department of Natural Resources West Central Region Office at (715) 839-3700.

You can also make a donation to the Central Wisconsin Prairie Chicken Festival by contacting the Golden Sands Resource Conservation and Development Council, Inc., at (715) 343-6215 or www.goldensandsrcd.org.

# 2

# Sturgeon: Spotting Those Who Spawn

## *Lake Winnebago, the Wolf River, and the Shawano Dam*

### STURGEON SPAWNING

"I was walleye fishing on the Flambeau River with my dad, and I was probably only ten or twelve years old," recalls Ron Bruch, the lead sturgeon biologist for the Lake Winnebago System, when I talk to him by phone and ask him to tell me his favorite fish story. "The Flambeau is a wild river up in Iron County, with pristine rapids. It's absolutely beautiful—just gorgeous! I'm way down on the river in a very remote spot, but there just happened to be some other guys— I think they were from Bulgaria—there that day, who were also fishing. I was standing only about ten feet away from one of these guys when he hooked into a sturgeon. So, he's playing this fish, and suddenly it jumps out of the water in front of us. I swore at the time that that fish was nine feet long! But remember, I was just little then. In reality, it might have been a seven-footer. But that fish certainly impressed me, and I'll never forget it. I thought, *Oh my God, it's a monster!* I just didn't think things like that existed then."

It was shortly after that that Ron caught his own lake sturgeon (*Acipenser fulvescens*) for the first time. In between then and now, however, he's probably fielded hundreds more fish stories and even more sturgeon—probably twenty thousand of them. All of this was not as a fisherman, but as the Wisconsin Department of Natural Resources (DNR) fisheries supervisor, based out of Oshkosh. And his "office" is the Lake Winnebago System.

## LAND OF THE BIG VOICE PEOPLE

A remnant of ancient, glacial Lake Oshkosh, the freshwater Lake Winnebago— at 137,708 acres—is Wisconsin's largest lake that lies entirely within the state and one of the largest inland lakes in the United States. Today, what's known as the Lake Winnebago System includes Lake Winnebago; Lakes Butte des Morts, Winneconne, and Poygan (collectively known as the Upriver Lakes); the Wolf River; the Upper Fox River; and the tributaries that feed into those rivers.

Says Ron, "Lakes Butte des Morts, Winneconne, and Poygan make up about thirty thousand acres combined. The Fox and Wolf Rivers flow into those lakes, then out of them through Oshkosh and into Lake Winnebago. From Lake Winnebago, the Fox River flows out through two outlets at Neenah-Menasha and then downstream toward Green Bay, dropping 140 feet in elevation before reaching that city. Right now, the Lower Fox River has fourteen dams on it. But at one time, it had to be one of the great natural wonders of North America. With that much natural drop, the waterfalls, chutes, and rapids must have been just spectacular."

In 1634, the French happened upon a Native American tribe living on the shores of Green Bay and inhabiting an area that stretched all the way to Lake Winnebago. Neighboring Potawatomi and Menominee people called the tribe *Winnebago* ("people of the filthy water") because in the summer, the big lake had a strong fish odor. But *Ho-Chunk* ("big voice") was the tribe's own name for themselves.

It's to the wild Wolf River and the great Lake Winnebago that I'm headed on this mid-April day, to encounter the oldest and largest fish living in Wisconsin— and to meet sturgeon wrangler Ron.

## ROLLIN' ON THE RIVER

I've been standing on the shore of the Wolf River for about two hours now, and I've come to the conclusion that sturgeon have a face only a mother could love.

With four catlike "whiskers" (called *barbels*) hanging off the front of their mouths—which they use to feel around on the bottom of lakes and riverbeds for food: shells, crustaceans, and small fish—alligator-like, round snouts, and shark-like tail fins, they almost look like a fantastic creature created from other animals' parts. Of course, I could be a little jaded because one of the sturgeon that Ron's crew just pulled out of the water managed to squirm away from his handlers and make a beeline toward me. The runaway fish promptly butted into my leg with his body and slapped me with his tail. The force of those hits almost took the pins right out from under me. It hurt like heck.

The reason the fish are being netted and pulled out of the water is to weigh, measure, sex, and inject them with a microchip (or scan them if they've already been microchipped). After these statistics have been recorded and the micro-chipping is complete, the sturgeon are allowed to roll back down into the river—

Barbels are efficient organs for detecting food, but they give a sturgeon a face only a mother could love. (Photo: Candice Gaukel Andrews)

today at a temperature of fifty-nine degrees—by way of a watered-down rubber mat.

Mid-April is the best time to catch sturgeon for tagging since during spawning season—typically mid-April through early May—the fish venture close to shore. Sturgeon spawning is dependent on water temperature—they prefer fifty-two to fifty-eight degrees Fahrenheit—and flow.

Each spring, as conditions become favorable, the males swim to rocky shorelines and wait for females. When they show up, the males will pound the water and hit the females' sides, stimulating them to lay eggs. The females will then lay their eggs on the rocks, a surface the eggs can adhere to.

"Sturgeon need a sticky, rocky substrate and aerated water to spawn," says Ron. "Their optimal spawning range for water velocity is about a foot and a half to two and a half feet per second. The riffle rapids on the Wolf River are the perfect habitat for spawning lake sturgeon."

Once the females have laid their eggs, the males drop sperm to fertilize them. In about eight to twelve hours, when they get done spawning, the females will start to move downstream, back to wherever they came from. The males, however, will hang around for a month or longer if there are females in the vicinity who haven't spawned yet.

"So," says Ron, "the males will spawn at a site until all the females have left it. Then they'll go upstream or downstream or even into a completely different river system and find females there that haven't spawned yet and spawn with them. They're very motivated! We've actually had males that died as a result of spawning stress; they literally spawned themselves to death. I've seen males with skull fractures and colored pink from lacerations caused by vigorously beating on the rocks and beating on the females."

Some of the sturgeon will then swim as far as the Shawano Paper Mill Dam, the end of the line. From there, they turn around and go back downriver.

## FOSSILS WITH FINS

It's a trip the male representatives of these stately fish may make every year—or every three to five years for females. Explains Ron, "About 83 percent of the adult sturgeon spawning here on the Fox River come from Lake Winnebago. About another 15 percent live their lives in the Upriver Lakes and 2 percent or so never leave the river—they live their whole lives here. So wherever they're coming from, most will migrate out in the fall of the year, move either into the Upriver Lakes or up the river, 'stage' for the winter, and then as soon as the water warms to the proper temperature, they'll find a spawning site. After spawning, they go back downstream.

"We used to think that the males spawned every other year, with just a small component that spawned every year," says Ron. "But new research is showing that the bigger males and the males that are in good shape will spawn yearly, and the smaller ones and younger ones will spawn every two years. If food resources are high and the sturgeon are able to build up a fat reserve in a short period of time, they'll spawn on an annual basis."

It's quite amazing that we're still learning new behavioral aspects about this "living fossil," as sturgeon are often called. Sturgeon made their first appearance about one hundred million years ago, in the Upper Cretaceous period of the Mesozoic era, at just about the time that dinosaurs abruptly exited the planet. But while sturgeon behaviors might seem like news because they're being freshly revealed, their looks would prompt you to place them somewhere back at the dawn of time.

Primarily cartilaginous, sturgeon lack a backbone with separate vertebrae. Instead, they have a continuous, flexible, cartilage-encased rod called a *notochord*, which runs the length of their bodies and ends at the tips of the upper lobes in their tail fins. They have two spiracles (or vents) located on top of their heads just forward of the gills.

Typically colored slate gray, olive-brown, or black with a milky or yellow-white underside, sturgeon are covered with bony plates (called *scutes*) rather than scales. Young sturgeon often have black blotches on their sides, backs, and snouts, which help to camouflage them on river bottoms. Lake sturgeon can be immediately recognized by their barbels, torpedo-shaped bodies, and sharply ridged backs. When its barbels, dragged over river and lake bottoms, detect food, this toothless fish will protrude its tubular mouth and suck it up, along with gravel and silt. The debris is then expelled through the gills.

Mature adults range from four to seven feet in length and twenty to two hundred pounds in weight, but they can occasionally grow larger than seven feet and up to two hundred fifty pounds. The only other species of sturgeon in Wisconsin, the shovelnose sturgeon—which is common in the Mississippi River—though somewhat similar in appearance, seldom exceeds four or five pounds.

Sturgeon are probably the longest lived of fish, some attaining one hundred years or more. A male doesn't reach sexual maturity until about fifteen years of age, while a female waits to mate until she is twenty-four to twenty-six years old. The combination of slow growth, slow reproductive rates, and the high value once placed on mature, egg-bearing females for caviar almost took sturgeon to the edge of nonexistence.

## BACK FROM THE BRINK

Lake sturgeon were once common in all the Great Lakes and in most of the large lakes in the northeastern United States. Today, however, their numbers have been drastically reduced. We in Wisconsin are fortunate: our Lake Winnebago System holds the largest single concentration of lake sturgeon in the world.

Says Ron, "In the late nineteenth century, when the commercial fisheries were really taking off in the Great Lakes, sturgeon were considered a nuisance because they ripped up the fishermen's nets. People really didn't know what to do with these fish: They were big, oily, and they didn't taste like lake trout, perch, or walleye. It wasn't until a few enterprising German immigrants arrived and showed people in the area how to smoke sturgeon flesh and process caviar that they realized sturgeon were very valuable fish."

Once people did appreciate the commodity that they had, however, things drastically changed for the state's sturgeon—and not for the better. "We went from killing sturgeon and stacking them up on the beach to rot to fishing them and processing them in earnest," Ron goes on. "Within thirty-five years, by 1915, the sturgeon population in the entire Great Lakes was driven close to extinction. Overfishing, the building of dams, and pollution on the spawning streams almost finished them off. But, luckily, there was a remnant population still left out there—and there was still a population in the Winnebago System."

The sturgeon in Lake Winnebago fared a bit better than their Great Lakes counterparts did, thanks to good—and timely—management. Says Ron, "The huge commercial fisheries were in the Great Lakes. While we know from anecdotal evidence that we did have some commercial fishing going on in Lake Winnebago, apparently the fishing effort here wasn't as ramped up as it was there. If we had had the Endangered Species Act back in 1915, I believe sturgeon would have been classified as endangered. But in response to the demise of sturgeon in the Great Lakes, that year the newly formed Wisconsin Conservation Commission closed all sturgeon harvest in the state of Wisconsin.

"That prohibition of harvest provided protection for the Winnebago stock that was remaining and allowed it to rebound much faster than the Great Lakes stocks did," Ron continues. "So that tells us that the Winnebago population must still have been in halfway decent shape in 1915. It would eventually support the winter spear-fishery that was reopened in 1932 on Lake Winnebago."

In fact, one hundred years of good management on Wisconsin's Lake Winnebago has produced not only the world's largest lake sturgeon population but also its healthiest. Says Ron, "There are twenty-five different species of sturgeon on the planet. Seven of them are found in North America. In our area, lake sturgeon exist in the Great Lakes, Lake Winnebago, the Mississippi River, the Wisconsin River, the Flambeau/Chippewa Rivers, and the Menominee River up on the border with Michigan; all the major river systems in Wisconsin have them. But Lake Winnebago is *the* absolutely perfect place for sturgeon. It has more than three hundred miles of tributaries with spawning habitat for adults and nursery habitat for the young. And the system has shallow, fertile, productive lakes, which provide a tremendous food base for the subadult and adult sturgeon to live their lives out. It's a big system that can handle a lot of basic food production and provide habitat for a big fish like a sturgeon."

Today, sturgeon may be legally taken in Wisconsin not only during a short winter spearing season on Lake Winnebago but also in a limited hook-and-line season on some Wisconsin rivers. In fact, on opening day of Wisconsin's 2010 sturgeon spearing season, a lake sturgeon weighing 212.2 pounds and at least a century old was speared in Lake Winnebago. The previous record was a 188-pound sturgeon speared during the 2004 spearing season.

## EVER VIGILANT

The Winnebago System has between forty thousand and fifty thousand adult sturgeon and another fifty thousand subadult sturgeon, according to current estimates. Ron credits a good share of that success not only to good management—historically and presently—but to the Sturgeon Guard program.

"Poaching is not as big of a problem today as it was in the past," says Ron. "But it was a very serious problem in the 1930s, 1940s, 1950s, and even into the 1960s. It had a significant negative impact on the population. In fact, by the mid-1960s, the Winnebago System population was down to a brand-new, very critically low level."

But because sturgeon are so long lived, it wasn't until the 1960s that the effects of what had started in the 1930s started to be noticed. "When you start chipping fish out of a population where individuals can live up to a hundred years, it takes a while for that to finally catch up with you," warns Ron. "For example, it took thirty-five years to decimate the sturgeon population of the Great Lakes. Although poaching in the Lake Winnebago System probably wasn't near the extent of what it was in the Great Lakes, it did happen. It created a 'hole' in the population, where there was a bunch of fish of a certain size that were missing. That hole was quite apparent when you looked at the ages and lengths of fish from the 1950s. Biologists at the time were at a loss to explain it. But with the hindsight of having sixty-plus years of data now, we're able to take a closer look at trends. And when we track back, we can see where that hole came from; it came from the poaching in the 1930s and 1940s.

"The other interesting thing," Ron goes on, "is that in the last ten years, we've seen a huge upsurge or increase in the number of what we call *trophy fish*, fish one hundred pounds or larger; we've actually had them over two hundred pounds. And when we traced that hole through time—seventy to eighty years later—we found that the hole has finally passed through the population. We're on the backside of the hole that was created by the illegal harvesting that was going on during the Great Depression."

Efforts to prevent any such future exploitation gaps were intensified starting in the mid-1990s. From 1993 to 2004, Wisconsin DNR staff worked closely with a citizens advisory committee made up of sturgeon spearers from around the area and interested members of the general public to put a new harvest-management system in place. Says Ron, "When that thing really started humming, it was about at the same time that these bigger fish were starting to show up in the population. So it all worked out as a perfect coincidence that we were providing the protections we needed to take advantage of this new surge of big fish that were starting to appear. That's what allows us today to now have fish that are in the 180- to 200-pound class on a regular basis."

Not only did thoughtful, timely management help diminish the devastating effects of illegal harvesting, but the Sturgeon Guard program played a significant role. Explains Ron, "Because of the spring sturgeon guards, poachers know that these fish are guarded twenty-four hours a day when they're spawning and vulnerable to being just jerked out of the river. There are not too many places where poachers can go and try to take a fish illegally now—at least in the spring when they're spawning."

As soon as fish start showing up anywhere on the Winnebago System during the spring spawning season, guards are immediately dispatched to those sites. Each year, three hundred or more people volunteer to work as sturgeon guards. "It's a bit of a nightmare coordinating the program because with so many people involved, you've got to plan way in advance," Ron says with a laugh. "And, you never know when the fish are going to spawn. So we schedule guards at various sites from April 15 to May 5. Everyone is assigned a twelve-hour shift, and shifts run around the clock, day and night. If April 15 comes and the fish aren't spawning, we start to cancel shifts. Then we keep canceling shifts until the fish come on. That's when the 'sturgeon camp' is opened and the guards go on duty."

Being a sturgeon guard means, basically, just that: you sit and you guard. Says Ron, "Hopefully, if it's a nice spring day, a guard will be able to enjoy the weather; usually, there are no mosquitoes because it's too early for that. Some of the sites are pristine, out-of-the-way places where there are no people to distract you. Those are the places where it's great to go and sit with a good book and just watch the fish spawn."

It's not all sunshine, peace, and bucolic moments, however. "It's also possible, if you're a guard, that you may be posted at a site where there are a thousand people or more looking at the fish," Ron cautions.

## A Trifecta of Spawning Activity

Thousands *do* come every year to see sturgeon spawning in the nation's most accessible places for watching this activity. And most of them visit at least one of three sites, according to Ron. The Wolf River Sturgeon Trail on County Highway X, west of New London, Wisconsin, is marked by a huge statue of a chainsaw-carved sturgeon. The trail has a paved surface alongside the river. And here, fish spawn within two to three feet of your feet. It would be hard to get closer to this phenomenon of nature than that.

The second popular place for watching sturgeon spawn is Bamboo Bend on Highway 54, just west of the village of Shiocton. "There's almost a half mile of shoreline that will be loaded with fish in the spring," Ron promises. "It's wheelchair accessible, and the 4-H sets up a brat-and-hot-dog stand," he makes sure to tell me.

A third sure-place is the paper-mill dam in the city of Shawano. On the east shore is a public ground called Sturgeon Park. "The Shawano Dam is as far upstream as the fish can swim," says Ron, when I ask him why the Shawano Dam is such a hot place for viewing sturgeon. "It was built at about the midpoint of one of the best natural spawning rapids for sturgeon on the Wolf River. The lower half of this spawning site is still available to fish migrating from the lakes 125 miles downstream, and they make good use of it! Every spring, it's used by the largest number of spawning lake sturgeon—numbering in the thousands. And it's historic: sturgeon have been traditionally spawning there for as long as the Wolf River has been flowing."

The sturgeon don't all go to the Shawano Dam, however. There are about sixty different spawning sites on the Fox River, and sturgeon will start dropping out at these various sites all along the route to the dam. "It's important to note that there are probably almost ninety miles of shoreline that have spawning sites on them, just on the Wolf River alone," says Ron. "Then you've got another fifty miles on the Embarrass River (a tributary of the Wolf River) and probably twenty miles on the Little Wolf River. So Shawano Dam is just one of the sites."

Collectively, however, at the three most popular sites—the Wolf River Sturgeon Trail, Bamboo Bend, and the Shawano Dam—thousands of people will stop to watch sturgeon spawning throughout the season.

"The average duration is seven days, but one year, it lasted over three weeks," says Ron. "It may not be consistent every day. You'll have little peaks and valleys in activity. But, usually, in a normal season at any given site, you'll have good viewing for about three days," he estimates.

## FESTIVAL FOR FISH

Prior to two dams being built on the Wolf River in the 1890s—the Shawano Dam and one north of Shawano but south of Keshena—sturgeon migrated from the Lake Winnebago System to traditional spawning grounds at Keshena Falls, now on the Menominee Reservation that was established by the Treaty of 1854. For the Menominee, sturgeon have a powerful spiritual and physical presence. After the long winter months, the tribe would wait for the sturgeon to return so they could replenish their food supplies. Sturgeon were also considered the spiritual protectors of wild rice—another important food source—and used in medicines. Historically, the Menominee would hold a sturgeon festival during the spring spawning, which recognized and celebrated the fish. Male members of the tribe would perform a fish dance, in which they mimicked the movements of the sturgeon as they traveled up the river to spawn. The dance was meant to ensure a productive season and a good harvest.

In 1993, Menominee tribal members who felt that the tribe should reconnect with the ancient fish reinstated *Maec Micehswan*, the sturgeon festival and feast that their ancestors had practiced every spring. The DNR, the U.S. Fish and Wildlife Service, and the U.S. Bureau of Indian Affairs then began to work with the tribe on a plan to reestablish a self-sustaining population of sturgeon in the Wolf River where it flows through reservation land. In spring 2012, more than 120 years after the construction of the dams, sturgeon began spawning once again at Keshena Falls.

## Live Long and Prosper

After bidding farewell to the sturgeon taggers on the Wolf River—and after stopping to massage away the pain in my leg from the sturgeon that slapped me— I head over to the Shawano Paper Mill Dam to see some sturgeon-spawning activity—and some avid sturgeon-spawning watchers—for myself. Ron, too, will be heading over there this afternoon, for more tagging.

Under the Shawano Dam, the water roils with shadowy, torpedo-shaped bodies. (Photo: John T. Andrews)

Sturgeon Park is brimming with people on this sunny Thursday afternoon. I begin to understand why as I make my way down to shore, just under the Shawano Dam. A more raucous group of fish I have never seen! Here in this roiling water, I can see packed, black, shark-like fins that face every which way racing, and huge, shadowy bodies darting about, splashing up a storm.

While witnessing this huge display of energy—and the smiles on the faces of the adults and children who came to see the show—I'm struck again by the strength of these fish, some of which could be quite elderly. I ask Ron for his thoughts about the number of years that could be represented by the individuals in this frothing, breathing body of fluid movement I see at my feet.

"We don't know for sure exactly how long sturgeon can live," says Ron. "We think the females may live up to 150 years and the males more than a century. But here's the deal: Every population of this species in North America has either been severely or substantially exploited in the last one-hundred-plus years. With a fish that can live over a century and with the exploitation rates being what they were, sturgeon have not had the opportunity anywhere in North America since presettlement times to show us their innate longevity or their innate ability for how big they can get. We have some old records that document fish weighing more than three hundred pounds and measuring eight feet in length, but you don't see too much of that anymore.

"However," Ron emphasizes, "on the Winnebago System, we're beginning to see fish weighing 230 to 240 pounds. These are the sturgeon that are just starting to appear from coming around the backside of that poaching hole. So I predict that within the next thirty to fifty years, we're going to finally see what lake sturgeon are really made of! And right here on the Winnebago System will be the first and best opportunity for them to show us that in any numbers because of the long-standing management program that we've had in place, some luck, and the fact that we have laws to protect them," he says proudly.

That's pretty big stuff coming from an expert such as Ron. And definitely something for sturgeon to splash about.

## SOUNDS ENCOURAGING

Although the sound that's ringing in my ears this day is the one of water being slapped over and over again by astounding numbers of rowdy and randy sturgeon, Ron has some other noise news for me.

"One of the lesser-known aspects of observing sturgeon spawning is that the males make a sound," says Ron. "We're not exactly sure how they create it, but we think it's with their swim bladders. It sounds similar to a ruffed grouse drumming. Although I published a report about this several years ago, we have just recently been able to capture the sound on a hydrophone. The noise is at an extremely low frequency; humans almost can't hear it. It's probably more accurate to say that you can feel the noise more than you can hear it. Its low frequency gives it a very long wavelength, which means that it can travel long distances through water. We're quite confident that this is a communication method that male sturgeon use to let the rest of the sturgeon world know that there's spawning going on. We'll be conducting further work to fully describe the sound," he says excitedly.

The theory is plausible. It's known that other animals make similar low-frequency sounds to communicate for mating purposes, such as elephants and humpback whales. But now by capturing the sound on a hydrophone, Ron and his team will be able to analyze it from a technical standpoint. Practically, then, in the future, this particular sound could be used to document—and then protect—other spawning sites.

Ron explains, "Say, for instance, that you have been stocking sturgeon as part of a sturgeon restoration program. You believe you have fish old enough to spawn, but have not been able to document spawning activity. Presently, that's not easy to do if you only have a handful of female sturgeon spawning. It could happen in a day, and then they'd be done. If you weren't at the right spot to see them, you might miss them. But once we fully describe the sound made by spawning males and how to capture that sound, you would be able to put a hydrophone in the water near what you think might be a sturgeon-spawning site and get hard evidence. You wouldn't have to be on site to *see* the fish—you could use the hydrophone to *hear* them for documentation."

Right now, however, the best way for you to hear this sound is by becoming a sturgeon guard. "If you're sitting on a quiet spawning site where you don't have a lot of road or people noise, much like some of the sites the guards are assigned to," says Ron, "and you're on the bank as these fish spawn right next to your feet, you can sense—that's probably the best way to put it, *sense*—the sound. It's a deep rumble, almost like thunder in the distance: *woe-woe-woe-woe-woe-woe-woe*. But it's not the weather: it's the sturgeon, spawning."

Sturgeon do, however, make other sounds. "They can make an orca-type sound that is very high pitched," says Ron. "That sound has been recorded as well. Russian researchers have determined that it's a prespawn sound when they're moving upstream. We don't know if it's just the females or the males that make it, but I suspect it could be the females, as if to say, 'Okay, boys, I'm in town, get ready.' Each female is on her own biological clock, and she has to communicate somehow to these males that she's there," he postulates.

It could be an efficient system for propagating the species. "After all," says Ron, "sturgeon have been around a long time. They've had one hundred million years to figure this all out."

## ANOTHER WHOPPER OF A FISH STORY

In his long career with sturgeon, Ron, too, I suspect, has had time to try to figure out just what it is about these fish that so intrigues him. "Why sturgeon?" I ask.

"Sturgeon are interesting animals because they're prehistoric, big, and their use and abuse around the world is a storied past," he replies. "Their course runs from the Russian caviar that was once the 'food of the czars' to the present day where the queen of England is still the rightful proprietor of all the sturgeon that are harvested within three miles of United Kingdom shores or washed ashore either dead or alive. Sturgeon are fish that have always had a high place of prominence in the fish world. You even see them in a lot of old masters' paintings. Often, if a waterfront market is depicted, you'll see a sturgeon somewhere in the painting," he says with a smile.

I can't say good-bye to Ron without asking him for just one more fish story. He pauses, as if he's rifling through a jam-packed mental file cabinet.

"Well, there's a favorite urban legend out here on Lake Winnebago," he begins. "The story goes that it was the winter spearing season, and there was a fellow sitting in his spearing shack. I don't know if you've ever been inside a spearing shack, but it's completely dark inside. In fact, spearing shanties are sometimes called darkhouses. The only light that comes in is an eerie, green glow from the hole in the ice, the result of sunlight filtered through the snow and ice on the frozen lake. So, you're staring down this hole, and most of the time you're staring down at nothin'. I mean, you have your decoy down there, but the odds of seeing a fish aren't good. There are guys who sit for twenty years of spearing seasons and don't see a single sturgeon. On the other hand, of course, there are the few who can go out and in ten minutes see a fish and spear it. But on average, you're sitting for days at a time, year after year, *not* seeing sturgeon.

"And so a fellow's sitting there in his shack, looking down at the hole in the ice," Ron goes on. "It's nice to have a little company at times like this, so most people usually bring a radio or some will bring their dogs along with them. So this one guy's got his black Lab out there, and the black Lab's watching down the hole, too. Every once in a while, a minnow or something else will swim by, and that keeps the dog's rapt attention.

"Well, a sturgeon suddenly glides past, and the black Lab jumps right into the hole, going after it! But the dog gets stuck under the ice, and he's down there for some time, swimming around. When you're under the ice and you look up, the ice looks white, but the ice holes look black, which is a bit confusing. So the dog is swimming around down there for a while, and he finally recognizes a hole and comes up through it. The only problem is, the hole opens up into a different guy's ice shack! The frantic dog, suddenly popping up out of the hole, scares the guy inside so much that he runs out, right through the side of his ice shack!

"Well, that's one of the more popular stories around here," Ron concludes. "I don't know if it's true or not. But I'm just saying."

### HOW TO HAVE A GENUINE STURGEON ENCOUNTER OF YOUR OWN

Start **watching for sturgeon** in the Winnebago System in mid-April. These sites are particularly accessible:

+ Shawano Dam: parking on the east side of the river at the end of Richmond Street
+ Bamboo Bend: on County Highway 54; parking on the north side of the highway
+ Wolf River Sturgeon Trail: about two miles west of New London on County Highway X; parking on the south side of the river about a half mile from the spawning site

The DNR website at dnr.wi.gov/topic/fishing/sturgeon/sturgeonspawning .html posts **sturgeon updates** during the spawning season. Also, check the websites of local communities, such as Shawano, Shiocton, and New London.

### HOW TO BECOME INVOLVED WITH STURGEON CONSERVATION EFFORTS

There are five chapters of Sturgeon for Tomorrow, a nonprofit organization dedicated to the conservation and propagation of lake sturgeon, in the Lake Winnebago area. Monies are raised through each chapter's annual banquets, held January through March. Since 1978, Sturgeon for Tomorrow has raised more than $750,000, which has been donated to the DNR, the Sturgeon Guard program, and other sturgeon projects and study groups.

Visit www.sturgeonfortomorrow.net or dnr.wi.gov/topic/fishing/sturgeon /sturgeontomorrow.html to learn more.

The five chapters and the areas they represent are:

- Main Chapter, southeast side of Lake Winnebago; annual banquet held in Kiel
- Northern Half Chapter, north end of Lake Winnebago; annual banquet in Darboy
- Southwest Chapter, southwest side of Lake Winnebago; annual banquet in Fond du Lac
- Upper Lakes Chapter, Upriver Lakes of Winneconne, Poygan, and Butte des Morts; annual banquet in Fremont
- West Central Chapter, west side of Lake Winnebago; annual banquet in Oshkosh

You can volunteer for the Sturgeon Guard program through the DNR. Go to dnr.wi.gov/topic/fishing/sturgeon/sturgeonguard.html or e-mail DNR SturgeonGuard@wisconsin.gov.

# 3

# Sharp-Tailed Grouse:
# Liking the Land Between

*Namekagon Barrens Wildlife Area in Northwest Wisconsin*

### A BLIND ON THE BARRENS

Pine barrens, no matter where they are located in the world, are strange countries. They can't be classified as grasslands, nor can they be considered forests. They have no backdrop of blue mountain peaks or foreground of turquoise seashores. They're not completely flat, but they're not exactly hilly, either.

Going to a barrens always leaves me feeling a little unsettled. Not quite sure of how to describe where I've been. Not sure of anything, really. Because even their name—*barrens*—tends to put me into a mode of feeling a little empty and lost.

So when I decided to go to the Namekagon Barrens Wildlife Area to encounter one of Wisconsin's native birds—the sharp-tailed grouse—I knew I'd need a guide to help me muddle through these mixed feelings in the middle lands.

And there's no one better to fill the bill than Gary Dunsmoor, wildlife technician at the Namekagon Barrens Wildlife Area in the northeast corner of Burnett County in northwest Wisconsin. This thirty-five-year veteran of "the land between" knows a landscape that's a little bit here and a little bit there, some of this and some of that, intimately.

### LEARNING TO LOVE A BARREN LANDSCAPE

I meet Gary for the first time at our arranged spot, a gravel pull-off near Hoinville Road off of Highway 77. I find him in his pickup truck, which has a huge fire hose mounted on the back. Gary has offered to give me a tour of the pine barrens (alternately referred to as just *barrens* or *pine-oak barrens*) this afternoon, prior to tomorrow's early morning outing to watch sharp-tailed grouse from a blind.

I park my car and jump into his truck. A bit surprised at the firefighting equipment on the back end, I ask him exactly what being a wildlife technician on a barrens entails.

"On the very first day that I came to the Namekagon Barrens Wildlife Area to work, more than three decades ago," he answers, "I was asked to go out and do some habitat maintenance jobs." And on this dry and windy April day, Gary tells me he's on call for fire control, since the pine barrens are now entering a three-year drought.

So from day one up to today, it seems, Gary has had his hands busy keeping the barrens . . . well, *barren*—a monumental task that many see as environmentally unfriendly. "In fact," Gary tells me, "shortly after I first started working here, I found a hand-painted sign that someone left on the barrens that read 'God created the land to grow trees.' I knew then that not everyone understands the importance of pine barrens habitats."

For most of us who have been trained to appreciate the green heights of old-growth forests and the red depths of canyons that we commonly see pictured in full-color wall calendars or dissolving screen savers, learning to love a barrens may be a hard sell. Pine barrens have little "poster appeal" and few groups devoted to saving them.

But around the world, pine barrens are rare and imperiled. And in Wisconsin, the Northwest Sands, where the Namekagon Barrens Wildlife Area is located, is listed as one of our sixteen ecological landscapes—regions to be appreciated for their distinct physical and biological characteristics, such as vegetation, climate, geology, soils, and water (see chapter 10, "Sandhill Cranes: Going Out for the Night, as They Come In"). The Northwest Sands also differs from the fifteen other landscapes found in Wisconsin by its management requirements and the uncommon bird and animal species it holds.

Although a "barrens community" might at first suggest a place bereft of flora and fauna, it is rich in both. From spring through late summer, prairie grasses and flowers paint the barrens in a spectrum of colors. Blue pasqueflowers, yellow hoary puccoons, purple prairie phloxes, orange butterfly milkweeds, and vermilion wood lilies bloom in a bright palette. Clemens Creek originates from springs on the North Unit and flows into the nearby Saint Croix River and is a classified trout stream. Megafauna, such as black bears, wolves, and coyotes, count on the pine barrens for their livelihoods. Grassland birds—such as Brewer's blackbirds, brown thrashers, Eastern bluebirds, Eastern towhees, gray catbirds, upland sandpipers, vesper sparrows, and yellow warblers—fill the scenery with music.

All of the Namekagon Barrens Wildlife Area's 5,050 acres are leased from Burnett County. The North Unit lies seven miles east of Highway 35 on the Saint Croix Trail Road, or eleven miles west of Minong. The South Unit is two miles to the south and west of the North Unit, on Namekagon and Spring-brook Trail Roads. The Saint Croix River flows within one mile west of the barrens, and the Namekagon River runs between the North and South Units; both are part of the protected Saint Croix National Scenic Riverway.

Although small, scattered, isolated populations of sharp-tailed grouse occur at a few other locations in Wisconsin, it can safely be said that this wildlife area is their last stronghold in the state.

And that's why I've come here to find them.

## AN APTLY NAMED BIRD

Native to Wisconsin, sharp-tailed grouse (*Tympanuchus phasianellus*) are large, ground-dwelling birds. Named for their sharp, pointed tails, which are edged in white, they may grow to eighteen inches in length. They have brown plumage above—mottled with white, buff, and black—with lighter-colored feathers below. (Greater prairie chickens are barred, not mottled, and show no white in their tails; see chapter 1, "Greater Prairie Chickens: Sitting Out the Dance.") White spots cover the sharp-tail's wings. The males have small, inconspicuous, yellow combs above the eyes and sport purple neck sacs, which are not generally visible unless they are inflated in a dancing display. Their legs are feathered to the base of their toes.

A female sharp-tailed grouse usually selects a nest site within a half mile of a dancing ground, which is typically a grassy opening with scattered brush. Here, she'll make a scrape (or depression in the dirt) hidden in tall grass or twigs and line it with down. Hens lay one drab, olive-colored egg per day until the clutch of ten to fourteen eggs is complete. Incubation lasts for about twenty-three or twenty-four days. Following hatching, the brood remains in cover to feed on insects and plants. In about ten days, the young will begin to fly. By six to eight weeks, they are fully independent and will then disperse; young sharp-tails often move several miles from their hatch sites.

Although not listed as "endangered" federally or here in the state, they are deemed a Wisconsin Wildlife Species of Greatest Conservation Need. Threats to their continued survival are housing development, conversion of barrens and jack pine forests to red pine plantations, invasive plants (such as spotted knap-weed), population isolation and loss of genetic diversity, and overhunting. But because the DNR estimates that our state's sharp-tails number in the hundreds, an annual limited hunt is usually allowed. Although it seems counterintuitive, hunting can actually help the population grow.

"By having a hunting season," says Gary, "we hope to maintain more interest in and more support for the birds. Hunting is, of course, very limited—to a three-week season, about mid-October to the first week in November. And people have to apply for and get a permit. That's why we do surveys. Lately, we're not seeing the number of birds we've seen in the last couple of years. We do know that, like ruffed grouse populations, sharp-tailed grouse numbers cycle up and down over a three- to ten-year period. But by doing surveys and finding out approximately how many birds we have here, we know whether or not to institute a hunting season in any given area and how many permits it's safe to issue," he explains.

## No Man, No Woman, No People

Gary and I have entered the North Unit of the barrens, and as he drives me along the sand and gravel roads, I'm struck by the subtlety of the landscape: muted browns and greens, a few trees that aren't too large or showy, only delicate rises and dips in the roadways. There are no signs of civilization all the way to the horizon.

It seems almost prophetic when we pass by a sign that reads No Man's Lake Road. I see no lake and no other man than Gary. Perhaps this is why the deer, black bears, coyotes, foxes, and songbirds find the Namekagon Barrens a good place to be. Gary has even seen evidence of wolves and perhaps a cougar, too.

Gary pulls off to the side of the sandy road we've been traveling on to give the dust a chance to settle. Idling the engine, he reaches over to pull a map out of the glove compartment. He unfolds the map and points to the locations where he's set up twenty-four bluebird and kestrel houses. One time, he tells me, he came upon some folks with a Colorado license plate driving through the pine barrens. They told him they had come all the way from the West to Namekagon just for a chance to see an upland sandpiper.

Gary begins driving again and says he wants to show me the location of the north blind, which I'll have to find in the early-morning dark tomorrow if I want a chance to see the sharp-tailed grouse dance. I try to memorize the route and make a mental map of the spot's location. Some people who sign up for a blind never manage to find it; they get hopelessly lost in the blackness of the barrens.

We get out of the truck so I can stand in the middle of the dancing ground, where the birds will be showing off tomorrow. I try to get a feeling for what it is that the sharp-tailed grouse like so much about this particular place. From the perspective of my height, I can't discern any elevation difference between here and the surrounding land, but I do get an impressive, panoramic view across the barrens. There is a small grove of trees off in the distance in front of me and scrubby vegetation to my sides and back.

Beginning in April each year, male sharp-tailed grouse gather on dancing grounds like this one, hoping to impress a hen with their displays and fancy footwork. They advertise their locations by cackling and "flutter-jumping," where a male will jump into the air, fly a few feet forward, and then land again. More vocal than greater prairie chickens, male sharp-tailed grouse emit *chilk* and *cha* sounds, squeals, whines, and gobbles. Their cooing is a version of the greater prairie chicken's booming.

Such notes accompany their visual presentations, the most complex of which is "tail-rattling." This display consists of a series of rapid stepping motions performed with the tail erect, the head held forward, and the wings outstretched. After assuming this stiff posture, the male "dances" in a small circle or arc. He vibrates his tail feathers, which make a clicking or rattling sound. When he has successfully attracted a female, they mate. The female will then leave the dancing ground for her nest site.

In anticipation of tomorrow's performance, I ask Gary to describe one of his most memorable viewings.

The dance of the male sharp-tailed grouse is an extravagant display. The birds strive to outdo each other and win the opportunity to breed. (Photo: John T. Andrews)

"One year," begins Gary, "as I was watching a group of sharp-tails from a blind, a goshawk came flying onto the grounds. It came down so hard and fast that the sharp-tails hardly had time to flush or run off. The hawk hit one of the birds, kind of knocked it over, made a quick little circle, then came back and grabbed it. He ate it right there.

"The rest of the birds then, of course, flew off," continues Gary. "But while the hawk was eating the sharp-tail that it killed, the other sharp-tails flew over at least twice—real low, right over the dancing grounds. Within minutes of the goshawk's leaving, the sharp-tails came back and started right up again as if nothing had happened," he recalls.

Sharp-tails are, in fact, so faithful to their dancing grounds that they usually return to the same ones every year. Says Gary, "The two main dancing grounds that are on the barrens—where the north and south blinds are—have both been around for about twenty years."

As if to provide validation for Gary's statement, a story that appeared on the National Audubon Society's website reported that in one case, a homestead was built over a sharp-tail dancing ground; the following spring, a grouse displayed his moves on the farmhouse roof.

## RARE GROUND

Although sharp-tailed grouse have never been in danger of being extirpated in Wisconsin and none had to be reintroduced, they have disappeared throughout many parts of their historic range due to habitat loss. And declines in their population and ranges are still occurring.

Luckily, today in Wisconsin, sharp-tailed grouse can still be found in eight areas:

+ Namekagon Barrens Wildlife Area
+ Moquah Barrens (within the Chequamegon-Nicolet National Forest in Bayfield County)
+ Douglas County Wildlife Area (located between Solon Springs and Gordon in Douglas County)
+ Crex Meadows Wildlife Area (in western Burnett County)
+ Pershing Wildlife Area (in west central Taylor County, south of Ladysmith)
+ Riley Lake (within the Chequamegon-Nicolet National Forest in Price County)
+ Kimberly Clark Wildlife Area (twelve miles west of Phillips in Price County)
+ Black River Falls area

"I want to stress that there *might* be a few birds in Black River Falls," says Gary. "But from what I saw on a map at a meeting I went to just last week, there was a big question mark over that area. Historically, there were birds at Black River Falls, just as historically there were birds in northeast Wisconsin as well."

That's most probably because the state once had far more prairies than it does today. Says Gary, "In the past, even southern Wisconsin had sharp-tailed grouse. But over the course of 150 years of intensive Euro-American settlement, the prairies and the habitat suitable for the birds has continually declined. In the early twentieth century, after the big cutover and with the wildfires that used to occur regularly, sharp-tailed grouse were doing very well in the state. But since then, between development and land fragmentation, fire control and a reduction of wildfires, maturation of regenerated forests and a general increase in woody cover, the population has been shrinking. Now, sharp-tails, for the most part, are found only on managed, state lands where we do a lot of prescribed burning for them. We're trying to help them hold on."

Prescribed burns are essential to keep lands habitable for sharp-tails. Some Native Americans even referred to sharp-tailed grouse as *firebirds*, due to their reliance on brush fires to keep their habitat open.

In the mid to late nineteenth century, large wildfires were a common occurrence. Fueled by huge amounts of pine slash left from the extensive logging of the period, wildfires would run for miles and set back vegetative succession. But by the early 1930s, a vast network of forest rangers, lookout tower personnel, and fire wardens had been put in place, and wildfires were attacked with everything we had. In fact, on August 2, 1915, Wisconsin became the first state to use an airplane for locating fires.

"Currently, in Wisconsin," states Gary, "all of the wildfires that start—whether by people or by lightning or by anything else—are suppressed immediately. The fear is that they'll grow so large that they can't be controlled and that they then will do major damage."

But the barrens are still burned. Right now, the Namekagon is broken down into thirty burn units. Approximately seven hundred to eight hundred acres are burned per year.

"We're on a rotation of every five, six, or seven years—depending on how bad the units need burning and, of course, the weather," explains Gary. "We conduct prescribed burns in the spring. However, last spring, for example, it was so snowy, rainy, and cold that we couldn't do any burning."

A lot of preparation is required before a unit is burned. If mature trees are present, the first step is to call in loggers to harvest anything that is merchantable. Following that, Wisconsin DNR staff may need to do some additional cutting of heavy vegetation. Firebreaks then need to be built around the area to be burned; typically, such work is done in mid-September by *rotovating* (similar to rototilling but on a larger scale) a fifteen- to twenty-five-foot track around the unit. This creates a "mineral (no vegetation) firebreak." Vegetation that is twenty to seventy feet inside the rotovated area is mowed down. Only then, and when the weather conditions are just right, is the prescribed burn allowed to take place.

"So, the land is not really forested when we burn it," says Gary. "We've already set back that succession using timber sales and heavy equipment. This way, we can safely burn areas without fire escaping and doing damage to people's properties and homes."

Because the state does not own the land the Namekagon Barrens is situated on, keeping the pine barrens from becoming a pine plantation took some fancy footwork—and this time, not by the sharp-tails. Gary tells me a bit about the political history of the barrens: "In the early 1950s, we started leasing land from Burnett County and doing management on it for sharp-tailed grouse in response to concerns about their diminishing habitat. There's a big difference between a *grasslands* and a *barrens*, which many people don't understand. Greater prairie chickens are a grasslands, open-prairie type of bird. Ruffed grouse are a species of the forest. Sharp-tails, on the other hand, live in an in-between habitat, a semi-open one, with shrubs, small trees, and scrub oak.

"When our last lease came due in 1992," continues Gary, "the county preferred not to lease it to us again and wanted to plant most of it to red pine. However, The Nature Conservancy stepped in, and with their help, we were able to acquire a new lease. This habitat is important not only for sharp-tailed grouse but for people—everyone from birders to hunters to eco-tourists. Our current lease expires in 2017, so by then we'll have to figure out if we can purchase the land, trade other lands for it, or lease it again."

Gary and I conclude our tour with a stop at the remnants of a building foundation almost buried on the barrens, where a school once sat. It's visual proof that the barrens want to remain remote and wild, free from our development.

Gary drives me back to my car, parked off of Highway 77, and we say our good-byes. Tomorrow, I will go back to the Namekagon Barrens to "settle" briefly, too, to watch from the north blind as the sharp-tailed grouse dance.

## FASCINATIN' RHYTHM

The barrens are bare of people at 4:00 a.m., even though Gary mentioned I would probably run into some turkey hunters. The prophecy of "No Man's Lake" has come to pass.

I now understand why some people give up looking for the blind in the dark. Even having had a tour to it in the light of yesterday afternoon, it takes me about forty minutes to find it once I've officially entered the barrens.

The blind is basic: a canvas covering drapes over a boxy framework, just large enough for two, one-seater wooden benches inside. There are a couple of "windows" cut into the fabric. It's primitive but cozy on this thirty-eight-degree, April morning.

Just as my watch registers 5:30 a.m., I began to hear low *coo*-ing coming from somewhere in the grass beyond my canvas walls. Then, in the still emerging light, several sharp-tailed grouse appear on the grounds. I watch as they dip their heads down low, splay out their wing feathers, and start drumming their feet.

I'm amazed at how they seem to be one with their landscape, their beautiful, brown feathers blending in perfectly with the brown barrens. Only the purple air sacs on the sides of the males' necks stand out—but still, purple is an earth color. It's almost Frank Lloyd Wright–esque, a natural blending of life and environs.

Then a most unusual thing happens: The males simultaneously freeze. They stand perfectly still in whatever stance they were in for what seems like forever, although it's probably only about seven seconds. Then at the same, precise moment, they start up their dances again. Shortly after, the phenomenon is repeated. By the third occurrence of this game of "statue," I can't help laughing.

I later ask Gary what that strange behavior is all about.

"That's just part of their display," he says. "When there's a female around, they'll start dancing very intensely. Then, as though someone turned them off by flipping a switch, they'll stop—sometimes with one foot up and one foot down and their wings spread out. It's like they're showing off for a photograph, saying, 'Just look at me now, in this action moment!'

"I've even seen them freeze in pairs," Gary continues. "They kind of get down on their bellies on the ground and just sit and stare at each other for five minutes or more. Sometimes, they actually flutter up in the air and battle each other. I think everyone should put watching sharp-tailed grouse on their life list of things to do!"

It's now 7:30 a.m., and things have significantly quieted down. There are only four or five sharp-tailed grouse left, although throughout the morning I've counted fourteen males and four hens on the grounds at one time. As I step out of the blind, the few remaining grouse flush. The rising sun has warmed up the April air, and I can already tell it's going to be a beautiful day.

After being privy to this early morning ball, I'm not feeling as if this landscape is empty and barren anymore.

The last grouse flush as I step out of the blind. Despite the name, the barrens are vital, so full of life. (Photo: John T. Andrews)

### Assigning a Value

When I return home, I call Gary to tell him about my sharp-tailed grouse encounter. He totally understands my transformation—from being a bit uncomfortable on the barrens with a feeling of emptiness to now seeing it as so vital, so full of life.

"I do think people have an appreciation for pine barrens landscapes more so today than they did just a few decades ago," Gary tells me, "especially when they receive more education about them and have experiences on them like you did watching the sharp-tailed grouse. But many still make comments such as 'The Namekagon would be a better place if it were planted in trees.' Some of that is economics, of course. People think that if trees grew here, there would be a monetary benefit to the county, as part of the tax base, in the production of fiber for wood markets. But it's harder to set a value on open land with sharp-tails on it. For me, that's got a very high value, but for the next person, unfortunately, that might rank pretty low.

"I'd like people to realize," Gary goes on, "that this type of habitat is extremely important in the state—and it's dwindling. Barrens habitats have trouble finding champions because managing them involves fire, and not everybody understands the role of fire in the ecosystem. If it weren't for doing prescribed burning on major properties that have sharp-tailed grouse on them, my guess is that the birds would be extinct here."

Sharp-tailed grouse supporters agree. Many of them believe that if more acreage is not transferred into state ownership soon and managed for the birds' benefit, the long-term outlook for sharp-tailed grouse in Wisconsin is bleak.

I still believe barrens are strange countries: "lands between." They are neither grasslands nor forests, neither flat nor hilly. But I know now that they are definitely not empty—not as long as odd birds with sharp, noisy tails still dance in the early hours of April mornings.

### HOW TO HAVE A GENUINE
### SHARP-TAILED GROUSE ENCOUNTER OF YOUR OWN

Blinds are put out in early April and brought in by mid-May. To reserve a spot in one of the **sharp-tailed grouse blinds,** visit the Friends of the Namekagon Barrens Wildlife Area website at www.fnbwa.org. Plan to arrive at least a half hour before sunrise and to stay for three to four hours. Gary suggests making your reservation early, starting in January. Peak times of the month and weekends, especially, fill up quickly.

If you have questions about the barrens or sharp-tailed grouse, contact a DNR wildlife biologist at (715) 635-4091 or a wildlife technician at (715) 635-4092.

### HOW TO BECOME INVOLVED WITH
### SHARP-TAILED GROUSE CONSERVATION EFFORTS

Become a member of the Friends of the Namekagon Barrens Wildlife Area by going to www.fnbwa.org. The purpose of the group is to "*protect and preserve* essential constituents of native species that inhabit pine barrens habitats, *restore* the critical connections and biological relationships within pine barrens ecologies, *conserve* the corporate integrity and diversity of natural pine barrens communities within a stable geographical land base so that they are not lost, and *consecrate* a legacy that promotes an intergenerational continuity of such effort."

# 4

## American Bison:
## Peeking into the Mountain

### *MacKenzie Environmental Education Center in Poynette*

BISON HERD

Strike you our land
With curved horns.
Bending our bodies,
Breathe fire upon us.
Now with feet
Trampling the earth,
Let your hooves
Thunder over us.

—OJIBWE BUFFALO DANCE

Once, nothing on our nation's great prairies was more powerful—physically or spiritually—than the American bison (commonly known as buffalo). Even though females weigh about a thousand pounds and males may be upwards of a ton, bison are extremely agile: They can turn and run so fast that most animals, including humans, are unable to outmaneuver them.

The Lakota of the Great Plains trace the spiritual origins of their culture to the visit of a white bison. Long ago, this "White Buffalo Calf Woman" visited the Lakota and taught them how to make offerings to Earth Mother, Sky Father, and the four directions. She promised that as long as the people remembered the proper way to make these prayers, bison would remain around their camps and give themselves to the people for sustenance.

On the Medicine Wheel—a symbol used by native peoples in North and South America for more than ten thousand years—bison represent the North: a place of cleansing and renewal, wisdom, and knowledge-based, personal power. The color associated with the North on the wheel is white, the hue of snow. For the Lakota, if the Medicine Wheel's color and animal manifest together in the physical world, the result—in this case, a rare white buffalo—will be considered a powerful message.

Historically, bison had a range that encompassed most of the continental United States, from the Appalachians to the Rocky Mountains, and from Georgia all the way up to Hudson Bay in Canada. And Wisconsin's own southern and western prairies teemed with buffalo. But in 1832, after the onrush of white settlement, the last two bison east of the Mississippi River were shot in our state.

Today there are no free-roaming bison herds left on their native prairie habitat anywhere in our country. America's last significant wild bison herd—which is made up of about 3,000 animals (fluctuating between 2,300 to 4,500 individuals, according to the National Park Service)—lives within Idaho, Montana, and Wyoming's Yellowstone National Park. Currently, however, the National Wildlife Federation is working to restore a wild bison herd on lands around Montana's 1.1-million-acre Charles M. Russell National Wildlife Refuge.

But fortunately for Wisconsinites, there are a few of their number closer to home: at Poynette's MacKenzie Environmental Education Center.

## SOME VERY BIG QUESTIONS

"There's been a bison herd here at MacKenzie going back probably into the early 1960s," says Derek Duane, as we stand outside the bison pen on this 250-acre property owned by the Wisconsin DNR. The bison enclosure occupies about twenty of those acres, running alongside the road that takes you into the grounds, off Highways CS and Q.

Derek is the environmental center's former property manager, now employed by the Wisconsin Wildlife Federation. "When environmental education became a focus here," explains Derek, regarding the history of the herd at the center, "the staff looked for ways they could teach people about wildlife management. It was thought that having an animal here that *was* native to Wisconsin but is no longer found in the wild would be ideal. It would provide an opportunity to talk about the reasons why certain species become extirpated, which is primarily due to mismanagement of a resource. So, having bison on the property fills the bill.

"Of course," Derek continues, "it helps that by being so large and being something people don't normally see, bison also tend to command people's attentions. They elicit a *lot* of questions," he says with a laugh.

I'm lucky on this May day because although the MacKenzie Center typically has two cows and a bull on site, before me now stand two cows, a bull, two youngsters born the previous spring, and a brand-new baby bison.

## Fur and Game

But historically or presently, bison are by no means the only animals here at MacKenzie. On the day of my visit, the center is also honored with the presence of bobcats, white-tailed deer, cougars, coyotes, a wolf, and several raptors, including a bald eagle. All of them have been injured, orphaned, or raised in captivity and confiscated. Incapable of being released into the wild, these native animals of Wisconsin are sent to the Poynette center—located just twenty-five miles north of Madison—to live out the rest of their days in safety.

Although the Wisconsin DNR owns the center, the Wisconsin Wildlife Federation (affiliated with the National Wildlife Federation) manages the education program, the wildlife exhibits, and the grounds under a ten-year partnership agreement, which became effective on July 1, 2006. And the Friends of the MacKenzie Center, a local group of volunteers, provides funding support for the center's activities and manpower for the maple syrup program, trail maintenance, and various other projects.

What is now the MacKenzie Environmental Education Center actually started out as a "different animal"; that is, it was once the Wisconsin Experimental Game and Fur Farm. Prior to the mid-1930s, Wisconsin's game farm was located in Door County. (See chapter 5, "White-Tailed Deer: Ferreting Out a Phantom.") But in 1934, Harley MacKenzie, a man who had ties to Poynette and was director of the Wisconsin Conservation Department (later the Wisconsin Department of Natural Resources), started purchasing property here to move the facility. He believed that a central location would benefit more people than the northeastern site.

Says Derek, "In about 1936, during the Great Depression, the Works Progress Administration constructed our buildings. So there's a tremendous amount of skilled labor represented here. Then, responding to public demand, a raise-and-release program began. A variety of birds, including ring-necked pheasants and fur-bearing animals—such as foxes, minks, and raccoons—were raised for hunting and trapping purposes. Pens and cages covered much of the five-hundred-acre property. The birds and animals would then be released in various places throughout the state. But as the conservation movement grew in the early 1960s, the environmental education center split from the game farm, which is still adjacent today," he explains.

The part that became the environmental center was named for Harley MacKenzie in 1971. Today (and since the 1950s), the neighboring game farm raises only pheasants. Supported by pheasant-hunting license fees and the purchase of pheasant stamps, the game farm still releases forty thousand to sixty thousand birds every year.

The modern MacKenzie Center serves both individuals and school groups with environmental education programs and hands-on learning opportunities. Among its assets are an arboretum, a picnic area, nature trails, prairies in various states of restoration, a nature study pond, an observation tower, two environmentally themed museums, a maple syrup finishing house and sugar house, overnight lodging and eating facilities, and live wildlife exhibits. The wildlife exhibits trace their beginnings back to the 1930s and 1940s when people began bringing sick and injured animals to the game farm for rehabilitation. Today, the center houses about twenty different kinds of animals.

And one of those twenty kinds is the American bison (*Bison bison*). It's believed that the first bison to arrive at the center came from the Sandhill Wildlife Area's captive herd in Babcock, Wisconsin. (See chapter 5, "White-Tailed Deer: Ferreting Out a Phantom.")

## RUNNING DOWN THE NUMBERS

Small captive herds such as the one at Sandhill just may be what saved our nation's largest terrestrial mammal from complete annihilation.

About twenty thousand years ago, America's earliest peoples had begun to establish villages. At that time, bison flowed over our rolling grasslands and forested hillsides. Although no one will ever know exactly how many bison once inhabited North America, estimates range from 25 million to 70 million. Wood bison (*Bison bison athabascae*) existed in smaller numbers (no more than 170,000 at their peak).

Many Native American tribes on the Great Plains, such as the Cheyenne and Lakota, depended almost completely on bison for their livelihoods. Though killing such formidable, quick animals was a challenging task—bison can run for long periods at up to thirty-five miles per hour—effective techniques were developed. Some tribes surrounded small herds with a human chain, giving archers a better shot at the tightly packed group. Others learned to stampede bison over cliffs. Harvested bison provided not only gifts of meat and hides; virtually every part of the animal was put to use, from horns to tail hairs.

For thousands of years, then, the huge bison herds were able to accommodate the loss of the relatively few animals taken by Native Americans. In the sixteenth century, however, Spanish explorers introduced their horses to the continent, and things dramatically changed. By the nineteenth century, some Native American nations had become adept at using horses to chase bison, which expanded their hunting range. They also gained access to guns, significantly improving their hunting effectiveness.

White trappers and traders made a deeper dent in the great numbers of bison. By the 1870s, they were shipping hundreds of thousands of buffalo hides to the East each year; more than 1.5 million were packed on trains and in wagons in the winter of 1872–73 alone. But it was the arrival of vast waves of white settlers—and their conflict with several of the Native American tribes of the prairies—that really spelled the end for our nation's bison.

As these tribes started to resist the takeover of their lands by whites, some U.S. government officials promoted the destruction of the bison herds as a means to defeat them. One army general quipped that buffalo hunters "did more to defeat the Indian nations in a few years than soldiers did in fifty." And Congressman James Throckmorton of Texas is quoted as saying that "it would be a great step forward in the civilization of the Indians and the preservation of peace on the border if there was not a buffalo in existence." Soon, military commanders were ordering their troops to kill buffalo—not for their own meals, but to keep Native Americans on the Great Plains from getting theirs.

Adding to the carnage were the train companies. They started to offer tourists the chance to shoot buffalo from their coach windows. In 1867, the Kansas Pacific Railroad hired "Buffalo Bill" Cody to slaughter the animals for the construction crew's meat. He is said to have killed more than 4,000 bison in seventeen months. And in 1873, in a "buffalo killing contest," a Kansan by the name of Tom Nixon was reported to have set a record by shooting 120 bison in forty minutes. Later in that year, he set another record for having killed more than 3,200 buffalo in just thirty-five days.

The World Wildlife Fund estimates that before 1800, there were 30 to 60 million bison living in North America. By the late nineteenth century, however, fewer than 1,000 survived on our Great Plains. The largest wild herd—just a few hundred animals—found sanctuary in the isolated valleys of Yellowstone National Park, newly created in 1872. Luckily, around 1900, the federal government took steps to protect and increase the herds of bison remaining. In Yellowstone and other national preserves, the bison were carefully protected by laws, and in 1908 a National Bison Range Wildlife Refuge was established in Montana.

Fortunately, during all this decimation, a number of people were also establishing small, captive herds. The United States Department of Agriculture estimates that there are now approximately 150,000 bison roaming both public and private lands in the U.S. today. The National Bison Association attributes that growth to conservation efforts and the increasing recognition of the culinary and health advantages of bison meat.

## A Wisconsin Miracle

In fact, many believe that it is bison meat that is partially responsible for North America's earliest people coming to our continent. During the Ice Ages, much of the earth's seawater froze into glaciers, lowering the sea level. Dry land appeared where once there was water. One of these "land bridges," called *Beringia*, joined Siberia and Alaska. Although the Bering Land Bridge theory is still hotly contested, proponents say that it is likely that the first people who came to North America were following herds of horses, woolly mammoths, and bison that crossed the bridge. When the Ice Ages ended, water once again flowed over the land bridges, and they disappeared. The woolly mammoths and horses eventually became extinct. Only the descendants of the ancient bison survived.

These early bison were enormous animals, weighing up to five thousand pounds. Their massive heads sported horns that spanned more than six feet across. Over time, however, North American bison evolved into a smaller, trimmer animal. Modern bull bison are about twelve feet long. Both sexes stand up to six feet tall at the shoulder hump, a complex of muscles supported by long vertebrae that allows the bison to use its head as a snowplow in winter. Swinging their heads side to side, bison are able to sweep aside the snow in order to find the vegetation underneath.

Being that big, of course, means that you can generally do *what* you want, *when* you want to do it. As Derek attests, "One time, after one of our bulls died, we procured another, new bull. He was brought to the center in the morning, about 9:00 a.m. or so, in the back of a stock truck. He was positioned with his head facing out, toward the back of the truck. We parked the vehicle in the middle of the upper bison field, opened the back, and put the ramps down. But we just *could not* get this bull to come out of the truck. We did everything we could think of to get him to leave it—and he wouldn't do it. We even tried to parade the females past him, thinking that would get his attention. But that didn't work, either. When you're that big, you can pretty much call the shots!

"So, we all went to lunch," continues Derek, "and we left the bull there. After we got back, I went back up to the field with Greg, one of our maintenance staff. Greg wanted to check in on the bull, so he stuck his head in the back of the truck. And all of a sudden, that bison shot out like a rocket! I guess he decided that that was the time to come out. It really scared us. After several hours of trying to get him to come out, all it took was just one peek!"

Modern adult bison are about six feet tall. The characteristic hump begins to appear at about two months of age. (Photo: John T. Andrews)

Not only are bison hardheaded; it turns out they are also very hardy. They can survive extreme weather conditions in which other large animals would perish. A bison's thick, shaggy underfur and long guard hairs are so insulating that snow can settle on its back without melting. In spring, when bison begin to shed their heavy winter coats, they often rub against large stones and trees. Travelers going across the Great Plains in the 1880s often wrote of seeing highly polished rocks and trunks with the bark rubbed off six to seven feet above the ground.

In summer, though, without the protection of those heavy coats, bison are especially vulnerable to insect attack. To escape such torment, they often wallow in dust or sand. Those on the Great Plains in the 1880s were also apt to see buffalo wallows that measured a foot or more deep and fifteen feet across.

The bison-breeding season is in July and August. Gestation may be from 270 to 285 days, with most calves being born in May.

One famous Wisconsin calf, however, made her first appearance on August 20, 1994. At 6:00 a.m., Janesville family farmer Dave Heider went out to check on a buffalo that he knew was about ready to give birth. When he reached the cow, what he found surprised him: she had with her a white calf with brown eyes, nose, and tail tip. Because Heider had never seen a white calf before, he called a journalist friend. Heider thought the baby bison might make a cute feature for the local newspaper.

But after the Associated Press picked up the story, members of the Lakota, Dakota, and Nakota Nations (along with representatives of many other tribes) started to arrive at the Heider farm. They brought gifts and prayers for the white calf. Soon thousands of people were coming to see her, and she was named Miracle.

Over her lifetime, Miracle's fur changed color four times, just as prophesied in many Native American legends. When her first winter coat grew in, she turned deep brown. In early 1995, she turned black; then in June of that year, her color turned to a deep red. In July 1997, she transitioned to a pale yellow. She was beginning to turn white again just before her death of natural causes on September 19, 2004.

The Heider farm saw a second female white buffalo calf (called Lady Miracle) born in 1996, but she died after four days. A third white buffalo calf, a male, was born there during a lightning storm on August 25, 2006. Named Miracle's Second Chance, he was killed by lightning during a storm on November 26 of the same year.

White buffalo are the exception, of course. Most bison calves vary in color from red to cinnamon. Normally, a cow will give birth to a single calf, but on rare occasions twins will be born. They show no sign of the characteristic hump until about two months of age. Both males and females will develop sharp, curved horns.

"Bison are very protective of young; all the adults will protect the calves, not just the mothers," says Derek. "I remember one time when we had a calf born here. A few days later, another staff member and I stopped to look in on it on our way home from work. We saw the bull standing next to the calf and the cow. Then, all of a sudden, the bull put one of his horns underneath the calf and threw it into the air several feet—just like it was a little, stuffed animal! The calf came down, and, luckily, it was fine. But we just looked at each other. Usually, the bison are very protective of the young. We just couldn't imagine why he did that. It's possible he wanted to get the calf away from us," postulates Derek, "or maybe he just goofed!"

Bison normally live fifteen to twenty years, but they are capable of achieving up to forty years of age. It is their athleticism, though, that astounds most people.

Says Derek, "I've always been amazed at how graceful and fast these animals are. In their twenty-acre field here at MacKenzie, most of the time the bison are

All the adult bison will protect the calves, not just the mothers. These two bison made sure they stood between me and the calf I was photographing. (Photo: Candice Gaukel Andrews)

just walking around, taking their time. But I think they get spring fever like everybody else. They don't do it often, but every once in a while they'll just take off. They're not running out of fear or out of anything else that's obvious; they just decide to run. They can go from one end of the field to the other in a matter of seconds. It's just a thrill to see that—two-thousand-pound animals running together, flat out."

### A Place for—and for Learning about—the Wild

While the sight of flat-out-running bison certainly makes the "environment" part of the MacKenzie Environmental Education Center thrilling, the "education" component is equally enticing. School-group visits are important to the mission of the place, and the bison are a key species for capturing not only the children's attentions but their imaginations as well.

Explains Derek, "When I ask the kids that visit here why Wisconsin doesn't have bison anymore, they typically answer, 'Because we shot them.' That's direct and to the point, but another reasonable response is that so many people came into the state in the 1830s, 1840s, and 1850s that we just didn't leave room for the bison anymore. And we didn't understand wildlife management strategies at all back then. Having the bison at MacKenzie is a great chance to get the next generation really engaged in that type of learning and caring."

Because parents today are worried about the copious amounts of time children now spend indoors in front of electronic media, the demand for outdoor education services—such as those found at MacKenzie—is growing. As a result, new programs to serve that need are constantly being instituted at the center.

"Four staff at the center have now been trained as instructors for the National Archery in the Schools Program," states Derek proudly. "We have learn-to-hunt programs for deer and turkey, and we're hoping to expand that into courses for hunting rabbits, squirrels, and pheasants. What's really cool is that we're also now teaching kids how to build fire by friction, with a bow drill. They don't usually start a fire, but they sometimes get a little smoke! Both kids and adults love *that*," he reports.

Another skill currently being taught is how to erect a "debris hut."

"When I was a kid," says Derek, "we called it 'building a fort.' Alex, one of our educators, is a pure environmentalist. He lives off the land as best he can and occasionally lives in a debris hut. At the center, he'll take kids outside to talk about survival skills and then show them how to build such a shelter out of sticks and leaves. Now, when I walk over to the lodge, instead of seeing kids outside just goofing around like they usually do, I see them adding to their huts and improving them. We've now got debris huts all over the place!"

This plethora of debris huts, however, isn't the only abundance that defines the Poynette area for Derek. "There's a tremendous amount of history here," he says, when I ask him what makes this parcel of Wisconsin so special, "that goes all the way back to the Native Americans and the fur-trading days. But the profusion of wildlife out here is what's truly phenomenal. It's just amazing what you can find: black bears, sandhill cranes, foxes, Canada geese, ducks, and even wolves."

But of the area's wild animals, the one that holds the topmost position in Derek's heart is the cougar. And that could be because of one particular, captive individual he met at MacKenzie. "We've had wild mountain lion sightings within five miles of the facility," says Derek. "And the mountain lions here at the center have always been pretty high on my list. We lost our male mountain lion to old age early in the winter of 2011. That was very difficult; all of us were pretty fond of that animal, mostly because of his personality and his size. He and his sibling came to us through a confiscation, about fourteen years ago. He was just very special," Derek tells me.

## Personal Protection Agency

Attachment seems to run deep at MacKenzie, for all animals—human and nonhuman alike.

"About five years ago, we had a bison calf that died right after birth," relates Derek. "The dead calf happened to be lying out in the field next to the road, where people could see it as they drove into the facility. It was a bit disturbing for visitors. So, we wanted to remove the calf, but the bison would *not* let us. For one thing, the mother wouldn't leave the calf. She stayed close by it for a couple of days. We tried to get near the deceased newborn with a tractor, but when we did, the other bison came flying at us. So rather than risk any injury to the animals, we backed off.

"About the third day, when the mother finally left the calf and went to the other end of the field with all the other bison," continues Derek, "I said, 'Now's the time. Let's go in and try to quickly remove the calf.' A few of us opened the gate and went in with a tractor. As soon as we got to the calf, all the bison started coming toward us! We hurriedly loaded the calf into the bucket and got out of there *just* in time," says Derek. "Their instincts are just amazing."

## Buffalo Mountain

Derek talks of another bison that got protective; only this time, it was over—of all things—a bale of hay.

"Shortly after I got here, some big, round bales of hay were donated to the center," recalls Derek. "We decided to give them to the bison, so the animals would have something to continually munch on. The bull we had at that time was extremely territorial. We got into an old Ford pickup and dropped one of the bales into the pen. All of a sudden, the bull began to butt the grille of the truck—while we were in it! He was banging away at it, trying to chase us out of there. It seemed as if he had decided that that bale of hay was *his* and his alone. He started to destroy it, tear it apart. After a couple of days, that whole round bale was just flattened out, and all the bison were lying in it. But trying to get it in there was a thrill ride, to say the least! I think he just wanted his space."

Space for bison to be bison is, perhaps, what they need from us the most.

The Kiowa tell a tale of a time long ago, after white people had killed thousands of bison, left their carcasses to rot on the prairies, and piled their hides high on railroad cars. The Buffalo became concerned and decided to hold a council. It was determined that they should go to a place where white humans could not find them. They offered to take the Kiowa with them, but the Kiowa opted to stay on their land, the place where they had lived for thousands of years.

The next morning, in the misty dawn, the Buffalo walked to the foot of a large mountain. The mountain opened up and swallowed them. However, it is said that when a new white bison calf appears, it will be the sign that the Buffalo will come back from inside the mountain and roam free on the land once again.

### EYE TO THE STONE

It could be that the *right* white buffalo calf hasn't been born yet, or that the days when great bison herds rippled over the grasslands and prairies like waves and sounded like thunder are over, never to return.

But in Poynette, Wisconsin, at least, it's possible to find a small crack in that Kiowa mountain, put an eye up to the cold stone, and take a peek at the past.

## HOW TO HAVE A GENUINE
## AMERICAN BISON ENCOUNTER OF YOUR OWN

Admission to the **MacKenzie Environmental Education Center** is free to the general public; however, donations are greatly appreciated. The center grounds are open daily, dawn to dusk. The museums and wildlife exhibits are open daily, 8:00 a.m. to 4:00 p.m., the first full weekend in May through the last full weekend in October; and Monday through Friday, 8:00 a.m. to 4:00 p.m., November through April. All of the wildlife exhibits and some of the trails are handicap accessible.

The **MacKenzie Environmental Education Center** offers classes to elementary and middle school students on a variety of environmental topics, including forest ecology, pond and stream ecology, outdoor skills training, and wildlife management. All programs include classroom instruction and field experiences. One-day or multiday camp programs can be designed to meet the educational needs of students. Call (608) 635-8105 to learn more about classes and the overnight program.

At the **Sandhill Wildlife Area** in Babcock (see chapter 5, "White-Tailed Deer: Ferreting Out a Phantom"), a small herd of bison resides in a 260-acre enclosure along the Trumpeter Trail auto tour. The trail is open seasonally, usually during the snow-free months, roughly from the middle of April to the end of October.

## HOW TO BECOME INVOLVED WITH
## AMERICAN BISON CONSERVATION EFFORTS

To help support the **MacKenzie Environmental Education Center**, you can deposit donations into boxes found throughout the facility. Or, to make a specific donation for the wildlife species of your choice, such as the American bison, contact the center at (608) 635-8105.

To become a member of the Friends of MacKenzie, visit www.mackenzie center.com/friends-of-mac-about.php.

At the **Sandhill Wildlife Area,** you can help restore the bison pasture to a native oak savanna—which will increase your chances of seeing bison in their native habitat—by donating to a special gift account. Funds will go directly to habitat restoration efforts. To make a contribution, use the donation box in the Sandhill Wildlife Area office during normal business hours or write to: Sandhill Wildlife Area, P.O. Box 156, Babcock, WI 54413-0156.

# SUMMER

(Photo: Candice Gaukel Andrews)

# 5

# White-Tailed Deer: Ferreting Out a Phantom

## Sandhill Wildlife Area in Babcock

### WHITE-TAILED DEER HERD

Enclosed by a nine-foot-tall, wire and wooden-post fence, the place looks intimidating enough. And the litany of regulations signs posted on the big gate makes me begin to wonder if I'll actually be allowed entrance. But looks can be deceiving.

All you really have to do to get *in* is get *out* of your car and swing open that large gate. Drive through, idle the engine for a moment while you get out of the car to close the gate again, buckle up once more, and you're on your way.

The other deception here is that because you're going inside an enclosed area, you'd assume the animals you'll encounter must know that they're captive. Nothing could be further from the truth. What's inside the 9,150-acre Sandhill Wildlife Area, located in Babcock, Wisconsin, is definitely wild.

This Wisconsin DNR property is currently home to about 218 wild white-tailed deer. I'm here on a late June afternoon, a couple of hours before dusk, to see if I can catch a glimpse of one. And according to Dick Thiel, currently a workshop leader at the Sandhill Outdoor Skills Center, I've come to the perfect place. He says the number one reason people come to Sandhill is to see white-tailed deer.

And, surprisingly, one of the best ways to do it here is from the comfort of your automobile.

## UNSEEN COMPANIONS

No other large, wild mammal lives and prospers so near to humans as does the white-tailed deer (*Odocoileus virginianus*). Although there are probably more than a million deer in Wisconsin—keeping in mind that numbers vary with the years and the seasons—a long and cherished hunting tradition in the state makes

The nine-foot-tall fence surrounding the Sandhill Wildlife Area seems, at first, to keep everything out. But once you venture inside, the animals you'll find are definitely wild. (Photo: Candice Gaukel Andrews)

them shy of having any contact with us. So, they choose to dwell just beyond the edge of our senses and streetlights. They drift through our yards when we're sleeping and raid our gardens. They are, for the most part, our unseen companions, our wild "familiars." Wild deer are graceful and shy, lingering at civilization's fringes, slipping back into the forest if we dare to look too closely. It is no wonder we like to spot them.

The word *deer* (in its original spelling, *deor*), in fact, was once the Old English word for *animal* in general. And *wilddeoren* once simply meant "the place of wild animals."

My path to finding a place with deer will take the form of the Trumpeter Trail auto tour that begins just inside Sandhill Wildlife Area's big gate. And according to a brochure titled *Trumpeter Trail Nature Interpretive Guide* that I picked up at the trailhead, this fourteen-mile route that winds through Sandhill should take about two hours. I hope that's enough time for a white-tailed deer—Wisconsin's official State Wildlife Animal—to show itself to me.

## CONTAINED, BUT CONTENT

The fenced-in portion of Wood County's Sandhill Wildlife Area covers an area of more than fourteen square miles. Managed as a "living laboratory" for wildlife

Restored prairies, large marshes, and several flowages add their beauty to the Sandhill Wildlife Area. (Photo: John T. Andrews)

management techniques, Sandhill holds large marshes; several flowages; low, sandy uplands; pine and oak barrens; and restored prairies.

But the best thing about Sandhill, if you ask Dick Thiel, a thirty-three-year veteran of the DNR and the former coordinator for the Sandhill Outdoor Skills Center, is that tall fence. "The animals don't know it's there," says Dick. "And that fence controls or limits human access. A lot of wildlife needs some sanctuary away from people. Certain species seem to be more comfortable here—less stressed—than they are in other nearby terrains where there are people all over the place.

"But," he admits, "some people get scared off by the fence; Sandhill almost looks like a prison! I've actually seen people pull up to the gate, take one look at all the signs there, get totally miffed, turn around, and leave. Even though all they have to do is get out of the car and open the gate, most people don't. It's rather interesting."

While Stop 1 on the auto tour is a brief welcome and Stop 2 lists some wildlife observation tips, by the time I reach Stop 3, Wetlands: A Valuable Wildlife Commodity, I'm extremely happy that I was one of the brave souls who ventured in. With all four car windows rolled down on this sunny summer afternoon, I soon hear the unmistakable prehistoric garbles that can issue forth only from sandhill cranes (see chapter 10, "Sandhill Cranes: Going Out for the Night, as They Come In"). I turn my gaze skyward. Just as I do, a flock of the big birds comes wheeling in, on approach to their marsh landing on my left.

At Stop 4, the Swamp Buck Hiking Trail, that green, wild marsh beckons me in, too, and I find I *must* get out of the car and walk for a while. Although I could keep trekking on this trail for three and a half miles and end up at a volcanic-rock outcrop called the North Bluff, it only takes a few paces for me to feel ensconced in the natural world and enveloped in birdsong. A few steps on, just beyond some marsh-side trees, I discover two sandhill cranes fishing, oblivious to my presence.

At Bison and Butterflies (Stop 6), I again put the shift in the Park position and exit the vehicle to climb the Bison Barrens Observation Tower. Bright yellows, intense oranges, and the pure whites of prairie wildflowers color this wide perspective on an oak barrens. Beyond Stop 11, Rock of Ages Past, I find myself climbing again, this time up a steep hill ascending to North Bluff, which rises two hundred feet above the surrounding landscape. From the observation tower on top, I can see more bluffs off in the blue distance of my twenty-mile vista.

## A Living Lab for Research—and Education

It turns out that Sandhill is a place not only of panoramic visions but of prominent visionaries as well.

At the height of the Great Depression, pioneer wildlife biologist Wallace Grange and his wife, Hazel, managed the property under the name of Sandhill Game Farm, Inc. Dick Thiel familiarizes me with some of the history here.

"The land that is now Sandhill was probably used by the Ho-Chunk until the 1830s," he tells me. "Sometime during the 1850s, the first white settlers established homesteads in the area and swiftly started taking out the white pine and other extractable commodities. They then transitioned into agriculture. We are aware of six or seven farmsteads here that may have lasted until the late 1920s. But by 1930, all of that land had been abandoned; it was tax delinquent. It reverted back to Wood County's ownership."

It was then that Wallace Grange started to acquire some of these tax delinquent lands from the county. Between 1930 and 1937, he was able to purchase about seven thousand acres.

"Wallace Grange was a wildlife biologist before there even really was a recognized profession of wildlife biology," explains Dick. "He was in that mix of people across the nation—such as Aldo Leopold and Adolph and Olaus Murie—that literally were the forefathers of professional wildlife management. Wallace was, by current terms, the first director of what is today the Wisconsin Bureau of Wildlife Management. In 1928, the Wisconsin Department of Natural Resources' predecessor agency, the Wisconsin Conservation Commission (later the Wisconsin Conservation Department), created a position with the title of director of Game Management Division and asked Wallace to fill it. His job was to survey all game distributions in the state and to work with game wardens and fire control personnel to establish areas to put aside for wildlife. With just one half-time secretary, he helped establish the first game farm in Wisconsin, which was located near Peninsula State Park in Door County." (See chapter 4, "American Bison: Peeking into the Mountain.")

In the early 1930s, a period of infancy for wildlife management, many populations of wild animals in the state—such as deer, pheasants, and ruffed grouse—had already been largely depleted. And for the wildlife that was left, habitats were quickly disappearing. The Manifest Destiny beliefs of late-nineteenth-century Americans led them to take out everything of value from the land: from minerals to forests, to turning prairies into farmlands, to almost wiping out the game populations for food.

"So," says Dick, "there was this scramble to figure out how to replenish Wisconsin's wildlife and how to do it rapidly. Wallace was right in the fray. He started to tinker around with different techniques for managing habitats, and that became his forte.

"After two years, though, he left his position with the Wisconsin Conservation Commission," continues Dick. "I think he probably had a high frustration level with what he thought were the molasses-type movements of government. He was totally passionate about wildlife, and I believe the reason why he acquired the Sandhill property was that he wanted to experiment with the concept we now know as 'habitat management.' In other words, he wanted to play with the landscape and see what kind of response he'd get in terms of populations of wild animals based on what he did to the land to enhance the food, shelter, and other components."

But Wallace also needed to earn a living after leaving his state job, so he came up with an innovative idea: why not supply wild game animals to government entities as a private-sector businessman?

Says Dick, "Essentially, the concept was this: if I can quickly quantity-produce pheasants, ruffed grouse, mallards, geese, and even deer—and do it efficiently— then capture these animals and release them out onto habitats that have been managed for them, maybe we can reestablish populations of these animals in the wild. So, he got all the permits that he needed from the state, constructed a fence around the whole fourteen miles of his acquisition in southwestern Wood County, and called it the Sandhill Game Farm, Inc. He opened the doors in 1937."

Over the next twenty-five years that Wallace and Hazel Grange owned their game farm, deer live-trapped on Sandhill not only were released in Wisconsin but were also shipped to and released in such far-flung places as Florida, Georgia, and Mississippi in order to jump-start the diminishing deer herds there.

"Wallace knew how to raise deer; he had a lot of them—probably kept them artificially high or higher than what the habitat could support," states Dick. "But he certainly knew how to manipulate habitats to produce things. Of course, today, deer management is exceedingly controversial among certain user groups, notably deer hunters. And, it was that way back then, too. So early-day wildlife researchers who were working with deer in Wisconsin desired and *needed* a place where they could manipulate deer herds, habitat, and even numbers of hunters to basically watch what happened to the deer herd as a consequence of such things. For instance, what would happen to Wisconsin's deer population in terms of age and sex ratios if we had a two-week season rather than a one-week season? Or, how do deer numbers respond to changes in forest habitat? So, essentially, all eyes were on Sandhill. Wallace was well known to DNR personnel, and there was discourse between them constantly, in terms of what he was doing. While the place wasn't run without controversy, a lot of people respected Wallace and what he did."

But by the late 1950s, interest in stocking deer faded as state deer herds began to rebound. And after running Sandhill for a quarter of a century, the Granges felt they were ready for retirement. They began to look for a buyer for their beloved game farm, one that would promote the ideals of conservation through research—and education.

Deer research biologists and many game managers were interested in acquiring Sandhill. They knew that with some improvements, the deer-tight (or as deer-tight as anything *can* be) fence surrounding the property would provide the perfect barrier or "contained laboratory." In such an environment, they would be able to test various management strategies in an attempt to answer pressing questions on deer herd management. They would gain a place where they could study the behavior of the deer hunters who used the site, as well.

The Wisconsin Conservation Department's Game Management Division (the Bureau of Wildlife Management's predecessor) decided to buy the property, and in 1962, Governor Gaylord Nelson signed a purchase agreement.

"Sandhill's size also made it extremely desirable for biologists," says Dick. "The deer on Sandhill don't even know they're captive. So they therefore are predisposed to behave normally. Even back then, there was an acknowledgment that animals in zoo settings display different behaviors *because* of being confined. Scientific research has to meet certain criteria. If you're studying a deer herd and you've only got a square mile to do it in, a lot of those animals are going to be exhibiting behaviors reflective of being confined. But if you've got a laboratory like Sandhill, which is fourteen square miles, most of those deer have never even seen the fence because they live in the interior."

Since the early 1960s, then, what is now the DNR has used the site as a deer research facility. But the Granges had a caveat as a condition of their sale: the land was to be also used to provide opportunities for wildlife education. To address that requirement, the Outdoor Skills Center was established at Sandhill in the early 1990s. Today, numerous programs appealing to a variety of interests are offered: from learning how to hunt and trap to studying wildlife ecology; from honing skills tracking carnivores to tagging turtles; and even how to use a dutch oven when cooking in the outdoors.

I get out of the car at Stop 12 on the Trumpeter Trail auto tour, just past the halfway point. The stop is titled Grange's Sandhill Game Farm. According to the brochure, Wallace's interest in wildlife started when he was a boy. On weekends, he would hike the ten miles home from the high school where he boarded during the week and write down notes about the wildlife he found along the way.

Wallace Grange died in 1987, and Hazel passed away ten years later. He was inducted into Wisconsin's Conservation Hall of Fame in 1993. I imagine Wallace and Hazel standing shoulder to shoulder here today, between the two small bodies of water where I now stand.

I watch as two elegant and curvy trumpeter swans float nearby on their wetland sanctuary, decorated with scores of lily pads in full bloom.

### Engineered to Disappear

By this time in the tour, I'm wishing I could stretch my legs out as long as a white-tailed deer's. Their graceful, long limbs—a well as their joints, bones, and almost all of their other features—are designed to get them quietly about the forest, so unlike my short, noisy appendages.

A whitetail's narrow, tapered hooves are specialized to allow minimal contact with the ground, reducing friction and increasing speed. Whitetails can run up to forty miles per hour. Those narrow hooves also allow a deer to easily place its feet quietly amid the forest floor's noisy leaves and twigs.

When a whitetail is moving at normal walking speed on flat ground, its hind prints will register a tiny bit in and slightly to the rear of its front footprints, leaving a track that shows that the hind and front feet are placed almost exactly on the same spot on the ground. The advantage of this is that once the front hooves have been safely and quietly placed, the deer knows that its rear steps will be equally as quiet.

Like many prey species, white-tailed deer have remarkably acute senses. It's said that a deer's nose is one hundred times more sensitive than a human being's nose. Not only can deer differentiate between animal species through just the use of scent, but there is evidence that they can also determine the age of an odor. A wolf scent that is old seems to cause a far different physical reaction than one that is fresh.

When it comes to danger, a deer's sense of smell is the ultimate warning system. A deer doesn't need to see a predator—wolf, cougar, or human—to know that it needs to disappear. One good whiff is enough to make a deer decide whether to stand or flee.

Researchers think that whitetails see some color, especially in the yellow and blue ranges. They also believe deer are least sensitive to long wavelengths—those in the red-orange range. Some studies have indicated that whitetails may see well in the ultraviolet range, which is invisible to humans.

But whether or not they see color, deer are remarkably adept at seeing motion. The slightest movement will cause a deer to focus intently. If you're the source of that movement, it will seem like an eternity that a deer can stand unblinking, waiting for you to move again. Often, they'll lower their heads for a moment, giving the impression that they are no longer observing you. But move a fraction of an inch, and they'll snap their heads back up and vanish in a flurry of bounds and snorts.

A whitetail's brown coat is designed to blend in with many surroundings. The darkest hair is on the top—especially along the spine—which gives the deer a shadowy look when light is cast from above. Grayish hair scattered through the shoulders and haunches of its winter coat also tends to make a deer appear ghostlike, helping it dissolve into the colors of the trunks of trees. White patches beneath the chin and along the entire underside help to break up a deer's own natural shadow, so it looks less three-dimensional to predators passing by. The white underside of the tail flashes as a warning when danger is sensed, and it waves when the deer runs.

It is the fawn, however, that takes first prize when it comes to camouflaging makeup. Reddish brown in color, the fawn's coat has two rows of white spots down either side of the spine and an array of randomly placed white spots elsewhere. While a fawn is lying motionless in hiding, it is almost impossible to see it, blending in with the dappled sunlight that drifts down to the forest floor through the leaves of trees. The fawn's spots disappear when it completes its first molt, at about five months old.

While a buck's antlers will serve as weapons against predators and other whitetail rivals, for the most part these elaborate ornaments are there so they *won't* have to fight. Social dominance for a male whitetail is largely determined by body and antler size. Since generally the largest bucks produce the largest antlers, this headgear is a visual display of status. Small bucks fear large bucks, so the rare combat that does occur is usually between rivals of equal stature. Thus, the antlers that we humans are so fascinated with mostly *prevent* fights.

Sandhill's deer are particularly known for their antlers. Says Dick, "Since the 1980s, we have been trying to manipulate our deer herd to have a slightly larger percent of the adult population as bucks. We've also tried to increase the age of those bucks. Increasing the age of bucks, up to a certain point, gives the bucks

The white-tailed deer is an animal of incredible beauty and power. The number one reason that people come to the Sandhill Wildlife Area is to see one. (Photo: John T. Andrews)

bigger racks. So in the last twenty or thirty years, Sandhill has become *the* popular place for seeing really big-antlered bucks. When we do surveys of why people come here, always the number one reason listed is to see white-tailed deer."

## CENSUS-TAKERS

Spotting those deer is also important to the staff at Sandhill, since to manage the herd, they need to know how many animals they have. Dick explains the census process to me.

"About every other year since the late 1960s—depending upon budgets— we have been doing a helicopter survey of the deer herd on Sandhill. We conduct the census usually in the month of February when the snows are deep and the oak leaves are starting to fall off the trees so you can see down through the forest. We attempt to count every deer. The helicopter works a system of strips, back and forth and back and forth, sequentially going through every square mile on Sandhill. Spotters on the ground keep track of any animals that get spooked and jump across to another section while the helicopters are working in a segment, in order to ensure that no deer is counted twice and the figures are as accurate as possible. Although we also use other techniques to count deer, the helicopter method is the gold standard for measuring our deer herd to this day," says Dick.

In fact, one of the reasons that Sandhill was acquired by the state is that it's the perfect place to experiment with how to most accurately count a deer herd. "Sandhill has figured prominently over the years in terms of that kind of research," says Dick. "What kinds of techniques can you play with to accomplish that task? Now, keep in mind that most years we have a deer hunt. Because the property is fenced and has a single gate, all of the hunters have to pass through that gate to exit the property. When a hunter comes out, the deer is taken from his or her car. It is weighed, sexed, and aged. That information becomes part of a database that is unsurpassed anywhere else in the world for white-tailed deer because we've been doing it for fifty-odd years. And with that data, we can reconstruct the white-tailed deer population.

"Let's say that I pull a doe out of the trunk of a car," Dick goes on to explain. "I open up its mouth to age it [by its teeth], and it was a six-year-old animal. Let's also say it was shot in November 2011. I can backdate it to when it was born, so that would be in the spring of 2005. Imagine that next year, a hunter exits with a seven-year-old doe. That deer was also born in 2005. So essentially, I can reconstruct the birth years of literally *every* deer that comes out of Sandhill. All I have to do is have patience and wait until that generation is extinct.

"For the 2005 tally, then," says Dick, "we would probably in 2011 have already accounted for some 85 percent of those deer. We know that because we not only have data on 2005, we have data on 1995 deer, 1985 deer, 1975 deer—and all of the years going back to Sandhill's acquisition in 1962. By using that data, we can construct a graph showing when you would expect to wipe out 85 percent of a particular year's herd, known as a *cohort*. Now that doesn't mean that we've actually—by a certain time in 2011—taken 85 percent; maybe it's 83 percent or 92 percent. On an average basis, however, we know what we can anticipate based on how many years have elapsed since the birth of that particular group of animals. Eventually, then, we know the size of that cohort. Say that in 2005 there were 200 fawns born. We might compare that with 1995 when there were only 140 born, or something similar.

"Only about 10 percent of the birth of a cohort doesn't come out in the trunks of cars," Dick states. "Those deaths would be attributed to things like accidents, coyotes, or disease. Each year is different. We try to get into those populations and look back retrospectively, figure out what was going on. For instance, what was the weather like that year? You can see how incredible the

Sandhill property is in terms of deer management. It's a side to Sandhill that people don't usually get to see; it's like watching how a doctor works behind the scenes. Sandhill gives us that kind of a laboratory."

## A CIRCLE OF SCIENCE

It turns out that that laboratory is one not only for professional biologists and researchers, but for amateurs—children—as well. And over the past thirty-three years, that's been one of the most rewarding things for Dick.

"Professionally," says Dick, I am a wildlife *biologist*. Before I came to Sandhill, I was doing research work. But quite frankly, when I became a wildlife *educator* for Sandhill, what I enjoyed most was working with kids and teaching them about the wild. Over the many years I've worked here, I've organized several youth hunting and trapping programs. And that's cool in itself. But teaching those very hunters how we get the information that allows them to do what they do is what's really interesting.

"As my job evolved at Sandhill," Dick recollects, "I think what I enjoyed the most was starting programs where high school and college kids participated in *actual, usable* wildlife research. I'd take the information derived from their work here and use it to work with succeeding school groups coming in. So the kids knew that their productivity was actually being used; that whatever they did at Sandhill wasn't a dead-end street; that we weren't going to just close the book on it when they left. I'd tell the next group that 'this is what the previous bunch did—I've actually used kids just like you to do this—and this is what they found. Now, let's build on that.' We even turned around and actually made adult workshops out of some of that stuff."

Straddling the worlds of research and education as he has for so many years at Sandhill has made Dick believe that you shouldn't have one without the other.

"My administrators would sometimes question me," says Dick with a laugh. "They'd say, 'You're doing research, when you should be concentrating on education programs.' I'd say, 'You know what? You can do all the research you want until you turn blue in the face, but if you don't *do* anything with that information, you're accomplishing nothing. The only value to doing research is to take that information and turn it over to the public. That process is called *education*.'"

## HATS OFF TO HUNTERS

Of course, no discussion about *watching* white-tailed deer in Wisconsin would be complete without also addressing *hunting* white-tailed deer in Wisconsin—

and Dick gives those hunters a lot of credit for providing the watchers among us with the subjects we so love to see.

"My salary at Sandhill, the whole education program, the supplies that I worked with, and the building itself were all paid for entirely with hunting dollars that came through license fees," states Dick. "I've always felt that Wisconsin's deer hunters are very generous. In fact, I *know* that they are, having worked with a lot of them.

"When I teach youths in the learn-to-hunt deer program," continues Dick, "I always use substantial data. In that way, I combine hunting with research. Sometimes, though, I have kids coming in that are interested in ecology and not interested in hunting per se—or might even be averse to hunting. So I'll say some things about deer and then tell them that this data is compliments of the deer hunters. Now, *they* can take this information and go out there and watch deer, see their sign, and benefit from the studies we're doing here at Sandhill with the hunters. But without the hunters here, we wouldn't be able to answer the questions that they're interested in. We wouldn't have the tools, the methodology, or the money. We wouldn't have the know-how, because hunting is what drives the system."

In fact, at Sandhill during most deer hunting seasons, the first permits are given to participants in the youth learn-to-hunt-deer program. To determine the number of permits to issue on Sandhill in any one year, a "deer committee" gathers two or three times annually to figure out what that number should be. Committee members analyze the data and discuss questions such as: How did last year's hunt go? What's the current composition of the herd? What is the size of the herd now, posthunt (taken from the census), and where do we want it to be next year? How many permits would it take to get to that point?

Says Dick, "We can factor in what our fawn improvements are going to be because we know approximately how many fawns are going to be born, on average, based on all the data we have. Then we consider competing forces, such as research project requests, which will adjust up or down the number of permits issued for the upcoming hunt. We try to reasonably accommodate research requests from outside groups because we feel that that's part and parcel of the property's mission."

## THE PHANTOM MAKES AN APPEARANCE

At Stop 14 of the auto tour, Ghosts from the Past, I get out again to stretch and move about. This is the former site of the Gallagher family homestead. Sometime around 1930, the farm reverted to Wood County, due to unpaid taxes. The stone foundation of one of the Gallaghers' buildings still rests among the cliff break ferns that now seem to be the real "owners" of the property. A tree grows in the middle of what I imagine would have been their home's living room floor.

I glance at my watch and see that what should have been a two-hour drive— at least according to the brochure—has turned, for me, into a four-hour quest. The sun will set soon, and it's time for me to leave.

I drive past Stop 16 (Winter Deer Lessons) and Stop 17 (Sandhill Deer Research and the Fence) without much further pause.

But then, just a half mile from Sandhill's exit, without warning, a white-tailed deer suddenly bounds away into the trees, on the edge of a small clearing on my left. How long had she been there, watching me approach? I didn't even notice her until she moved, until the moment when she vanished before my eyes.

I realize that this afternoon, Sandhill has taught *me* a lesson. Just like the big gate at the entrance/exit, when it comes to white-tailed deer, looks can be deceiving.

## HOW TO HAVE A GENUINE
## WHITE-TAILED DEER ENCOUNTER OF YOUR OWN

Dick Thiel recommends **two times of the year to look for deer:**

+ May: Watch for them especially in the evenings, two to three hours *after* the heat of the day, but two or three hours *before* sundown, in marsh margins. White-tailed deer like succulent, emergent vegetation, such as arrowhead, that has a high sodium content. In the winter months, a deer's sodium gets depleted, so it will search for those kinds of plants.
+ October: This is the time when bucks are running, so racks are fully developed. They are also a little less wary because they're occupied with the rut.

Be aware, however, that the Sandhill Wildlife Area is open to the public only from dawn to dusk. There is a gratis period, typically of a half hour either way. Please honor the time periods posted on the gate. In early November, special deer hunting seasons are offered by advance permit applications. Only those with hunting permits are allowed access during these November times.

The **Trumpeter Trail auto tour** is open seasonally, usually during the snow-free months, roughly from the middle of April to the end of October.

## HOW TO BECOME INVOLVED WITH
## WHITE-TAILED DEER CONSERVATION EFFORTS

To donate to the Sandhill Wildlife Area, contact the property manager by going to dnr.wi.gov/topic/lands/wildlifeareas/sandhill.

There is a donation box at the Trumpeter Trail auto tour trailhead. Monies help to keep the trails maintained and purchase supplies.

# 6

## Loons: Counting on the Croix

### Saint Croix Flowage in Gordon

FIVE-YEAR LOON COUNT

In their long and illustrious careers, movie stars Henry Fonda and Katharine Hepburn made only one picture together. It was titled *On Golden Pond*, and when it came out in 1981, my mom went crazy for it. She was drawn to what she felt was an honest depiction of an older couple in love; but more than that, she fell in love with the film's loons.

The movie was set in a small New England town, mostly in and by a cabin on the shores of the named pond. The unmistakable and haunting cries of the loons were important "characters" in the film—perhaps as much as the two famous stars themselves were. After seeing the flick, my mom went out and bought loon books, loon decoys, and a loon windsock to hang off her home's back deck.

Loons have a way of casting that sort of spell on people, especially in Wisconsin. The lake country of the Northwoods is almost synonymous with loons. You could even say that their wild calls put a stamp of genuineness on a northern-lakes experience as much as the howl of a wolf confers authenticity on a wilderness-forest outing (see chapter 15, "Gray Wolves: Tracking and Howling"). But with loons, there's an added dimension: It's probable that if you hear loons, you'll also see them, which isn't always the case with the wild canids.

And so, I'm going to northern Wisconsin—to the Saint Croix Flowage in Douglas County—on this July weekend to spot and listen for loons. I'll be participating in Saturday's five-year LoonWatch count, a census conducted by the LoonWatch program, which is part of the Sigurd Olson Environmental Institute, located at Northland College in Ashland, Wisconsin. The data from the census is analyzed by LoonWatch personnel with the help of Wisconsin Department of Natural Resources staff. The five-year loon count utilizes many volunteers on a specific set of 258 lakes, originally selected in 1985. And loon advocates and enthusiasts Lorna and Roger Wilson, counting veterans of more than ten years, have agreed to let me pontoon-ride along with them as they survey the entire Saint Croix Flowage.

## Free to Be on the Flowage

Before meeting Lorna and Roger, I had always thought of flowages as flat, man-made, *un*natural areas, created by the bane of so many free-flowing rivers: dams. But I was soon to find out that the line between what's "natural" and "unnatural" isn't always crisp and clear. There are some fuzzy edges.

Lorna and Roger live right on the shore of the Saint Croix Flowage. As I drive onto their property, I can see that off the back of their home is an elevated deck, which overlooks the lake. In the front yard, the side toward the road, I pull up to park near a serene pond, complete with fish and a short waterfall over several rotund boulders. This is where the previous owners had once had a swimming pool. The sound of the gurgling water when I step out of the car washes away the last few hours of highway noise that had built up in my ears during my 290-mile journey from my home in southern Wisconsin. I feel cleansed. There are hummingbird feeders everywhere, and I particularly notice one large feeder off the back corner of the deck near the shore that is filled with oranges for the chipmunks.

My first sight of Lorna is of her down by the water, bent over the native plants she has so carefully moved here to restore her frontage on the flowage. I walk down to meet her as Roger comes out of the house to join us there.

"It's true that the Saint Croix Flowage was 'helped along' by the Gordon Dam," affirms Roger when I tell him how surprised I am that the flowage looks so wild, undeveloped, and untouched. "But there was a small, *natural* lake here before the dam was even built."

A *flowage* is a lake formed upstream from a dam. The town of Gordon's dam formed what we know today as the Saint Croix Flowage—sometimes called the Gordon Flowage or the Gordon–Saint Croix Flowage to distinguish it from Upper Saint Croix Lake, which is a few miles upstream at Solon Springs. But from what historians have been able to reconstruct, prior to the arrival of Europeans, there was a natural lake here rich in fish. A Chippewa village was located on its shore, and these early people, too, appeared to have created a dam, using rocks and sticks to improve the fishing.

In 1854, white settlers then built other small dams in this shallow area of the Saint Croix River to raise its level in order to allow logs to float downstream. Thirty years later, a logging company built a larger dam—with eighteen-foot-high gates—to facilitate the transportation of the region's now-harvested virgin pine trees.

By 1912, the last log drive was history. A few years later, the wooden dam caught fire, and it was replaced with a walkway made of timbers to allow foot traffic to cross the river. By 1935, it had been determined that a dam was needed here to maintain the water levels of thirty area lakes. In 1937, the Works Progress Administration completed the current dam, constructed of wood, concrete, and steel. In 1988, the dam was upgraded and an eight-foot-wide walkway was installed on top.

Roger and Lorna suggest a drive over to the Gordon Dam on this Friday afternoon so that I can take a look at it for myself. Wanting to understand this flowage better, I readily take them up on their offer.

Standing on the broad top of the dam with the rushing waters spilling over the concrete and steel beneath my feet, I'm struck by how deep the flowage looks from up here. In reality, though, the maximum depth anywhere on the flowage is twenty-eight feet, while the mean depth is only seven feet. Roger tells me that there are more than two hundred aquatic plants in Wisconsin, and in the most recent aquatic plant survey of the Saint Croix Flowage conducted by the DNR, at least fifty-eight of them had been found here.

This shallow depth and aquatic vegetation are part of what makes the 2,247-acre Saint Croix Flowage one of the most undeveloped and quiet lakes in northwest Wisconsin today. "Silent sportsmen," such as anglers and paddlers, love it, while motorboaters and water-skiers tend to avoid it. It helps that most of the flowage's twenty-nine miles of shoreline (about 85 percent) is on public lands, which are protected from development (the land along the shore is so low lying that it wouldn't be suitable for development anyway).

A wide assortment of mammals, reptiles, and birds have noticed the lack of people here and have moved in: beavers, otters, muskrats, deer, bears, fishers, foxes, minks, weasels, coyotes, wolves, frogs, turtles, trumpeter swans, blue herons, sandhill cranes, terns, kingfishers, sandpipers, pelicans, bald eagles, ospreys—and common loons.

## COUNTER, COORDINATOR, AND COUNCILOR

Most people recall their first experience with loons—especially the first time they heard loon music—and Lorna is no exception. It was the loons, in fact, that

Because of its shallow depth and plethora of plants, the Saint Croix Flowage is one of the most undeveloped and quiet lakes in northwest Wisconsin today. Several pairs of loons, eagles, and ospreys nest in this relatively undisturbed place. (Photo: John T. Andrews)

inspired her to become a permanent resident of Wisconsin's Northwoods. A native New Yorker, Lorna spent her childhood summers on a lake in Burnett County. When she and Roger retired, they relocated to the shores of the Saint Croix Flowage.

"As a girl visiting Wisconsin in summer, I used to lay in bed at night and hear the loons," recalls Lorna. "To me, they were just an integral part of being here. That childhood connection is probably responsible for why I got involved with LoonWatch as soon as I moved here in 2002."

Not only is Lorna a LoonWatch volunteer, but she's also the coordinator for that organization's speakers' bureau and a member of the LoonWatch Advisory Council. The five-year count isn't the only loon census; there's also an annual count.

"What we call *loon rangers* conduct the annual surveys," explains Lorna. "A ranger is someone who volunteers to watch a certain lake for loons periodically throughout the summer. Usually, the lake is the one the loon ranger happens to live on. At the end of the year, then, the ranger sends in a report to the LoonWatch program, documenting when the loons arrived in spring, how many were spotted on that particular lake, where they nested, whether they had chicks, if the chicks were successful, and when the loons left in fall.

"But the five-year count," Lorna continues, "is done on a specific set of 258 predetermined lakes. Both the Wisconsin Department of Natural Resources and the Sigurd Olson Environmental Institute are involved. The five-year count is done specifically to ascertain loon population numbers. Five-year census-takers, who are also volunteers, are sent precise instructions. They must be on their assigned lakes—whether they live on them or not—not earlier than 5:00 a.m. and not later than 10:00 a.m., to lower the possibility that a loon counted on one lake could fly to another lake and be tallied again. The count is always done in July because by this time, the loons typically have hatched their chicks. So, the five-year count is a little more scientific and concentrated."

Lorna and Roger are the loon rangers for the Saint Croix Flowage during the annual count. "But it just so happens that the flowage is also one in the set of 258 predetermined lakes for the five-year count," says Lorna, "so we'll be responsible for the five-year census on the Saint Croix Flowage tomorrow."

## A Long Runway for the Red-Eye

Loons (*Gavia immer*) have such dramatic and distinguishable physical characteristics compared with other birds that they will be hard to misidentify tomorrow morning. And one of their standout features is their red eyes.

We in Wisconsin are lucky: the Badger State is one of the few that have loons in summer (other states include Minnesota, Michigan, Maine, Massachusetts, Vermont, New Hampshire, Montana, and Washington), and it is *only* in summer that loons have those red eyes and their distinctive black-and-white plumage. Those who live in the areas of their wintering grounds on the ocean coasts encounter them only as drab-gray birds with gray eyes that rarely make noise.

Interestingly, no one really knows why a loon's eyes are red in summer. One theory states that water filters out the red, orange, and yellow ends of the color spectrum first, allowing the blues and violets to become dominant. A loon's eye looks red to us because it reflects red light back. By reflecting red light, a loon's eye eliminates it before it enters the eye, in effect doing the same thing as the water. Beyond a depth of fifteen feet or so there is no red anyway, so having an eye that filters it out is advantageous.

Also in the summer breeding season, both male and female loons wear their arresting black-and-white plumage, which in winter is a much plainer gray. The bird's basic-black back is decorated with an extensive white-checker pattern— each one unique. Summer loons have shiny black heads and bills and black-and-white, vertically striped "collars" and small "chin-straps." The bird's breast is white.

We in Wisconsin are lucky, for we have loons in summer—and it is *only* in summer that these birds have red eyes and their distinctive black-and-white plumage. (Photo: Bob Leggett)

Unusual for the bird world, loons have dense, solid bones. This makes them heavy—six to thirteen pounds, or weighing as much as a bald eagle. The common loon measures about thirty inches from head to tail and has a five-foot wingspan.

Built for diving, a loon can flatten its feathers in order to push out air and become less buoyant. With its pointed wings pinned to its side, a loon will plunge below the surface, paddling with webbed feet for propulsion. It can dive down to 250 feet in search of fish and stay below the surface for five minutes. Adult loons eat up to two pounds of fish per day; however, those fish are small—only 0.35 to 2.50 ounces.

Loons engage in a behavior called *foot waggling*, or stretching a foot out of the water and shaking it. Researchers are unable to determine if this is done to regulate temperature or is a way of preening.

A loon lives most of its life—which can last twenty-five to thirty years—on the water, coming ashore only to nest. Preferred nesting sites are shorelines, islands, or floating bog mats (a floating mass of vegetation) where they can keep chicks away from predators. You may see chicks hitching a ride on a parent's back, which not only keeps them warm but is also a safeguard against muskies, northern pike, and snapping turtles.

Because a loon's legs are located so far back on its body and because its body is so long, loons do not walk on land but scoot. They have trouble taking off on water and require a long runway to get airborne. In order to achieve liftoff, a loon has to "run" across the water for up to a quarter mile, beating its wings. That's why you'll rarely find loons on lakes under nine or ten acres.

## CALLS OF THE WILD

While their distinct looks and strange behaviors are part of what makes loons so fascinating, it is probably their vocalizations that truly define the bird for most of us. Sometimes they sound like howling wolves. At other times, their calls approximate the prehistoric warbles of sandhill cranes.

Loons make four, easily identifiable sounds:

*The tremolo.* This is the call that is most associated with loons. Because of its three to ten even, rapid notes, some say the tremolo sounds like a quavering laugh. This call is typically used when loons are disturbed or excited. A variation of the tremolo is the *flight tremolo*, which is often given over lakes and is a loon's way of requesting clearance for landing. If a loon that's already on the lake responds with a yodel, the one in the air will usually fly on to the next lake.

*The yodel.* Only uttered by male loons, the yodel is a territorial call. This vocalization begins with three notes that rise slowly and are followed by several undulating, repetitive phrases. Like your own voice, the yodel of a male loon is one of a kind. It says to any loons in the area that "I'm a male loon, I'm on my territory, and I *will* defend it."

*The wail.* This most frequently heard call is similar to the howl of a wolf and is used to locate other loons. It can carry for miles and is often heard at night.

*The hoot.* The hoot is a soft, one-note call used to communicate with other loons, chicks, or mates who are in close proximity.

### KNOWING THE WAY

That proximity for loons increases during late July and August, just before the fall migration. Loons will then gather in small groups, called *rafts*, on large lakes, calling and swimming in what may seem to be repetitive patterns. This is called the *circle dance.* The Great Lakes function as one of the main migration staging areas.

Migration takes place from September to ice-over. The adults will leave first, singly or in loose groups. The chicks will stay four to six weeks longer to gain strength—especially if they are late chicks—but they, too, will leave before the ice is in. No one knows how the chicks know where to go. They've never been south before and the adults have left, yet amazingly they find their way to their winter grounds.

The chicks and loons from Wisconsin and other areas of the Midwest will migrate to the Atlantic Coast, from North Carolina to Florida and the Gulf of Mexico—just over a thousand miles away. (Common loons in the West over-winter on the Pacific Coast from Alaska to the Baja Peninsula and the Gulf of California.) The young will stay south for about three years, until they become mature enough to breed. After that, they will migrate every year. At the time of their first migration back to their summer lakes, the chicks' gray-to-brown feathers will change to the dramatic black-and-white ones. By visiting the U.S. Geological Survey's Common Loon Movements and Migrations website, you can follow the migration paths of midwestern and New England loons.

The loons return to their Wisconsin lakes in April to early May. "It's amazing," says Lorna. "The day the ice goes out, loons will be on the Saint Croix Flowage."

Nesting begins in May and goes through June. Loons will use the same nest from year to year if they were successful the previous year. Loons typically lay one to two eggs and on rare occasions, three. Both males and females sit on the nest, alternating in shifts of about forty-five minutes. The average incubation period is twenty-eight days. If disturbed, loons will slip off the nest, leaving the eggs exposed to overheating or cooling and to predators such as bald eagles, gulls, and raccoons.

The eggs will hatch one day apart. The chicks stay in the nest for twenty-four hours, and then the parents will coax them—or the chicks themselves will hop—into the water. The birds are never on land again until they breed three to five years later.

Once they leave the nest, the chicks are taken by their parents to a "nursery" area, which is likely a quiet, undisturbed bay with little wave action where both

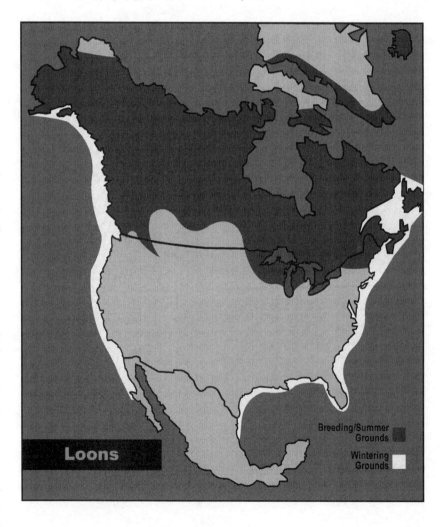

The dramatic white-checker pattern on every loon's back is unique. (Photo: John T. Andrews)

parents can feed them bugs and crustaceans. Chicks can't dive when they are little; they bob like corks. As the chicks mature, the adults will leave them on their own for longer periods of time. In twelve weeks, the chicks will be ready to fly.

According to Lorna, the majority of nesting loons in Wisconsin are north of Highway 29. But they are on the move. Says Lorna, "The greatest density of breeding loons is found in Vilas and Oneida Counties, with an additional cluster in the northwest portion of Wisconsin. But just in the last couple of years, as their population has grown, loons are making their way to places like cranberry bogs in the southwestern part of the state.

"I guess loons like the same things people do," she muses. "A home on the lake, clean water, good fishing, and peace and quiet. But suitable habitat around the lakes is increasingly getting hard to find as more and more people are building their homes there and taking their lawns all the way down to the shore. Some, thankfully, are putting out artificial nesting platforms, which work sometimes. But the loons are finding they have to start spreading out to less desirable habitats to the near south. So, on the cranberry bogs is where they go."

As loons and people come in closer contact with each other, it's good to remember that as a migratory bird, loons are protected by the Migratory Bird Treaty Act, which prohibits the harassment or killing of loons, eggs, or chicks. It is also illegal to possess loon eggs, nests, feathers, or entire birds.

## GETTING THE LEAD OUT

But lakeshore development isn't the only thing that today poses a threat to loons, which are currently listed as a species of "special concern" in Wisconsin. It seems as though there are more people out on our lakes every summer. As long as we stay two hundred yards away from loons, loon chicks, and loon nests, we'll be able to coexist. What's more troublesome, though, than our being *on* the water is what we put *into* it.

Phosphorous from lawn and agricultural fertilizers that runs off into lakes may encourage the growth of blue-green algae blooms, which can be toxic to loons. Oxidized mercury produced by coal-fired power plants and municipal waste incinerators can be washed into local water bodies by rainfall. A potent neurotoxin, mercury accumulates in the bodies of adult loons, affecting their behavior and ability to care for their young during prime breeding years. And mercury can kill loon eggs. It's lead tackle, however, that is particularly deadly.

Lead, which is found in fishing jigs and sinkers, is a toxic metal. In sufficient quantities, it has adverse effects on the reproductive and nervous systems of animals, fish, and birds. Loons often mistake lost fishing weights for the pebbles they ingest to help grind their food. Loons die within two to three weeks after swallowing a single lead sinker or jig.

According to the Minnesota Pollution Control Agency, lead poisoning from lead fishing tackle is responsible for 12 to 50 percent of adult loon deaths. Several states have already banned the use or sale of lead sinkers, and the U.S. Fish and Wildlife Service is planning restrictions on lead sinker use in over two dozen national wildlife refuges.

Says Lorna, "We realize that everyone can't totally get rid of his or her whole tackle box at once, although that would be ideal. But gradually, you can. You have to be an advocate when you go into gear stores; say that you'd like to start buying nonlead tackle and ask that they stock it. Fishing tackle made of tin, bismuth, steel, or tungsten are good alternatives. Eventually, we hope lead tackle under a certain weight—less than 1.76 ounces—will be banned in Wisconsin.

"Last year," Lorna continues, "we picked up a trumpeter swan that had lead poisoning. And people often casually mention that 'a bird struck my window last night and died.' It's so easy to prevent these kinds of deaths. There are stickers you can apply to your windows to let birds know they are there. It's important to be environmentally aware of what we're doing to all the creatures, not just the loons. Do the things that you can do to ensure animals live as well as we do."

## THE IMPORTANCE OF BEING LOON-HEARTED

Saving the lives of loons would be no less than what we owe them, at least from an Ojibwe perspective. According to one of their legends, it was Loon who saved the life of the first man.

In the legend, Loon was the first act of Creation. The voice of the Creator echoed across the void and became embodied in a gray and black shadow, the spirit of the Loon. Later, Sun threw light on the shadow, giving Loon his striking white markings. Loon loved Anishinabe, the first man. And it was Loon who saved Anishinabe when he tried to fly, fell into a lake, and sank straight down. Anishinabe's long, black hair became entangled in some old, underwater trees; Loon untangled every strand, freeing the man and saving his life.

The Native Americans living in Wisconsin's northern lake country could hardly *not* have noticed loons. The males arrive just after ice-out, yodeling their loud, complex songs, heard by everyone within miles. And the same loons come back to the same lakes every summer. It's estimated that only 20 percent of the loons monitored each year do not return to the same territory. This is due to winter mortality, choice of another lake or mate, or loss of territory to larger and stronger loons. If a loon loses its territory, its mate will stay there and mate with the intruder loon. It seems the birds are more faithful to their lands than to their "loved ones."

Native people would have watched as the same males—identified by their unique songs—returned to the same nesting spots year after year. They would have taken note of the fact that a loon's first allegiance is to its home place; but if both loons in a pair return, they mate for life. It is easy to imagine how witnesses to such loon behavior might have taken to heart the lesson of first being bonded to one's home ground and, secondly, being bonded to each other.

The Ojibwe people are divided into a number of clans, five of which are Crane, Bear, Martin, Fish, and Loon. The head of the Loon Clan is known for wisdom, honesty, fidelity, and bravery. The Loon Clan is one of two leadership clans of the Ojibwe (see chapter 9, "Whooping Cranes: Saving a Spirited Species"). To be described as "loon-hearted" is a great compliment.

## THE SAINT CROIX COUNT

On Friday after our excursion to the Gordon Dam, Roger and Lorna offer to let me stay overnight in their home so that we can get an early start for tomorrow's five-year count. I get the lower-level "apartment," which comes complete with companion cats, Spock and Turbo.

After a peaceful night's sleep amid the purrs of felines and the soothing whispers of shorelines, I awake to the smell of homemade blueberry scones and coffee. By 7:30 a.m., we're out on the water in Roger and Lorna's pontoon boat.

This day on the Saint Croix Flowage couldn't be more perfect for spotting loons: clear, in the sixties, with only a slight breeze.

I look over the side of the boat and gaze down into the water, hoping to gauge the depth. I see what looks like an underwater forest, with undulating, leafy branches "blowing" in the gentle waves.

Not long after we get into the main part of the flowage, there's a sound on my right. It's unmistakable: a flight tremolo! Living in southern Wisconsin, I'm not used to hearing such a bone-thrilling noise firsthand, yet I know it the instant it's uttered because I've heard it so often on "loon music" CDs and in films. Then to the left, followed quickly on the heels of the tremolo, comes a yodel. It seems the flowage is flowing with loons.

We quietly motor to almost every corner of this lake, and by 9:00 a.m., Lorna tells me she's counted nine loons. Sadly, though, we spot no chicks. From shore, a white-tailed deer stares at us momentarily and then quietly lowers her head again to browse as we move on. Bald eagles go about their livelihoods, too, fishing all around us. An osprey sits on her nest in a high tree.

By 10:00 a.m., we stop counting and head back home per the LoonWatch instructions. Lorna announces this five-year's final count for the Saint Croix Flowage: adult loons, seventeen; chicks, zero.

## Survey Says

Back at Lorna and Roger's home, we have a true breakfast. My gracious hosts fill me with toast and chokecherry jam, eggs, venison sausage, and a baked tomato dish. We have oranges—much like the chipmunks that frequent Lorna and Roger's deck—before I get in the car for the long drive back to southern Wisconsin.

A few months after I get home, I receive the complete results of the year's official five-year loon count. Volunteers had surveyed 244 of the 258 preselected lakes. The adult loon population was estimated at approximately 4,000 adults and 600 chicks. Five years earlier, the adults had been estimated at 3,373 and the chicks at 805. This year's number of adults represents the largest since the five-year census was started in 1985. Researchers at the Sigurd Olson Environmental Institute theorize that this year's lower number of chicks is linked to increased territorial aggression. As the loon population grows, the birds are fighting each other for the prime locations, with some being pushed into subprime nesting habitats. Both of these behaviors lead to fewer chicks being produced. Loons that do not have territories of their own will often attack a loon on a prime territory in an attempt to win it and the mate that is there. Typically, these are male-on-male or female-on-female battles. If an intruding loon wins, it will mean that the current nest or chicks will be abandoned.

After reading the results, I phone Lorna for her thoughts on the report. She tells me that she's already been involved in a follow-up count—this one to assess whether the BP oil spill on the Gulf Coast has had a negative effect on the loon population of Wisconsin. She happily tells me that in this brand-new count, she's seen two chicks.

That news is good. Contemplating it, it seems right that it be so. Loons go back a long time in history; they are one of the oldest types of bird still in existence (see chapter 10, "Sandhill Cranes: Going Out for the Night, as They Come In"). Their skeletons closely resemble that of *Hesperornis*—a toothed, flightless bird of the Cretaceous period, some 65 to 144 million years ago. Despite the degradations to the environment that we humans have perpetrated, it looks as if the loons are continuing to hold on.

We *Homo sapiens* have been walking around on Earth for only about two hundred thousand years. So for three hundred times longer than that, loon-like birds have been laughing, yodeling, wailing, and hooting their music.

As our extreme elders, then, we shouldn't want them to regret their decision to save us.

## HOW TO HAVE A GENUINE
## LOON ENCOUNTER OF YOUR OWN

+ **When:** In the Upper Midwest, the season for loon watching begins shortly after ice-out, usually in late April or early May. When the loons arrive in spring, their first activities are typically to establish their territories and their pair bonds. Territorial behaviors include aggressive running and splashing and the "penguin dance," when a loon taps his wing tips on the water and tries to get higher. Male loons also defend their territories with yodels. You may spot loon pairs enhancing their bond with behaviors such as bill dipping, synchronized swimming, and nest building.

  Unfortunately, people watching loons in early spring can easily disturb them and cause nest abandonment. While loons with a history of nesting on more developed lakes can acclimate to human activities, loons on remote lakes can be very sensitive to human presence. Remember to stay two hundred feet away from loons, chicks, and nests and view them with binoculars, a spotting scope, or through your telephoto camera lens. If they sound alarms such as the tremolo call, do the penguin dance, display a "hangover posture" (with head hanging low over a nest, trying to hide or be inconspicuous), or hunker down in the water so you can't see them (termed *snaking*), you are too close and should leave the area.

During June, most loons are incubating eggs. It is important not to frighten the birds from the nest during this period. Do not disturb loon families in nursery areas, which are usually quiet bays. The state has instituted no-wake or slow-wake zones since large wakes can drown chicks or wash out nests.

Perhaps one of the most interesting times to observe loons is during the fall migration. Large groups of loons will stage on the Great Lakes or inland lakes. Adult loons begin to migrate in September, followed by juveniles in late October and early November.

♦ **Where:** Lakes larger than five hundred acres are more likely to support loons, although the birds may be more difficult to find on large bodies of water. While some lakes may be accessible by foot, a small boat such as a canoe or kayak may optimize your chances of seeing a loon.

In Wisconsin, look for loons north of Highway 29. Vilas County and counties west of Vilas have large numbers of loons. The Turtle-Flambeau Flowage in Iron County and the Chippewa Flowage in Sawyer County have the largest densities of nesting loons. In the northeastern part of the state, lakes near Minocqua, Eagle River, and Mercer are prime locations. In the summer, it is possible to find nonbreeding loons on Lake Superior, particularly around the Apostle Islands.

## HOW TO BECOME INVOLVED WITH
## LOON CONSERVATION EFFORTS

If you visit lakes in the Northwoods frequently, consider becoming a loon ranger for LoonWatch and participate in the annual loon-monitoring program in Wisconsin. If you are a less frequent visitor or have limited time, you may choose to assist with the five-year survey in Wisconsin. If you would like more information about volunteering, contact LoonWatch at (715) 682-1220 or go to www.northland.edu/sigurd-olson-environmental-institute-loon-watch.htm.

To improve and encourage healthy loon habitats, work for healthy lakes and the banning of the sale of lead tackle less than 1.76 ounces. The quality of the lakes all the way up and down the migration route is important for loons and other migratory birds.

To track loons as they migrate, access the U.S. Geological Survey's Common Loon Movements and Migrations website at www.umesc.usgs.gov/terrestrial/migratory_birds/loons/migrations.html.

# 7

## Monarch Butterflies: Playing Tag

*The Ridges Sanctuary in Baileys Harbor*

CATCHING AND TAGGING ON THE RIDGES

The National Geographic Society counts it as one of the greatest migrations in the world, alongside that of the wildebeest of the Serengeti and the wild salmon of the Pacific Northwest. Placed next to their mammal and fish counterparts, however, the migrants who undertake *this* particular journey look diminutive and frail, weighing in at less than a hundredth of an ounce. But these tiny travelers are just as capable as their African and Northwestern brethren, traveling on the wing for up to three thousand miles.

Who are these great fliers? They are nothing more than insects. But just as with their looks, don't be fooled by their classification. These bugs are one of the most colorful, elegant, and charismatic creatures on Earth.

They are monarch butterflies.

### A SECRET WINTER REVEALED

Like bees, mosquitoes, and ladybugs, monarchs (*Danaus plexippus*) are one of the most identifiable insects. Big and flashy, they are found mainly on the North American continent; they are widespread in the United States, Canada, and Mexico (except in the high elevations of the Rocky Mountains).

There are two major populations of monarchs, with the Rocky Mountains acting as the dividing line. Every fall, the monarchs west of the Rockies (about 5 percent of the total monarch population) migrate to numerous locations along the coast of California. The vast majority that is east of the Rockies, however, travels to central Mexico. After flying as far as three thousand miles from Canada—gliding on wind currents and stopping to sip the nectar of plants such as aster, goldenrod, ironweed, clover, and alfalfa for energy—millions of them

One of the greatest migrations in the world is undertaken by one of the planet's smallest creatures. (Photo: John H. Gaukel)

arrive at a small, mountainous area in the state of Michoacán. There, they cluster tightly for the winter on their favorite oyamel fir trees, ten thousand feet
above sea level, on steep, southwest-facing slopes.

The mountain forests of Michoacán provide an ideal microclimate for the
monarchs. Temperatures hover just above freezing, letting the colorful insects
slow their metabolism down to a semidormant state. Fog and clouds help provide a cool environment so that they don't use up their energy reserves too
quickly, while sunny days warm them enough so that they can briefly leave their
roosts to visit nearby water sources.

For years, the monarchs' wintering grounds were a mystery. It was known
that they disappeared every fall, but no one knew where they went. In 1935, a
Canadian entomologist named Fred Urquhart set out to discover the answer.
Forty years later, he found it.

Fred realized that the first thing that was needed was some sort of method
to track the butterflies. Although leg bands had worked for birds, Fred's requirements were a bit more stringent: for his smaller subjects, the "tags" would have
to be lightweight, adhesive, extremely easy to attach, capable of carrying on a
tiny surface legible information that would not fade or wash, and not interfere

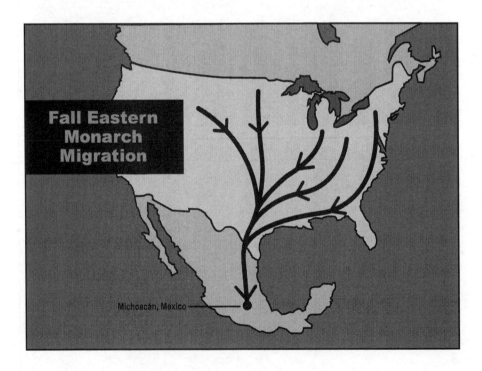

with a monarch's flight. After twenty years of trying different methods that failed, Fred Urquhart and his wife, Nora, finally found a workable solution in the 1950s: a tag much like the sticky price tags that grocery stores then used on jars and canned goods.

The Urquharts then began to write articles in naturalist magazines in an effort to muster volunteers to tag monarchs in different parts of the country and to watch for butterflies already tagged. By 1964, a few hundred volunteers had placed stickers reading "Return to Museum, Toronto, Canada" on about seventy thousand monarchs.

From what he was able to plot on a map using returned specimens, Urquhart was the first to identify the two populations of monarchs. He was also among the first to postulate that Mexico was the likely winter destination for the biggest group of migrants.

Recalling a drive through a sudden "storm" of monarch butterflies during a trip he had once taken through the volcanic mountains west of Mexico City, an American engineer from Kenosha, Wisconsin, named Kenneth Brugger—who was living in Mexico City at the time—wrote to Urquhart. Fred helped to convince Kenneth that he should return to the area to search for them. On January 2, 1975, Brugger and his wife were exploring an area near the summit of Cerro Pelón when they began to see dead butterflies on the forest floor. Soon, they entered a thick grove of oyamel trees.

After their eyes had adjusted to the dark, the Bruggers realized that the trees they were looking at were covered with monarch butterflies—millions of them, cloaking every branch and trunk. A few years after the Bruggers' initial discovery, one of the world's leading experts on monarchs, Dr. Lincoln Brower, a research professor of biology at Sweet Briar College in Virginia, and his colleagues found another dozen wintering sites: all in thick oyamel forests, all at altitudes of about ten thousand feet above sea level, and all within a radius of fifty miles of Cerro Pelón.

Finding the monarchs' wintering grounds was hailed as one of the greatest discoveries of the twentieth century, the zoological equivalent of unearthing Tutankhamen's tomb.

## Bagging a Butterfly

Scientists speculate that this particular Great Migration has been going on since the start of the Pleistocene era, about two million years ago. At that time, monarch butterflies lived in Central and South America. But with a changing climate and evolutionary adaptations, milkweeds—the exclusive food of monarch butterfly larvae—began to spread north. Just as the monarchs began following the milkweeds to more temperate latitudes, drier winters developed in Mexico. The milkweeds withered in the now dry Mexican winter air, and the monarchs found they could survive this period only by going into a semidormant state. This combination of shifting vegetation and changing climate most likely produced the migration pattern we see today, where monarchs take advantage of the abundant food in the United States and Canada each summer but must go back to Mexico to avoid freezing every winter.

Today, the timing of the monarchs' migration seems to be linked to the length of daylight rather than temperatures. Monarchs at the north end of their range—in Canada and in northern Minnesota—begin their migration the soonest, about mid-August. In the southern part of their range, in Texas and Oklahoma, for instance, the monarchs may not migrate until the middle of November. In Wisconsin the migration peaks in the first week of September.

So it is here, in the Badger State in the eighth month of the year, that monarch butterflies begin to gather before the big trip, in places such as The Ridges Sanctuary in Baileys Harbor in Door County. And on this Saturday morning in August, The Ridges is holding a special monarch butterfly-tagging outing. This could be the closest I'll ever come to having the often-quoted, most exciting job in the world: "tagging sharks for Jacques Cousteau."

I intend to go after the mighty monarch.

### FLYING WITHOUT A COPILOT

Inside the Marshall Cabin, an 1853 structure originally built in Fish Creek and now situated on The Ridges Sanctuary property, naturalist Karen Newbern gathers us thirteen adults and one seven-year-old girl named Ella who have signed up to attempt to tag our first monarchs. She explains the daunting journey that these particular butterflies—which we hope to see and catch today—face.

"From tracking studies," begins Karen, "we know that the Wisconsin monarchs and those on the Canadian-U.S. border that migrate south will stop to congregate in Texas, Oklahoma, and Louisiana. Then, they'll pretty much go straight on to Mexico. There, they will hang out in the trees until February. As the weather starts to warm up, they'll get the urge to mate.

"Soon after they leave Mexico, pairs of monarchs do," she confirms. "As they reach the southern United States, females will look for available milkweed plants to lay eggs. Then, that generation dies. Their caterpillars will emerge, develop, and turn into adults, and it is that generation of monarchs that continues the migration back to places such as Wisconsin, Illinois, Minnesota, and Michigan. They arrive in the Midwest around the end of May."

This generation of butterflies that arrives in Wisconsin in the spring, however, is still not the one that will fly back to Mexico in the fall—nor will their children. It is their grandchildren or great-grandchildren (or great-great-grandchildren, depending on the weather and how far north they live) that will make the return flight to Michoacán.

Says Karen, "When a butterfly emerges from his chrysalis, he has one of two urges: to mate or migrate. For the butterflies that emerge in August in Wisconsin, the switch is set to 'migrate.'"

The big question, though, is how the generation that flies south to Mexico— and the one that makes it back north again—knows where it's going, without the guidance of parents going along to model the route. We know that monarchs use the sun's position as a critical navigational tool in finding a destination thousands of miles away that they have never seen. Some entomologists believe that the earth's geomagnetic field may also have a role in orienting the butterflies. But *how* the monarchs are able to process that information has been a mystery—until recently.

For years, scientists have known that monarchs are very adept at sensing ultraviolet (UV) light, a wavelength of light that is invisible to the human eye, allowing them to detect the sun's angle even on a cloudy day. Lately, though, researchers have found evidence that the butterflies rely on *polarized* ultraviolet light (light that oscillates in one plane instead of in all directions), which enables the migrants to accurately navigate under a variety of atmospheric conditions.

But that's not all: Scientists have found that the monarchs' light-detecting sensors are hard-wired to the butterflies' circadian clocks, allowing them to compensate for time of day. Because the sun moves in the sky from east to west throughout a twenty-four-hour period, by knowing what time of day it is, monarchs can determine in which compass direction at any particular time the sun is located. Key genes responsible for the monarchs' circadian clocks' molecular "ticks" are expressed in a region of their brains called the *dorsolateral protocerebrum*, where tiny neural fibers connect the clocks to polarization photoreceptors in the eyes. This particular pathway has not been found in any other insect. That may be part of the reason why North American monarchs are the only butterflies that make such a massive journey.

"To me," says Karen, "the monarch butterfly migration is nothing short of a miracle. It just amazes me that something with such a tiny brain has the know-how to make such an extensive trip. I'm also surprised at how many people recognize monarchs and know a little bit about them, but don't know *anything* about this incredible migration and how it all works."

## OF MONARCHS AND MILKWEED

To understand how it does all fit together, you first have to understand the inextricable relationship between monarch butterflies and milkweed. While adults will sip on the nectar of many plants, their larvae exist exclusively on milkweed. In fact, butterflies will fly only as far north as milkweed plants grow.

Female monarch butterflies need milkweed for successful egg laying. Each mother has roughly two hundred to five hundred pearly-white, ridged eggs to deposit; optimally, the eggs should be laid separately, among a number of milkweed plants as a protection against sibling cannibalism. Usually only one egg per leaf per monarch is laid, although a leaf may have many eggs from different monarchs.

For three to nine days, then, the larva inside the egg matures. When the egg is ready to hatch, it will get a gray "bull's-eye," which is actually the caterpillar's head. The caterpillar chews its way out of its eggshell, devours the rest of it, and then turns its jaws to the leaf beneath its feet. It will greedily consume any unhatched monarch egg in its path, but the milkweed is its true meal. Eating milkweed also provides some protection. Since the plant's milky essence is full of glycosides that are distasteful to other animals, the milkweed-infused caterpillars are made unpalatable to most potential predators.

The newly hatched, eighth-of-an-inch-long caterpillar has a black head with a whitish body. It will spend its first two weeks feeding ravenously on milkweed and bulking up. As it eats and grows, it will shed its skin five times. The periods between molts are called *instars*.

When the caterpillar has stored up enough energy and it's big enough, it will crawl to the ground and go on a quest, looking for a well-protected site for the final molt. Once it finds a suitable place, such as below the overhang of a fence rail, in the eaves of a building, or in the angle where a thick tree branch joins a trunk, this searcher will consider its wanderings completed.

Now, on its carefully chosen site, the caterpillar will deposit a button-sized pad of silk, which it spins from a gland inside its body. On this anchor, it will situate its rear end and secure itself by using anal claspers. Then, much like a thrilling trapeze artist performing in a circus, the caterpillar will unfold its body and hang head down in a slightly curving J-shape.

The next stage of life is called the *pupa*. Underneath the caterpillar's last larval skin, the pupa is already forming. When the caterpillar's skin splits and sheds for the fifth and final time, it will push that discarded envelope along its suspended body and up to the silk button. Its fresh, new skin is soft and pale green, a jade-like color with golden markings.

Over time, the pupa's cuticle slowly hardens and darkens into what is called a *chrysalis*, from the Greek term for the word *gold*. Inside this nugget the monarch will be almost completely broken down into a "cell soup." From that liquid, a butterfly will be created. Cells morph into wings, long legs, a mouth tube to replace jaws, and all-new internal organs.

The chrysalis eventually turns to black. But within a day of the color change, the casing will thin, and through it, the monarch's characteristic reddish-orange wings will become visible. The chrysalis will start to twitch and twist, causing cracks and fractures. Then, in a brief minute, the fully formed butterfly emerges.

When it first comes out, the butterfly's head is down, just as the caterpillar's was. Pushing its long legs through the casing's rift, the butterfly slowly drags itself free. But far from the lithe and lovely insect we recognize, this new butterfly has a fat abdomen and crumpled wings.

For the next fifteen minutes, the butterfly's abdomen pulsates as it pumps fluid into the branching tubes that run through each of its four wings. The wings grow larger as the abdomen grows smaller. When finally fully stretched, the wings will span about four inches.

Usually, the butterfly will remain clinging to its perch for the rest of the day and overnight. Early the next morning, as the sun rises and its body warms, the butterfly will open and close its wings a few times, drop from its resting place, and flutter off to explore the world.

There is very little difference in appearance between male and female monarch butterflies. One distinction is that the male monarch butterfly has a black spot at the center of each hind wing. Another marker is that the veins on the wings of the female tend to be thicker and darker.

When butterflies emerge, the mate-or-migrate switch Karen mentioned is already functional. Those that come out of the chrysalis in late summer and early fall have a different propensity than those that do so during the longer days and warmer weather of early summer and midsummer. The fall monarchs are born to fly and know that they must prepare for a lengthy journey.

Migrating monarchs live for eight or nine months, compared with just two to six weeks for other monarchs. By the time the following year's winter migration begins, several generations will have lived and died. Yet these new generations know where to go and follow the same course their ancestors did—sometimes even returning to the same tree.

## BUILDING A BEACH

Karen has finished her talk, and our group's members are now anxious to see if we can actually catch, hold for a moment, and tag one of these marvelous migrators before their tour of a lifetime. Karen hands out butterfly nets to each of us and offers for purchase mini tagging kits, produced by Monarch Watch. Based at the University of Kansas, Monarch Watch enlists citizen scientists to track monarch butterflies. The kits include five monarch tags for the small fee of two dollars. Armed with my net and kit, I step outside the Marshall Cabin into a sunny, seventy-five-degree day. I catch up with Karen as the fifteen of us walk the boardwalk trail toward the ridges and swales on Lake Michigan. I ask her to tell me about the history of this sixteen-hundred-acre property.

"It actually had to do with the range light buildings," says Karen, as we approach the location of the front range light, one of two originally built in 1869 and operated by the U.S. Lighthouse Service to guide ships into the shallow waters of Baileys Harbor. "The U.S. government built the range lights on a forty-acre piece of land that they had here. After the range lights became automated and electrified in the late 1920s, there was no longer any need for a lighthouse keeper or human help. So, the acreage became surplus property. The U.S.

Equipped with butterfly nets, we go in search of monarchs—all the while listening to a great lake's soothing waves and feeling the light touch of a summer breeze. (Photo: John T. Andrews)

Department of Commerce deeded the land to Door County in 1935 with the intent it would be established as a park.

"Then, the idea started gaining ground that this would make an excellent trailer campground," continues Karen. "So plans were put in place to build a road that would go between the two range light buildings for easy access to the campsites. But some local residents who had come to care about the unique natural plant communities here caught sight of gravel being dumped into some of the swales to prepare for the road building. They started to investigate, found out about the project, and went to the parks board with their concerns."

It was then that the curator of botany at the Milwaukee Public Museum, Albert Fuller, got involved. "He had done a lot of studies in the area and had written a book on the orchids and plant life surrounding Baileys Harbor," says Karen. "He argued for protecting the biodiversity of the place. There are more wildflowers and more rare plants in this small area than anywhere else in Wisconsin, and we have one of the greatest concentrations of rare plants in the Midwest."

In fact, The Ridges Sanctuary is our state's oldest private nature preserve. When it was established in 1937, it became Wisconsin's first area set aside to protect native flora. It was designated a State Natural Area in 1953, a National Natural Landmark in 1967, an Important Bird Area by the National Audubon Society, and a Wisconsin Wetland Gem by the Wisconsin Wetland Society.

The sanctuary's name comes from the rare topography here: ridges of vegetation, separated by wetlands (or *swales*), created by the ebb and flow of Lake Michigan over time. Each ridge represents a former beach line, which occurs every thirty to fifty years. More than 475 plant species live among these bumps and hollows, including twenty-five of Wisconsin's forty native orchids. Nearly five hundred vascular plants find footing in the adjacent boreal forest.

Says Karen, "Jens Jensen was the other person who was really instrumental in starting The Ridges. He was a landscape architect, and he argued that you couldn't re-create a landscape like this. You've got to protect it in the first place. He helped to convince the parks board that this area shouldn't be developed as a trailer campground. In 1937, shortly after the plans for the campground were scrapped, the folks that had worked so hard to protect the place were the ones who founded The Ridges Sanctuary, Incorporated. They went back to the parks board and asked if they could manage this area as a wildflower sanctuary. The board agreed to that. Then, the founders of The Ridges Sanctuary started developing hiking trails, taking groups out, and introducing people to this spectacular topography and its natural plant communities."

The founders of the sanctuary had an original goal of one thousand acres in protection. They reached that goal in 1987, just short of the fiftieth anniversary of the organization. Today, the nonprofit Ridges Sanctuary organization, which is member supported, manages more than sixteen hundred acres, which it keeps open to the public.

"The natural diversity is what makes this place so special," says Karen. "A lot of that ties into the ridge-and-swale formations. There are wet areas, dry areas, sunny spots, and shade, and the youngest ridges provide a very different habitat than the older ones do."

And just as we reach the white sands of The Ridges beach, we see our first monarch butterfly.

### BLOWIN' IN—AND BATTERED BY—THE WIND

Ella, the seven-year-old in our group, carefully places her net over the resting butterfly, which has stopped to linger on the native grasses sprouting from one of the sandy ridges. Karen slowly comes up, shows Ella and the rest of us how to properly remove a butterfly from a net, and places the insect on Ella's arm.

The tagged monarch butterfly rests briefly on little Ella's arm. If you're careful, you can easily press a tag onto the butterfly's hind wing in the mitten-shaped section. (Photo: John T. Andrews)

The butterfly rests on its new perch, while Karen pulls one of her pencil-eraser-sized stickers out of her pocket.

Although it might seem that a butterfly's wings are too delicate to handle, if you're careful, you can briefly secure a monarch by holding its wings together between two of your fingers without damaging or hurting the insect. Karen writes down the number of the sticker, the date, the time, and our location on a data sheet and gently presses the tag against the butterfly's hind wing in the large, mitten-shaped section. She then lets it go. Ella's eyes light up and her smile grows large as the monarch lifts off.

Watching Ella's joy reminds Karen of her own childhood wonder at watching butterflies.

"I grew up on a farm in northern Wisconsin," she says. "Caterpillars were fun for me to play with. I could let them crawl around on my fingers, and compared to a lot of other wildlife, they were harmless. There was a railroad track that ran right in front of our house. And along the sides of the track, a lot of milkweed grew. That's where all the caterpillars hung out.

"When I was eight or nine years old," Karen goes on, "I had a caterpillar that went into the chrysalis and never came out. I waited and waited and waited. The chrysalis was dark, just like it was supposed to be. But after a while, it was obvious that the butterfly wasn't ever going to emerge. I'm sure that I had a lot of successful monarchs that came out, took off, and were just fine. But I remember that particular one because I kept wondering, *What happened?* Children are curious beings, and you never know what will ignite a lifelong interest in and passion for nature."

Karen catches another monarch in her net, but because it has a damaged wing, she lets it go. These strong monarchs can withstand a lot of battering; they can fly with even as much as half of their wing area gone. These remarkable appendages flap five to twelve times a second, depending on the flight mode. They are able to glide, cruise at about eleven miles per hour, or—when alarmed—speed away at up to thirty miles per hour.

Our group splits up to go searching for monarchs on our own. After more than an hour of listening to a great lake's soothing waves, feeling the light touch of a summer breeze, and leisurely seeking butterflies, we head back to the Marshall Cabin to return our nets. On the trail back, one man catches another monarch, which he tags, and just outside the cabin, another group member catches a third one, which is quickly equipped with a sticker.

A bigger breeze kicks up, and I hear the old trees that are nearest to the boardwalk begin to "moan" and crackle. I imagine them sounding like the creaking masts of wooden ships from a hundred years ago, bobbing in Lake Michigan's formidable waves.

## LOSING GROUND

Preserves such as The Ridges Sanctuary are becoming more and more important for monarch butterflies. Although they are not currently listed as endangered, there is concern about their recent downward population trend.

In the United States, land development is responsible for the pavement of more than 2.2 million acres per year, removing the milkweed the monarchs need for egg laying and the nectar-producing plants they require for food. And the use of herbicide-resistant, genetically modified soybeans has eliminated another 100 million acres of habitat since 1997.

Says Karen, "Here in Wisconsin, we don't have the numbers of milkweeds that we used to have due to the increase of commercial agriculture and Roundup Ready crops. It's a lot easier for farmers to go out and spray their fields if they know their corn or their soybeans aren't going to be affected. And corn pollen from transgenic hybrids blowing onto milkweeds can kill feeding monarch larvae. The Midwest is one of the biggest reproductive areas for the monarchs, so agricultural practices are a big issue."

Mowing along roadsides can also be detrimental. Although milkweeds do grow back after being cut down, if a community's road crew happens to mow at the time the monarch eggs are hatching, local populations can be lost.

In Mexico, illegal logging has completely eliminated some overwintering sites. And since almost all of the monarchs gather in one fairly small region in Michoacán, one snowstorm in central Mexico could wipe out huge numbers of the monarch population in one year. In fact, in January 2002, about 70 percent of wintering monarchs froze to death as a result of two days of rain; in January and February of 2004, two storms wiped out 70 percent of the monarchs in Mexico; and in 2010, an estimated 50 percent of the monarchs in Michoacán were lost due to torrential rains, high winds, and light freezes. Climate change is another threat to the insects, since it could disrupt the monarchs' temperature-sensitive life cycle.

Monarch population numbers are determined by measuring the hectares in Mexico that have trees that contain monarchs. There is no consensus on how many monarchs can be in a hectare, but researchers say the number may be as high as fifty million. Unfortunately, since the mid-1990s, there has been a fairly steady decline in how many hectares they use. From 1994 through 2003, the monarch population averaged 9.62 hectares (22.9 acres), and from 2004 to 2010, that average had dropped to 4.34 hectares (10.7 acres).

## Reconstructing an Epic Journey

It's clear that since 1992, when Chip Taylor, a professor of entomology at the University of Kansas, founded the Monarch Watch program, the size of the monarch butterfly's winter colonies has shrunk significantly.

In order to learn more about the challenges monarch butterflies face and their phenomenal migration, the Monarch Watch program pays about five dollars to local people in Mexico for every butterfly that is returned with a tag affixed. Donations to Monarch Watch and money acquired through the sale of the tagging kits (about fifteen dollars) are used for these payments. The wages are hard earned; sometimes it's necessary to sort through millions of butterflies to find one with a sticker, since in any one year, only thousands will have been tagged.

When an expired butterfly is sent to Monarch Watch, the number on the tag is recorded along with the location, date, and circumstance of the recovery. The tag number is then searched for in the data that was originally sent in on the tagging sheet records. The distance the monarch traveled can then be calculated according to latitude and longitude to obtain the straight-line course (a minimal estimate for the distance the monarch covered). Both the tagger and the person who recovered the tag can then review that monarch's travels online and print out a certificate.

But the biggest benefit of the Monarch Watch program may be that it brings at least one hundred thousand people into close contact with one of the world's most amazing natural events each fall.

## Soulful, but Songless

It's said that the Greek word *psyche* means both "butterfly" and "soul." But even before the Greeks' time, there were stories about how butterflies are intrinsic to our well-being.

To Native Americans in Mexico, butterflies were a symbol of rebirth, regeneration, happiness, and joy. The Blackfeet in the United States believed that dreams came to them from a butterfly. Their sign for a butterfly was a design roughly in the shape of a Maltese cross. This cross was painted on a lodge to indicate that the style and method of decorating the lodge were taught to the artist in a dream. It was also the custom for a Blackfoot woman to embroider the sign of a butterfly on a small piece of buckskin and tie it in her baby's hair when she wanted the infant to go to sleep. But one of the most intriguing butterfly stories comes from the southwestern Tohono O'odham Nation (or the Papago tribe).

Not long after Earth-Maker shaped the world, Elder Brother was sitting and watching some children play. He saw the beauty of their surroundings and smelled the fresh fragrance of the trees and the flowers. He heard the tunes of the birds and gazed at the blue of the sky. He watched the sunlight shine on the hair of the women nearby who were grinding cornmeal. He witnessed the joy and the youthfulness the children displayed, and he felt happy. But then Elder Brother realized that this would not last forever. He knew that the children would all grow old, weaken, and die. Feeling sad and troubled, he decided to give the children some of the wonderful things he saw.

Elder Brother took out his bag of Creation and began to place inside it some blue from the sky, some whiteness from the cornmeal, a few spots of sunlight, and the blackness of a beautiful woman's hair. He took the yellow of the falling leaves and the green of the pine needles. From flowers, he collected red, purple, and orange. He even gathered some songs from the songbirds.

He called the children together and told them to open the bag. When they did, hundreds of butterflies flew out. The children were enchanted, and the butterflies sang to them. But one songbird perched on Elder Brother's shoulder and said, "These pretty things have all of the colors of the rainbow already. Must they take our songs, too?"

Elder Brother replied, "You're right. I made one song for each bird, and I must not give them away to any other." So butterflies were made silent, and they are still silent to this day.

By looking at little Ella's face this morning, however, I'd say it could be argued that a butterfly still elicits songs, of the praise and joy kind.

## THE URGE FOR GOING

Their silence, their lightness, their chrysalis-like transparency—all conspire to make us think that monarch butterflies are ephemeral creatures, about to disintegrate or blow away at any moment. But we now know what strength lies beyond that appearance.

Says Karen, "Monarchs are frail when they first emerge, at least until their wings harden up a bit. But it's amazing what they're capable of. I've seen monarchs with wings that look as if a bird took a bite out of them, and yet, they keep on going! They're a lot tougher than we realize."

But the important question may not be how strong *monarchs* are, but whether they can withstand *human* frailties. They have stood the trials of epic journeys for eons, but will they survive our penchant for blacktop, chainsaws, and pesticides?

Dr. Lincoln Brower fears that the monarch migration may be "an endangered biological phenomenon." Could stories of a remote, mountainous region in Mexico that once had trees "made" of millions of butterflies become only a legend?

I think if Ella had her say, she'd prefer that this Great Migration continue on as one of the most daring feats of the natural world.

## HOW TO HAVE A GENUINE MONARCH BUTTERFLY ENCOUNTER OF YOUR OWN

+ **Attract butterflies to your backyard:** To draw adult butterflies, provide food and water for them. Plant flowers with lots of nectar, such as goldenrods, asters, joe-pye weeds, or coneflowers.

    To ensure the appearance of caterpillars, plant milkweeds: common milkweed, swamp milkweed, or butterfly weed (known as *orange milkweed*). But be aware that caterpillars eat milkweeds, so the plants will look unattractive during that time. Milkweeds, however, are adapted to being eaten by caterpillars, so they will grow new leaves.

    Beetles and crab spiders also eat milkweeds. Some other insects you may find on milkweeds are assassin bugs and some spiders, which can be caterpillar predators. If you want to raise monarch caterpillars, make sure your milkweed branch has no other bugs on it.

+ **Tag butterflies:** To purchase a tagging kit, visit shop.monarchwatch .org/store. Tagging kits cost fifteen dollars. You will receive instructions, tags, and a data sheet when the migration is about to begin.

    Then, catch a wild monarch or one you've raised from a caterpillar. On the data sheet, write in your name, address, and the requested information (tag number, date of tagging, whether the monarch was male or female, whether it was reared or wild, and tagging location). Apply a tag to a back wing (in the cell that looks like a mitten). Release the butterfly. When you are finished tagging butterflies, mail the data sheet and all unused tags to Monarch Watch at the address provided on the sheet. Or attend a monarch butterfly tagging workshop, such as the one held at The Ridges Sanctuary every August, where you can purchase a mini tagging kit.

## HOW TO BECOME INVOLVED WITH
## MONARCH BUTTERFLY CONSERVATION EFFORTS

The Ridges Sanctuary's naturalist Karen Newbern says that the best thing you can do for butterflies and insects in general is *not* be obsessive about having a perfect yard. By allowing some weeds to grow, you provide a range of diverse habitats for wild species.

Do not overuse insecticides and avoid them totally if possible. Strong chemicals will rid your plants of everything—the good bugs as well as the bad.

Consider becoming a member of The Ridges Sanctuary by going to www .ridgessanctuary.org/support-us/membership.

The Monarch Larva Monitoring Project (MLMP), developed and managed by the University of Minnesota, is a citizen science project, started in an effort to collect long-term data on larval monarch populations and milkweed habitat. You can sign up to participate at www.mlmp.org. As an MLMP volunteer, your work will help to conserve monarchs, protect their migration, and gain an understanding of butterfly ecology.

# FALL

(Photo: John T. Andrews)

8

# Elk: Heeding the Bugler's Call

*Chequamegon-Nicolet National Forest in Clam Lake*

ELK BUGLING AND THE ROCKY MOUNTAIN ELK FOUNDATION
BUGLE DAYS RENDEZVOUS

I've always been a traipser of trees, a fan of forests. And if you live in Wisconsin, you can't help but be conscious of the giant in our midst, the one that takes up more than 1.5 million of our acres and lies in the upper portions of our boundaries: the vast and beautiful Chequamegon-Nicolet National Forest, the only national forest in Wisconsin.

The western, Chequamegon side of this behemoth comprises about 849,000 acres, and on this fall Saturday afternoon, I've just entered the northern section of it, in the Clam Lake area. For this is where one of Wisconsin's greatest reintroduction efforts took place less than twenty years ago: elk are once again bugling in our woods.

Every September, the Rocky Mountain Elk Foundation (RMEF)—an organization whose mission is to ensure the future of elk and other wildlife in healthy habitats—holds a Bugle Days Rendezvous weekend, an event for RMEF volunteers, partners, and friends. I've been invited to tag along on one of this weekend's Elk Range Tours led by Wisconsin Department of Natural Resources (DNR) elk biologist Laine Stowell. We'll be looking and listening for bugling elk—starting in the dark hours before dawn tomorrow morning.

### ELK AGAIN

If anyone has an insider's perspective on how the idea to restore Wisconsin's elk came about, it would have to be Laine Stowell. At the very beginning, back in 1980 when bringing back elk was still just a wild dream, Laine was a graduate student in wildlife ecology in the College of Natural Resources at the University of Wisconsin–Stevens Point. He was then working on his thesis.

"The brainchild for elk restoration in Wisconsin was Dr. Raymond K. Anderson, and I happened to be one of his graduate students," begins Laine. "My thesis was on a wildlife resources inventory and management plan for the Apostle Islands National Lakeshore. As part of my paper, Dr. Anderson insisted that I look into the feasibility of restoring woodland caribou, moose, and elk to the Apostle Islands.

"Unfortunately, I was probably a disappointment to Dr. Anderson because I concluded that it was *not* feasible or desirable to restore those three animals there," he says with a smile.

Dr. Anderson, however, was not a man to give up. In 1989, he and a few others convinced Wisconsin state senator Joseph Strohl to put a directive in the biennium budget for the Wisconsin DNR to further investigate the advisability of—and, if feasible, to develop a management plan for—restoring woodland caribou, moose, and elk to Wisconsin.

"A graduate student named Linda Parker was then hired to prepare the study," says Laine. "In her treatise, she did not recommend restoring woodland caribou or moose because those two species are very susceptible to brainworm, a parasite indigenous in our deer population. Although brainworm does not affect deer, it is fatal to woodland caribou and moose. Elk have some susceptibility to that parasite, but not as much as those other two species. At that time, other eastern elk populations that live with abundant deer numbers had done okay in Michigan, Pennsylvania, and Arkansas. So, they went ahead with developing a management plan for elk," explains Laine.

In her publication *Feasibility Assessment for the Reintroduction of North American Elk, Moose, and Caribou into Wisconsin* (1990), Parker laid out a management plan for an elk reintroduction on the Bayfield Peninsula. But when local residents heard about the plan, they rallied to show their disapproval. Snowmobile clubs assumed that having elk would result in the closure of trails, and apple and berry growers in the vicinity of Bayfield, who had a long history of crop damage due to deer, went to their county board of supervisors and convinced them to pass a resolution opposing the reintroduction of elk. The plan for that area was subsequently dropped.

"But what happened next," says Laine, "is that a group of interested people that included Dr. Anderson, Martin Hanson, Neil Paulson, and Dr. Orrin Rongstad convinced Governor Tommy Thompson to go ahead with the project. Orrin Rongstad and Ray Anderson had done a lot of wildlife work on white-tailed deer and bear, respectively, in the Clam Lake area, and they had a close affinity to the local people. That environment also has a sizable degree of forage habitat because of the ELF transmitter," states Laine.

The site of the ELF (extremely low frequency) transmitter is associated with more than twenty-eight miles of overhead signal transmission line operated by the U.S. Navy. The line forms part of the "electrical" antenna that radiates the ELF signal, which communicates with deep-diving submarines around the world. Because of the ELF line, the forest near Clam Lake has about four hundred acres of openings, where elk like to browse.

The group was able to convince Clam Lake residents that restoring elk to their area would be beneficial for them and their environment. The U.S. Forest Service then gave its support to the project. By 1994, Governor Thompson had included funding for a research study to look into restoring elk to the Clam Lake area in the biennium budget. And because of Thompson's good relationship with the governor of Michigan, a fortuitous "gift" was offered: the people of Michigan agreed to give twenty-five elk to the people of Wisconsin.

"Another party that became involved in lobbying for the restoration was the Rocky Mountain Elk Foundation," says Laine. "Bernie Lemon, the state volunteer chairman for the RMEF-Wisconsin, helped convince Tommy Thompson that if he provided some seed money, the RMEF would work on fund-raising to get the *major* share of monies for this project. So, the governor allotted fifty thousand dollars—or twenty-five thousand dollars for each year of the biennium. The Rocky Mountain Elk Foundation stepped in with almost half a million dollars, over four years, to help pay for feasibility studies and research conducted by the University of Wisconsin–Stevens Point, under lead investigator Dr. Ray Anderson," says Laine.

In February 1995, twenty-five elk were trapped in Michigan. They were held in quarantine for ninety days, during which time they went through a rigorous disease-testing schedule, in particular for brucellosis and tuberculosis. They were then shipped to Clam Lake, Wisconsin. After being held in a pen for a two-week acclimation period, the elk were released into the mighty Chequamegon-Nicolet National Forest on May 17, 1995.

Wisconsin had elk again.

## A Railroad Record

As far as we know, the last time the forest—or any place in Wisconsin—saw elk hoof prints in its soil was in 1886.

Says Laine, "Several years ago, an almost complete, bull-elk skeleton was found in Middle Eau Claire Lake in Bayfield County. It was carbon-dated to be five hundred years old. So before Jean Nicolet ever stepped ashore in Green Bay, that bull was already in the bottom of Middle Eau Claire Lake. About the same time that that bull was found, an original elk antler shed was found by a fisheries biologist on one of the feeder streams into the Brule River. So we know that historically, for hundreds of years, elk were here in northwestern Wisconsin. Dr. A. W. Schroger, who was an eminent wildlife historian in the 1950s, and Dr. Hartley Jackson, who wrote the book *Mammals of Wisconsin* [published in 1961], felt that elk were probably once found throughout the whole state."

But the end of the era of elk in Wisconsin came in the late nineteenth century, when unregulated hunting extirpated them from the state.

Explains Laine, "The last documentation that there were elk in Wisconsin was found by Dr. Schroger. It was a shipping report from a railroad station in Chetek that listed six elk. These particular animals had apparently been killed near Lake Superior. One would assume if they had been killed in Minnesota, they would have been shipped to Duluth, where they would have been either marketed right there or shipped elsewhere on the Great Lakes. But because they were shipped by railroad from Chetek, it's more likely that they came from the south shore of Lake Superior and were in Wisconsin Territory.

"Of course," clarifies Laine, "that doesn't definitively mean that these were the last six elk in Wisconsin. Obviously, the territory had some remote areas, and folks don't always bother to document what they eat! But we know they were here, at least, until 1886."

## One Species; Several Eco-Types

The reason the RMEF holds its Bugle Days Rendezvous in the month of September—and the reason I'm here now, in these northern Wisconsin woods on this Saturday afternoon—is that elk become eloquent then. Or, at least, elk become more vocal. As the bulls prepare to mate, they will emit squeals, barks, whistles, and bugles as part of the annual ritual.

Elk make other notable sounds—ones that come not from their mouths but their bones. When they walk, their joints make cracking noises, much like the sound we produce when we crack our knuckles. This cracking tells elk that other elk—rather than a predator—are nearby.

While some scientists claim that there are five subspecies of elk, Laine believes there is only one: *Cervus elaphus.*

Says Laine, "Currently, the trend is to think of just one species of elk in North America. And it's a relatively young species, only about ten thousand years old. Elk researchers have done a fair amount of DNA testing of elk across North America, and they've found that there's no significant difference between any of what we now consider are eco-types.

"Separating elk into eco-types rather than subspecies means that the environments in which the individuals live have an influence on what those particular animals will look like," Laine goes on to explain. "For example, if an elk lives in an area where there's a longer growing season, it will tend to be larger in body size than an elk that lives in a region with a shorter growing season. While environmental differences provide for slightly different appearances of the elk, their behavior is the same in all areas and genetically they're the same. *Species* and *subspecies* tend to refer to genetic differences, not just morphological differences. These animals freely interbred with one another and definitely respond to each other's calls."

Our Wisconsin elk eco-type, then, has dark, thick coats, which help to absorb sunlight for warmth. The legs and necks of Wisconsin elk are often a darker color than their bodies. They are seven to ten feet long and weigh from five hundred to a thousand pounds. An average bull stands five feet at the shoulder.

Male elk develop large, branching antlers during the summer in time for the fall breeding season. As their antlers grow, they extend behind the elk's head, rather than growing tall and pointing forward, such as those on white-tailed deer (see chapter 5, "White-Tailed Deer: Ferreting Out a Phantom"). As the daylight increases, changing hormones cause the antlers to grow faster. The antlers do not turn into bone until late summer. Until then, they are covered in velvet—a soft, protective layer that aids in blood flow. When the antlers become fully grown in August, the velvet either falls off or is rubbed off. Elk joust during the rut, clashing antlers to establish dominance.

Elk are chiefly grazers, feeding on a variety of plants, including lichens and woody material. Newborns rely on their mother's milk for at least a month, gradually moving on to a diet of vegetation.

Gestation in elk lasts for 250 days. In the spring, after the white-spotted calves are born, they will hide for a couple of weeks to avoid predators, similar to the behavior of white-tailed deer fawns.

"Elk almost never have twins: 99.7 percent of the time, they'll have a single calf, unlike their smaller, white-tailed deer 'cousins,'" says Laine. "And also unlike white-tailed deer, elk are gregarious. Their strategy to prevent being eaten by predators is to be in a group and to have a warning system set up, composed of multiple eyes, ears, and noses. Their birthing strategy is to 'put all their eggs in one calf,' so to speak, and then try to protect that calf in a communal fashion. On the other hand, white-tailed deer use the numbers approach. A single doe defending a territory will have two fawns instead of one. If she loses one to a bear, she still has the other one. So she plays the strategy using the numbers game, and the elk do it by communal protection."

The main body of an elk herd consists of cows and their calves, while bulls tend to herd together at the fringes of the group. "Typically, yearling bulls will hang around the cow-calf group," says Laine. "At two years, however, the bulls become sexually mature. They'll try to stay in proximity of the cows, and, in some

While a white-tailed deer's antlers grow tall and point forward, an elk's antlers stretch out behind the animal's head. (Photo: John T. Andrews)

cases, the cows might even tolerate them. It depends on how well they behave. If they start to become aggressive with the calves, the cows will chase them away."

A bull who joins a cow-calf group and establishes a "harem," however, will not tolerate a male who is two years old or older. Explains Laine, "A bull will chase another sexually mature male away. Now, that's not to say that those 'satellites' won't stick around in close proximity. They just won't be allowed to be in with the group of cows. And, harems vary in size. One harem might be a bull with a single cow, or with a cow and a calf. Another harem might have half a dozen cows in it or even more. Whatever the size of the harem, a bull will aggressively protect his cows. We have had one verified mortality due to two bulls fighting, so it does happen."

## Moving Day

It's about 3:30 p.m. on this warm and windy September Saturday when I arrive in the community of Clam Lake, located within the national forest. I easily make my way to the Chequamegon's Day Lake Campground, just one mile north of Clam Lake on County Highway GG. A white tent has been set up on the grounds, where later the RMEF will provide a picnic supper. Laine is scheduled to give a talk at 4:30 p.m. on the status of the Wisconsin elk herd. Since I'm about an hour early, I decide to take a hike on the trail that winds down toward the shore of the 632-acre Day Lake.

As I walk along the water's edge, I can see the reflections of birches and tall jack, white, and red pines on the lake's surface. Fishermen often pull largemouth bass, muskies, pike, and panfish from these depths, while campers are frequently visited by eagles, loons, and white-tailed deer. At some point in the near future, they may also routinely spot elk.

Presently, there are three named groups of elk on the Wisconsin range: the Wayside Group, the 208 Group, and the 1265/1029 Group. Recently, however, as I'm about to learn from Laine's talk, the Wayside Group has started to transform into what will soon be called the Day Lake Group.

Now, back at the campground, I listen as Laine begins his presentation with an update.

"Over the last two years, the Wayside Group has shifted its activities about three miles north," he says. "And so we've renamed them. The 208 Group is still associated with Forest Road 208, and the 1265/1029 Group is affiliated with Forest Roads 1265 and 1029."

But what's even more encouraging for the Wisconsin elk restoration effort than the shifting of an established group into an unused portion of the elk

Towering pines surround peaceful Day Lake. Campers here are frequently visited by eagles, loons, and white-tailed deer. Soon, they may also spot elk. (Photo: John T. Andrews)

range is a new group being formed at Moose Lake, about twelve miles south of Clam Lake.

Says Laine, "When I first arrived here in 2000, the elk were occupying about 45 square miles of their 1,112-square-mile range. That was in the five years since they had been reintroduced. Since 2000, they've only expanded another 45 square miles, for a total of 90 square miles in the Clam Lake area.

"Over by Butternut," he continues, "we have about twenty elk that occupy about another 25 square miles. So, that's still only about 115 square miles of that elk range that is being occupied, or about 10 percent of the area that's been identified for them. That's why we've proposed and have gone forward with an assisted dispersal project," announces Laine.

In January 2011, with the help of a grant from the RMEF, eight cows (four yearlings, two two-year-olds, and two three-year-olds) and four yearling bulls were captured and moved to an acclimation pen southeast of Moose Lake in an area that was analyzed to ensure that it had abundant quality forage and winter habitat for elk. The animals were held in the pen until May 18, after green-up. Then, a section of the pen was opened, and the elk were set free. "The elk have continued to stay within about a mile of the pen," reports Laine happily, "which is what we wanted them to do."

One reason why elk here have pretty much stayed put is the quality of the landscape. "In the western United States in the Rocky Mountains," says Laine, "elk summer up near tree line, in the alpine meadows, where high-quality forage habitat, cooler temperatures, and fewer bugs are found. But their winter range is on grassland openings down in the valleys. So they migrate from winter range to summer range. But here in the East, from an elk's perspective, they have everything they need—from winter habitat to summer habitat—relatively interspersed and close together. They do not migrate on this type of habitat. In Michigan, Pennsylvania, and now Wisconsin, elk stay in the same area almost all year-round.

"That's why we're encouraging them to spread out into their range with assisted dispersal projects," continues Laine. "While they were in the Moose Lake pen, they developed a hierarchy within their new group. Leaders arose. And when the pen door was opened and they moved out onto the landscape, they basically had a whole new social system already developed. And it's been maintained over time—or for at least the first three to four months that they've been out. It looks like they've decided that *this is a good place; this is where we're going to stay.* The good news is that we've now got two little pockets and one big pocket of elk: about 120 to 140 in the Clam Lake area, about a dozen to twenty over by Butternut, and about a dozen over by Moose Lake."

## Elk Originals

While the formation of the brand-new elk group is exciting news, Laine's listeners are equally anxious to hear about what's happened with the original twenty-five.

"We know of four of the original twenty-five elk that are still alive because we're still getting signals from their radio collars," Laine reports. "Cow numbers 2, 9, 13, and 18 are still with us."

The original bulls, however, have not fared as well. "We don't know of any original bulls still out there," says Laine. "We did lose one of the original bulls in April 2010. Bull number 10 was killed by wolves. His radio collar had stopped working in 2001. The only reason we know about him is that, by luck, a turkey hunter saw him after he was attacked. He had fought the wolves to a standstill and was still alive.

"The turkey hunter contacted us," Laine goes on with the story. "We went out there, and we found the bull. He was fully alert but recumbent. He had chased the wolves off, but they had seriously injured him. He looked like he could potentially recover, so we left him. Unfortunately, he stiffened up, and the wolves came back. The next day, there wasn't much left of him. His recovered ear tag identified him as bull number 10, one of the originals. That placed him at sixteen years old, which is actually an abnormally long life for a bull in a nonhunted population *without* wolves, much less ours *with* wolves. Typically, bulls live to be about fifteen years old in a nonhunted population without wolves. Cows living without wolves tend to reach about twenty-one years old. But because of the abundant number of wolves on our elk range, cows here live to be about eighteen to twenty years old."

Generally, however, the only elk that can be definitively accounted for are the ones that are wearing working radio collars. Says Laine, "When the original elk were released, they all had radio ear tags on them. This was something that Dr. Orrin Rongstad had advised Dr. Anderson to use. Rongstad had used them with good success on white-tailed deer. Unfortunately, elk are much more social, and they communally preen one another. So they were chewing the radio ear tags out of each other's ears, and pretty soon few elk had them. So they put some hay back in the acclimation pen, and eighteen of the twenty-five original elk went back inside. Those eighteen were fitted with radio collars.

"Bull number 10, a yearling at the time, was one of the eighteen that had been recaptured and radio-collared," continues Laine. "But his radio collar had been dead since 2001. It was actually a pleasant surprise to find out that the radio collar was *not* on him when we found him. Apparently, it had gotten worn out and had fallen off. It was gratifying to see that these collars do eventually degrade."

While wolves account for most elk mortalities, they are not the only elk harvesters. Black bears and vehicle collisions take their share. About half of all elk deaths can be attributed to wolves (33 percent) or vehicle collisions (18 percent), while black bears take about another 16 percent. Assisted dispersal, away

Radio-collared elk in the Clam Lake area provide Wisconsin biologists with valuable data they can use to monitor, help grow, and disperse the herd. (Photo: John T. Andrews)

from known wolf pack territories and busy highways, should drastically improve the productivity of the herd.

The warning lights on Highway 77, which flash when elk are near and are triggered by the animals' radio collars, have also helped with preserving elk numbers.

Says Laine, "Over the last four or five years, we've added a reflective, orange color to the radio collars, and we've put them on sixty-one animals so far. Most of the elk in the past have been hit either in the early morning or late evening. Headlights shining on those orange, reflective collars have now made the elk more visible."

## BALANCING THE NUMBERS

Currently in Wisconsin, the elk herd stands at about 166 animals. For the past two years, thirty-four to thirty-eight calves have been born per year. To monitor population growth—or lack of it—elk are counted on what's called an *elk year* basis. Laine explains the system.

"An elk year starts with the start of calving season," he begins. "The date is determined by when we find our first calf. If the first calf we find is two days old, for instance, and we catch it on May 22, then the elk year for that particular year begins on May 20. Elk numbers are at their very lowest at that point. They're at their very highest about a month and a half later, after calving season. Then, over the next ten months or so, the numbers get slowly whittled down until just before the next calving season.

"So, you take the number that you had at the beginning of the previous elk year and the number you have at the beginning of the current elk year, and you subtract the two and divide by what you started with, and that's your percent of growth," says Laine by way of further explanation. "For example, last year we started on May 13 with 131 animals, and we ended on May 19 with 151 animals. So we gained 20 animals, which results in a 15 percent growth for that elk year."

Once the Wisconsin population of elk reaches two hundred, a limited hunting season on bulls could be instituted.

Says Laine, "Once we reach that benchmark of two hundred elk, there would be a very *limited* bull season for about 5 percent. So if we had two hundred animals, ten bulls would be allowed to be harvested. It would be done through a lottery system. Since we are in ceded territory, however, 50 percent of any harvestable quota goes to the Ojibwe tribes. So if we had a quota of ten animals, the Ojibwe would get five allotments, and five would be selected through a lottery."

For now, though, Laine focuses his attention on building the herd, rather than culling it. "My favorite time of year is the calving season," he tells me. "Seeing all those new elk coming on gives me hope for the future. Even though we have more than 150 elk right now, I still view them as being vulnerable."

### Elk on the Road, and . . .

As the sun begins to set, Laine finishes his talk and answers a few additional questions. We Bugle Days Rendezvous participants all agree to meet at the U.S. Forest Service guardhouse on the north side of Highway 77 at 5:00 a.m. tomorrow, before breaking off for a short night's rest.

On such a beautiful fall evening, however, I opt for an additional chance to see elk by cruising Highway GG for a bit. Some elk-spotting veterans have told me I might get lucky if I hit the highway just before dark. They were right.

Within ten minutes of cruising down the road, I spot a bull, a cow, and a calf crossing the pavement just ahead of me. It is my first sighting of elk in Wisconsin! Even though I have traveled through the Chequamegon-Nicolet National Forest several times before, this is my first encounter with this hulking Wisconsin mammal.

I slow my speed a bit and turn off Highway GG onto an intersecting forest road. I pull over to the side, and, using my car as a blind, I watch the family of three for about forty-five minutes. They seem not to mind me much at all, as they munch on leaves and twigs just off the shoulder of the road. It's gratifying to learn firsthand that as long as I stay quiet and inside my car, these massive mammals are willing to tolerate—at least for now—my presence in their old, familiar world.

### . . . Elk All around Us

In the dark of an early Sunday morning, cars begin to pull up one by one outside the U.S. Forest Service guardhouse. With steaming coffee cups in hand—and java-filled thermoses—we start to exit our vehicles and gather in the small parking lot. I'm pumped to tell my fellow elk-range tour-takers about last night's experience. What surprises me is that others have had sightings, too; most of them were Day Lake campers who watched as an elk wandered through the grounds late last night.

Laine organizes a caravan of just a few cars so that we may travel in as small a "profile" as possible. I am selected to ride with Laine in his truck, which has an antenna large enough to contact space aliens—or at least that's what it looks like to me. As he drives, Laine maneuvers a lever, which swivels the antenna around as it tries to "hear" bleeps from any radio-collared elk in the area.

Laine takes us to one of nine openings in the forest that have been constructed with financial support from the Rocky Mountain Elk Foundation and volunteers from both the Wisconsin DNR and the RMEF. In these high-quality forest opening areas (which total thirty-five acres in all), many cows have chosen to have their spring calves.

When Laine pulls over, we quietly get out of our vehicles. He instructs us not to talk and to move as silently as we can through both the openings and the woods.

About a half mile in, we hear the distinctive whistle of an elk bugling from somewhere off to the left. Soon after, a huffing chuckle—fast and undulating— is heard from away in the distance in front of us.

Laine walks to the side of the trail and begins rattling some bushes. Similar snapping is soon heard from not far off to the right. We smile as we hear this evidence of elk in the vicinity. We linger for about thirty minutes, but hear no more. Back at the spot where the cars are parked, Laine interprets what we just witnessed.

"The first bugle came from a young bull," says Laine. "It was answered by a chuckle, so the second bull was in a talkative mood. But while the response was in one area, the sounds of brush occurred in another. So the second bull was shifting his cows away from the other bull all the time that they were communicating."

Back in the truck, Laine picks up another signal with the enormous antenna, and we drive to the likely spot. Scrambling up an embankment and making our way through brush that is waist-high, we can just make out the shape of an elk standing near a tree trunk. We take turns hopping up on top of a nearby log to take a peek.

## A Higher Calling

By 9:00 a.m., our caravan heads back to the guardhouse, where our chilly cars await from almost four hours ago. On the ride back, Laine articulates why he feels having elk in the state is important.

"I think that restoration of indigenous wildlife could probably be the highest calling of any wildlife biologist," he says. "And that's because we're basically righting past wrongs. Elk were once very abundant here in Wisconsin. They were part of our landscape and part of our wildlife heritage. Our ancestors squandered that resource. Now, thankfully, we're able to help bring these animals back and make them part of the Wisconsin wilds again.

"Certainly, wolves do have an impact on our elk herd," he goes on to remind me, "but they, too, were here once upon a time. I would say whether you're talking about wolves or trumpeter swans or whooping cranes or wild turkeys or elk, we have to remember that they were here—and they belong here."

As a fellow bush rattler and traipser of trees of this great forest, I couldn't agree more.

## HOW TO HAVE A GENUINE
## ELK ENCOUNTER OF YOUR OWN

The **Clam Lake elk range** is in the Great Divide Ranger District of the Chequamegon-Nicolet National Forest. If you travel along **Highway 77 near Clam Lake,** you'll have a good chance of spotting elk. Elk-crossing signs along this stretch flash when elk are near.

Other good places to look for elk include along **Highways GG and M and Forest Roads 174, 175, 195, 208, 336, 339, 342, 1265, and 1275.**

When visiting elk country, remember that you must not disturb the animals. If you are trying to spot elk in the spring, keep in mind that during calving season, the elk are very sensitive to noise.

### Elk-spotting tips:

* Look near locations that have water, food, and shelter for elk, depending on the season. Elk prefer to forage in young timber harvests and grassy openings.
* Consider the time of day. Elk usually feed an hour after sunrise and an hour before sunset, and they rest in seclusion during the day.
* Listen for bugling sounds during early fall.
* Keep your distance.

By becoming a member of and volunteer for the Rocky Mountain Elk Foundation, you will be invited to the **annual Bugle Days Rendezvous in fall.** Go to www.rmef.org and www.rmefwisconsin.org to learn more.

At times, the Wisconsin DNR depends on **volunteers to help with calf searching and other research.** To learn more about elk and volunteer opportunities, visit dnr.wi.gov/topic/wildlifehabitat/elk.html or call the DNR at (888) 936-7463.

## HOW TO BECOME INVOLVED WITH
## ELK CONSERVATION EFFORTS

According to Laine Stowell, one of the best ways to help elk in Wisconsin is to become a member of the Rocky Mountain Elk Foundation.

"A great share of the funds needed to study the feasibility of restoring elk to Wisconsin, to do subsequent elk research and monitoring work, to purchase radio collars, and to make the Moose Lake dispersal project possible has come from grants from the Rocky Mountain Elk Foundation," he says. "By becoming a member of the RMEF, you support Wisconsin elk."

9

# Whooping Cranes:
# Saving a Spirited Species

## Necedah National Wildlife Refuge in Necedah

### WHOOPING CRANE FESTIVAL

In 1831, according to contemporary report, the whooping crane was common in the fur countries of Canada, and was even then so tenacious of life that there were known instances "of the wounded bird putting the fowler to flight, and fairly driving him off the field." This information will be of small surprise to people familiar with this spirited species. . . . The most statuesque of North American birds, standing over five feet tall, the whooping crane moves nearly a yard with each long graceful stride; its fierce, fiery eye and javelin beak, backed by a mask of angry carmine skin, might well give pause to any creature wishing harm to it. . . .

The whooper was one of the first birds remarked upon by the explorers of this continent, and the wild horn note of its voice . . . contributed to its early legend. Its dislike of civilization was evidenced by its swift disappearance from the East Coast. . . . During the nineteenth century it retreated west of the Mississippi, and by 1880 was a rare bird everywhere. It was last seen in Illinois in 1891, and a nesting in Hancock County, Iowa, four years later, was the last recorded in the United States.

—PETER MATTHIESSEN, *Wildlife in America*, 1959

When nature writer Peter Matthiessen wrote the above account more than fifty years ago, it was true that no whooping cranes were in evidence in the United States. Happily, that is no longer true, and Wisconsin has been a major player in the comeback of these sonorous birds.

Still, the Whooping Crane Eastern Partnership, a group of nonprofit organizations and government agencies working together to reintroduce a migratory population of whooping cranes—which currently stands at about ninety-four individuals—to eastern North America, estimates that there are no more than 500 whooping cranes anywhere in existence (captive or wild). Only about 240 birds are in the wild population that migrates between northwestern Canada and the Gulf Coast of Texas. Whooping cranes' "dislike of civilization"—which Matthiessen references above—may be the reason why this secretive bird is having so much trouble. As Richard King, biologist at Wisconsin's Necedah National Wildlife Refuge, puts it, "The biggest difference between sandhill cranes [see chapter 10, "Sandhill Cranes: Going Out for the Night, as They Come In"] and whooping cranes could be that sandhills have adapted very well to existing side by side with humans—and whooping cranes, well, not so much."

Today, whooping cranes stretch out their seven and a half feet of wingspan in America's skies in the two migratory flocks and in one smaller, nonmigratory flock of about twenty-four based in the Kissimmee Prairie Preserve State Park in Florida. And one of the few places where you can see whooping cranes in the wild—and one of a handful known worldwide for its dedication to their recovery—is right here in Wisconsin: the Necedah National Wildlife Refuge.

### Reconnoitering on the Refuge

The Necedah National Wildlife Refuge, one of seven national wildlife refuges in Wisconsin, occupies part of the ancient lakebed of Glacial Lake Wisconsin. When that vast, seventy-mile-long and 160-foot-deep lake drained for the last time, a flood of water rushed down the Wisconsin River, carving the famous rock cliffs around Wisconsin Dells and leaving behind a load of sand. The wind later sculpted that sand into dunes and ridges. The Ho-Chunk called this area *Necedah*, meaning "land of yellow waters," due to the high iron and mineral content in the soil that stained the left-behind marshes.

I've come to this place of raw sienna and ocher on this particular mid-September Saturday for two reasons: to see if I can discover one of the rarest cranes on earth in the wild and to learn about their struggle for survival at the Whooping Crane Festival, an annual event that is being held this year at Lions Park, just two miles east of the refuge.

The 43,656-acre refuge, located northwest of the village of Necedah, off of Highways 21 and 80, was the reintroduction site for an experimental population of whooping cranes for ten years starting in 2001. For every one of those years, young "whoopers" were brought to the refuge from the U.S. Geological Survey's Patuxent Wildlife Research Center in Maryland. From June through the first week in October, the young whooping cranes were trained at the Necedah National Wildlife Refuge to follow ultralight aircraft. Since 2011, rearing and training of the whooper chicks has been conducted at the White

River Marsh Wildlife Area in the northwest corner of Green Lake County and northeast corner of Marquette County.

After training, the youngsters are led by the plane down to one of two wintering locations in Florida: Chassahowitzka National Wildlife Refuge or Saint Marks National Wildlife Refuge. By the following April, these same birds migrate back, unassisted, to central Wisconsin, where they breed. This new migratory population in eastern North America augments the only wild migrating flock, the one that travels from Wood Buffalo National Park in Alberta and

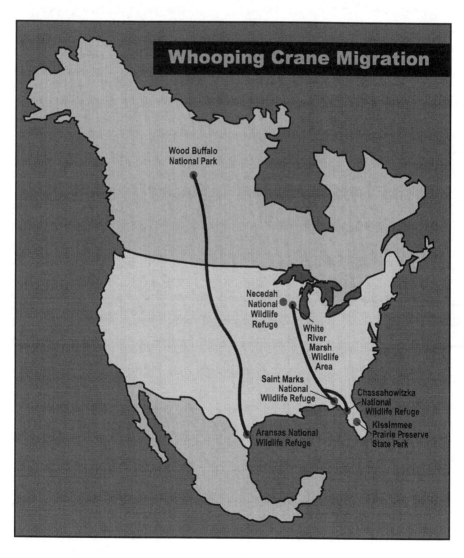

the Northwest Territories in Canada down through Manitoba, the Dakotas, Nebraska, and Kansas; and then down to the Aransas National Wildlife Refuge in Texas. Helping the cranes to establish this second migration route requires the partnership of more than sixty organizations, sponsors, and donors.

My first stop on the Necedah National Wildlife Refuge is at the Visitor Center. It sits on the edge of Rynearson Pool No. 1, a water management impoundment constructed in 1936. Occasionally, Rynearson Pools No. 1 and No. 2 are drawn down, to expose mudflats and provide a buffet of fresh vegetation and invertebrates for more than 245 bird species and the several species of mammals that frequent the refuge.

I make the center my first stop so that I can hike the Observation Tower Trail, just to the east of the building. A little under a mile, the looping trail meanders through woods and wetlands. Halfway through, I find an open-air blind and sit down to soak in the sounds, smells, and sights of a September day in Wisconsin. Within minutes, from somewhere in the nearby reeds, I hear the throaty, rattle-like utterances of sandhill cranes.

Once at the tower, I climb its two stories. I'm awed by the number of water bodies spread out below me as far as I can see, way too many to count. In fact, there are more than thirteen thousand acres of wetlands on the refuge property. This is a waterfowl's paradise.

## Fire and Water

In the early twentieth century, more than 120 miles of ditches were dug on what would become the Necedah National Wildlife Refuge. Bonds that were to be paid off with increased property taxes, which were supposed to result from the drainage improvement, funded the project. In his book *A Sand County Almanac*, conservationist Aldo Leopold wrote about the government-sponsored drainage while sawing through the growth rings of an old oak: "Now the saw bites into 1910–1920, the decade of the drainage dream when steam shovels sucked dry the marshes of central Wisconsin to make farms, and made ash-heaps instead."

By the 1930s, however, those high property taxes, intense peat bog fires, the Great Depression, biting insects, and a frost-prone landscape had caused most of the farms here to be abandoned. The federal government, under the authority of the National Industrial Recovery Act of 1933 and the Emergency Relief Appropriation Act of 1935, now found itself the owner of 114,964 acres of Wisconsin land.

A Civilian Conservation Corps (CCC) crew moved in to build dams and dikes to reflood drained areas, plant pines, construct firebreaks, and battle wildfires. On March 14, 1939, by Franklin D. Roosevelt's Executive Order 8065, a portion of the almost 115,000-acre parcel was designated as the Necedah Migratory Waterfowl Refuge. In that same year, Aldo Leopold started the Department of Wildlife Management at the University of Wisconsin. It was the world's first academic department dedicated specifically to the emerging field of wildlife management.

According to the refuge's Richard King, "Aldo Leopold first came here to do research with his graduate students in 1936. It's interesting that the history of this property weaves together with national figures such as Aldo Leopold and Franklin D. Roosevelt. Our mission, determined by the Refuge Improvement Act of 1997, is to restore habitats as much as we can to their original, pristine conditions and to help develop an appreciation for such wild places. It's really that 'land ethic' principle that Aldo Leopold talked about all those years ago. And it started right here, at the Necedah National Wildlife Refuge," he proudly says.

In 1940, the Necedah Migratory Waterfowl Refuge was renamed the Necedah National Wildlife Refuge and transferred from the Department of Agriculture's purview to the Department of the Interior.

To slow the encroachment of willows onto wetlands and oaks onto prairies, refuge personnel conducted the first prescribed burn on the property in 1946. Since then, more than seventy-five thousand acres of habitat have been pre-scribed burned. By the 1980s, habitat management included not only fire but water. Since that time, the flowages created by the CCC crew have been period-ically drained under a plan that is now known as Moist Soil Management. Draining, which occurs in May, exposes two plants with dense seed heads: smartweed and millet. They provide food for migrating waterfowl—more than one hundred thousand annually. The flowages are then reflooded in six-inch increments at two-week intervals beginning in mid-September.

Today, the Necedah National Wildlife Refuge is a mix of pine, oak, and aspen forests; wetlands and open water; grasslands; and rare savannas. It is one of the largest stopovers in the state for migratory sandhill cranes and has the distinction of supporting one of the world's largest populations of endangered Karner blue butterflies.

## AN ORCHESTRA OF SOUND

But it is the whooping crane (*Grus americana*) that people most associate with the refuge.

While sandhill cranes and whooping cranes are the only two crane species native to North America, it is the whooping crane that takes the top spot for the tallest bird on the continent. They are almost entirely white, with black wing tips, black facial markings, black legs and feet, and a bare patch of red skin on the top of their heads. Their eyes are yellow.

Whooping cranes are extremely territorial, both in their nesting habitats and in their winter range, where they defend feeding areas. They are omnivorous and will eat just about anything.

The birds' unusual name comes from their distinctive calls. The "unison call" (or "whoop") is a duet given by both members of a pair. While not executed at precisely the same time, the two birds' vocalizations are very closely coordinated; so closely coordinated, in fact, that it sounds like a single bird is making the call.

That call is also just one unique facet in a distinctive display of courtship behavior. Not only do the birds throw their heads back and let forth a whoop, but a pair will also jump up and down and kick their legs out in a wild dance.

All birds have very powerful breast muscles for flying. Because of that, they have large sternums with a *keel*, a bony partition that pushes out from the body, to which these powerful breast muscles attach. But in the whooping crane, that keel is hollow with an inordinately long trachea coiled up inside it. This long windpipe accounts for the volume of their whoops, which sound like tubas or French horns—except that the cranes' notes can be heard from two miles away.

### From Sixteen—Hopefully—to Success

That orchestra of whooping crane song was once much more abundant on the North American continent. Historically, whooping cranes made use of a breeding range that extended from Alberta, Canada, to the southern end of Lake Michigan. Their wintering grounds included parts of northern Mexico, the Texas Gulf Coast, and parts of the Atlantic Coast. There were groups of non-migratory whoopers that lived in Louisiana and possibly some other parts of the southeastern United States.

After my climb to the tower, I head over to the Whooping Crane Festival at Lions Park, where I know John French Jr., the research manager at the Patuxent Wildlife Research Center in Maryland, is scheduled to speak. I can't think of a better way to get a crash course on everything related to whooping cranes than directly from the leader of the country's whooping crane restoration program.

Several large tents are set up around the grounds, containing food concessions, arts and crafts exhibits, and raptor shows. The events schedule lists presentations from wildlife photographers, U.S. Fish and Wildlife Service experts, and Operation Migration pilots. I find a seat in the tent where John is just beginning his talk, titled "Whooping Crane Biology and Restoration."

Throwing their heads back, two whooping cranes send out a closely coordinated "unison call" (or "whoop"). It sounds as if a single bird is making the cry. (Photo: John T. Andrews)

"By the time of the widespread prairie settlement after the Civil War," begins John, "whooping cranes had become uncommon, with no more than fourteen hundred scattered birds. The draining of marshes and the plowing of prairies for agriculture destroyed most of the birds' nesting habitat, and given whooping cranes' inability to adjust to us, their numbers declined dramatically. Hunters, hobbyists, and museum collectors then scrambled to acquire some of these remaining birds and their eggs for their collections, further adding to their demise."

By the turn of the century, whooping cranes no longer bred in the United States, and by the 1930s, they were gone from Canada's prairies. By 1937, only two small flocks remained: one nonmigratory flock in southwest Louisiana and one migratory flock that nested somewhere in Canada and wintered in Aransas, Texas. In that year, the Aransas National Wildlife Refuge was established on the Gulf Coast to protect the migratory whooping cranes' wintering grounds.

By 1939, however, the migratory population's numbers dwindled to only about sixteen birds, with just six remaining in the nonmigratory flock. Severe hurricanes soon decimated the Louisiana population, and the last individual from that flock was taken into captivity in 1950.

"Of those sixteen birds, only three to five were breeding females," says John. "So all whooping cranes alive anywhere today have derived from them. That's an extremely small base. Imagine the great loss of genetic diversity with only about four breeding females. That's important to understand when it comes to managing this restored population."

With such a small migratory flock left, it was feared that there were far too few whooping cranes remaining to overcome inbreeding—in addition to the many hazards of a long, arduous migration. Nor was there a way to protect the flock once it left Texas, since the whooping cranes' breeding grounds, far north beyond Saskatchewan in the continent's vast sub-Arctic territories, remained a mystery.

Then, beyond anyone's expectations, years later the cranes brought six young south, and by 1950, their numbers had started a slow climb back up to thirty-three. They plummeted again during the next three years, however, when twenty-four were killed during migration, mostly by Saskatchewan farmers who complained that the Canadian Wildlife Service and other groups committed to bringing whooping cranes back from the brink of extinction were wasting money on a bird that was doomed anyway and that was destructive to their crops. The farmers were shooting the "pesky things" on sight.

With the real possibility that this magnificent bird would vanish from the earth, the National Audubon Society solicited public support by broadcasting the cranes' dramatic story all along their known migration route: in Texas, Oklahoma, Kansas, Nebraska, the Dakotas, Montana, and Saskatchewan—and especially in the environs of known resting places, such as the South Saskatchewan, Platte, Niobrara, Cimarron, and Red Rivers. The campaign was successful, and the shooting of whooping cranes stopped.

By chance, in 1954, a Canadian crew flying over Wood Buffalo National Park on their way back from fighting a fire noticed some white birds on the ground. The crew had accidentally discovered the whooping cranes' nesting place. That discovery provided a means to save the birds from imminent extinction. Because whooping cranes lay two eggs per clutch but usually succeed in raising only a single chick, scientists believed that they could go in and safely remove one egg from each nest without decreasing the productivity of the wild flock. Eggs collected from 1967 to 1996 became the foundation for all captive breeding-and-release programs in North America.

But in at least one case, eggs weren't the only things recovered.

"The first bird taken in captivity was captured up in Wood Buffalo in the mid-1960s," says John French. "The Canadians were doing a survey of the nests, and they were there after the chicks were flying. They spotted one chick that was with its parents. When the parents took off, he didn't fly with them. When they looked a little closer, the chick appeared to have a broken wing. They caught the chick, and with his capture, interest grew in starting a breeding program. The chick was named *Canus*, a contraction of *Canada* and *U.S.* His name was meant to signify the cooperation between the two countries in working to conserve and restore whooping cranes.

"Canus came to Patuxent in 1966," continues John. "We learned a lot from him about general whooping crane biology: how to keep these birds in captivity, what their nutritional requirements were, and how to design a pen that would work well for them. He was very important to the establishment of captive flocks and really took restoration efforts up to the level where they are now."

John believes that except for Canus, all but one of the other birds now in captivity came from eggs that were collected from the Wood Buffalo nests. "It's by far the easier and safer way to bring birds into captivity," he affirms.

In 1975, a captive whooping crane breeding program was started at the Patuxent Wildlife Research Center. To reduce the likelihood of a catastrophic event wiping out the entire captive population, Patuxent transferred twenty-two whooping cranes to the International Crane Foundation (ICF) in Baraboo in 1989 with the intent of establishing a second migratory flock. The ICF and Wisconsin were chosen for this recovery effort for several reasons: Wisconsin is within the historic breeding area of migratory whooping cranes; a reintroduced Wisconsin flock would be sufficiently separated from the existing migratory flock; suitable habitat on federal, state, and private lands was available; and— perhaps the main reason Wisconsinites can be proud of their selection—Wisconsin's long tradition of environmental commitment and support from the public would increase the chances for success.

### OPERATION MIGRATION

In the wild, young cranes learn migration routes by following their parents. But when trying to establish a brand-new migratory flock from scratch, parent surrogates with migratory know-how are needed. In Wisconsin, an ultralight aircraft fills that requirement. And the first step in conditioning the cranes to see the aircraft as a "parent" occurs while the chicks are still in the egg.

As mentioned, in the wild, cranes usually lay two eggs, but only one chick typically fledges. In captivity, however, the cranes' eggs are removed as soon as the birds lay them, upping productivity from two eggs to five to eight. The eggs are then incubated under sandhill cranes for the first two weeks and in artificial incubators for the second two weeks. The eggs are not allowed to hatch under the sandhills to avoid having the whooping crane chicks "imprint" on that species. Just before hatch, the eggs are exposed to sounds of whooping crane calls and ultralight aircraft engine noise. Whooping crane–costumed biologists at Patuxent then rear the chicks until they are forty to sixty days old. They are never exposed to an uncostumed person or the sound of a human voice.

The chicks follow a disguised biologist around much as they would their parents. Soon, the biologist climbs into the ultralight aircraft, and the chicks begin to follow the plane on the ground. Both the crane costume and ultralight play recorded whooping crane calls, communicating with the chicks in their own language. When the chicks are about six weeks old and have learned at Patuxent to run behind the aircraft on the ground, they are boxed up in crates and sent to the White River Marsh Wildlife Area for "flight training camp" behind the ultralight.

The cranes develop flight capability quickly and soon are able to fly short distances behind the ultralight, operated by personnel from Operation Migration, Inc. The flights become progressively longer, until the chicks are ready to begin the long autumn journey. Operation Migration pilots then lead them on a twelve-hundred-mile trip from the White River Marsh Wildlife Area in Wisconsin to either the Chassahowitzka National Wildlife Refuge or the Saint Marks National Wildlife Refuge in Florida.

In October 2001, the first group of reintroduced whooping cranes departed Necedah National Wildlife Refuge and began their southeast migration. Every fall since then, juvenile whooping cranes have followed ultralights from Wisconsin to Florida, a trip that can take two to three months to complete. The birds spend their first winter on the Gulf Coast of Florida, where biologists monitor them. When spring arrives, they undertake the return migration north—unaided by ultralights. In subsequent years, the reintroduced cranes migrate without assistance. On their own, the birds are able to fly more efficiently and cover greater distances by riding thermals and soaring, making the journey in only a few days or weeks.

Starting in the fall of 2005, the ultralight Operation Migration Program was supplemented with the Direct Autumn Release (DAR) project, where some crane chicks are released into the company of older cranes—both whooping cranes and sandhill cranes. For their first migration, these chicks follow behind elders that know the migration route from Wisconsin to the southeast United States.

Says John, "Once the cranes get to Florida, we stop managing them quite so heavily. We put them in a big, open pen where they are protected from predators,

Young whooping cranes follow an ultralight to Florida, a journey that can take up to three months to complete. Once on their own, however, the birds can make the trip in a few days or weeks. (Photo: Bob Leggett)

such as bobcats. We provide them with a little bit of food. But they are free to fly out for other habitats and learn to forage for themselves. If they haven't learned quite enough to be independent, they can come back and get a little food and then try to go out again. As the winter goes along, they spend more and more time away from the pen. Then at the right time of year, March or so, they fly back to central Wisconsin on their own, in groups of two to five, or maybe even alone.

"Today," continues John, "the eastern migratory flock is growing, but very slowly. And the estimated 240 birds in the wild, migratory population produce about twenty to thirty chicks a year. The nonmigratory flock in Florida, however, has not been reproducing well, and mortality rates have been high, primarily due to the bobcats."

## No Medals for Best Nester

Trying to get a handle on how many wild whooping cranes there might be just in the state of Wisconsin during an average summer has been difficult. Before coming to Necedah, I had asked Richard King for his opinion on how many pairs of the cranes he thought could be nesting here.

"It depends on how you define *nest*," answers Richard. "Some younger pairs build a nest but they don't lay an egg. So if you say, 'built a nest *and* laid an egg,' in 2011 we had twenty-two nests, from twenty different pairs [two were re-nests].

"But cranes live a long time," he goes on to explain. "Their strategy is 'We're not going to have a lot of chicks in any one year, but we don't need to because we live so long.' In the wild population in Canada, birds in their thirties are still reproducing. If you think about it from a very practical standpoint, if you are a member of a population that wants to sustain itself, in your lifetime, you only have to replace yourself once. So, if you nest for thirty years, does it really matter if you don't nest or fledge a chick in any given year if you only have to replace yourself once? This year, although we had twenty-two nests, they only resulted in four chicks. Of those four chicks, none of them survived to fledge. So the 2011 production was zero. Most people think that sounds very bad for the whooping cranes as a whole. But they don't need to replace themselves every year, if you multiply it out.

"You also need to account for the fact that this population has just recently moved into this area," Richard adds. "Most of the birds that are in this population came from eggs that were collected from wild nests in Canada. And then those eggs were transported to Patuxent Wildlife Research Center in Maryland, where the chicks were raised in pens. And then we brought them to Wisconsin.

So, of course, there's a learning curve. There's nothing about their history that would teach them to survive in the wilds of central Wisconsin. When we look at nest success and production, we would expect that it would be very low in the beginning. And that's what we're seeing."

In 2012, twenty pairs of whooping cranes bred or attempted to breed on the Necedah National Wildlife Refuge. They fledged two chicks. While future releases of young, captive-bred whooping cranes will take place at the White River Marsh Wildlife Area and the Horicon National Wildlife Refuge (see chapter 12, "Canada Geese: Dealing with Dueling Attitudes"), it is hoped that the Necedah population will grow as the birds from all three Wisconsin sites mix, breed successfully, and disperse.

"I started working with whooping cranes at the Necedah National Wildlife Refuge in 2009," says Richard. "By that time, the reintroduction project had reached some stumbling blocks. There was a bottleneck with nest success. The birds appeared not to be interested in their eggs. They would just leave their nests unattended. People on the project were having trouble honing in on the problem, so the Fish and Wildlife Service asked me if I would bring some of what I had learned figuring out similar problems with red-headed woodpeckers, eastern massasauga rattlesnakes, and Karner blue butterflies to help solve this mystery."

Although there isn't a definitive answer yet, one is getting closer. "The first thing we did," Richard says, "is look at the successes we've had with other reintroductions. And here in Wisconsin, we have the example of the trumpeter swan. In the first ten years or so of that project, nobody really knew if it was going to work. We tried cross-fostering, with mute swans raising trumpeter swans. Costume-rearing, with the trumpeter swans imprinting on a decoy, was also used. The trumpeter swan program took a similar route to the one the whooping crane project is now taking. And despite one early nesting success in 1995, we went years without having another successful trumpeter swan nest here. People started asking the question 'Is central Wisconsin just not suitable?' It wasn't until the number of wild-produced birds exceeded the number of captive-produced birds that growth really took off. But, the population had to reach that critical mass, and the birds had to get a certain amount of experience under the belt. That's the same thing we're seeing with whooping cranes."

Currently, whooping crane nests are being closely monitored by the use of surveillance cameras. "Is it an issue of predators coming in, is it related to weather or biting insects, or could the number of generations the birds have been in captivity be an influence?" asks Richard. "All of those things have to get factored in when we're looking at predicting whether or not a whooping crane nest will survive from one day to the next, let alone an entire thirty-day incubation."

What Richard has discovered is that whooping cranes don't seem to be as committed to their nests as other birds that nest in similar habitats are. "Trumpeter swans, sandhill cranes, and common loons will very rarely leave their nests," he says. "They also have about a thirty-day incubation period. For that month, they just tend to that nest. If they're feeding, they're not far from that nest. Whooping cranes will sometimes just leave. If a crow, a mink, or a snapping turtle happens to find those eggs before they get back, well, so be it. There are lots of theories about why that is, and my job as a scientist is to test them one by one. It takes a lot of time and a lot of discipline."

One theory is that the whooping cranes show up in Wisconsin in poor health. It could be that the energetic requirements of migration are so large that they can't stay on the nest because they have to go eat. Or, does it start further back, with the winter habitat? Are they leaving the winter grounds already in a very weak condition?

"In 2009, I tried to test that hypothesis," says Richard. "I put corn out for half the pairs. Unfortunately, the pairs that ate the corn didn't have any more success at nesting than the pairs that didn't eat the corn. So while that doesn't exclude that theory, it does point to the greater possibility that something else is going on."

Could biting insects in a Wisconsin spring force whooping cranes to leave their nests? "In 2011, the cranes themselves sort of disproved that theory," says Richard. "We had four cranes that nested and hatched a chick. Shortly after they left that nest area, we went in. There were lots of biting insects at the nest. But yet, these cranes were successful."

There is some evidence that age and its attendant experience have an effect. Generally speaking, the older a nesting pair and the more nest attempts they've made, the more likely they are to incubate full term, hatch an egg, and rear a chick. "Underlying all of this," adds Richard, "is the fact that these birds have been out of the wild for two or three generations. In captivity when they nest, their eggs are taken away to improve their productivity. As a result, there's no natural selection, no reward for being a really good nester. So it becomes very difficult to tease any one thing out of what is most likely a very complex issue affected by multiple variables."

## Still in the Balance

While whooping cranes are on the federal Endangered Species List, in Wisconsin they are deemed "experimental/nonessential." Approaching the end of his lecture, John French turns his attention to the topic of the threats whooping cranes face as they struggle to rebuild their populations.

"The Wood Buffalo flock has plenty of territory in northern Canada," says John. "For as far as the eye can see in that region, there's wet marsh interspersed with spruce forest. However, down in Texas, it's a different story. Aransas has beautiful coastal marshland and estuarine habitat. But development is creeping closer and closer to the edge of that refuge. And a lot of the upland areas where some of these birds feed are now being developed, so the habitat is really getting constrained. In addition, the inland waterway goes right through the refuge. If there were ever a spill from a tanker or a chemical boat, it would destroy that habitat—the *one* habitat that this flock uses."

## A Witness to the Struggle

The Ojibwe call the whooping crane Echo Maker or Speaker for the Clans and revere and admire it for its oratorical abilities. Among the five clans or totems of Crane, Bear, Martin, Fish, and Loon, it is *Ah-jii-jak*, or Crane (more specifically, the whooping crane is *Wabishki Ah-jii-jak* or White Crane), who shares the chieftainship with Loon (see chapter 6, "Loons: Counting on the Croix"), but it is Crane who sits in the place of honor, nearest the water drum and the east door of the Grand Medicine Lodge.

For Richard King, whooping cranes deserve respect for another reason. "These birds face a lot of obstacles," he says. "Some of them migrate over a thousand miles from Florida and have to contend with winter, power lines, bobcats, bears, and vehicles. Once they make it all the way up here, they have to build a nest, lay eggs, and tend to those eggs—rolling them every hour or so and keeping them warm and at the right humidity—for a *month*. On top of that, they have to feed themselves while they're doing it. And the bugs are not pleasant— I've been out there. Then, when they finally manage to hatch a chick, they have to take that chick out into the world and find food for it, too.

"It's a tough struggle *every* day," Richard reiterates. "Every critter out there has the same plate. But because we watch whooping cranes so closely, we get to *see* them in that struggle. I think that's what is most striking about them. They're on our screens, and we get to witness it."

## What Wisconsin Is Supposed to Be

After John French's lecture, I decide to head back to the Necedah National Wildlife Refuge for one more opportunity to find a rare whooping crane—in the wild. Besides, the refuge is such a scenic and bird-filled place that I want to stay here until the last of the September sunlight fades. I remember what Richard had told me about why the refuge is so special for him.

"I find myself motivated by some child who is not yet born," he had said. We restore habitats and bring animals and plants back to the landscape so that someday some young child can come here and get inspired by nature and know what Wisconsin is supposed to look like. This place can give them that little bit of wildness. Because if we don't preserve that for them, my fear is that there won't be any wild places left for young people to go to for inspiration and to connect with nature. At that point, people will stop caring about the natural world. And if they don't care, then we should all just pack up and go home."

This time on the refuge, I decide to drive on Bewick Road, which runs between Sprague Pool and Goose Pool. Using my car as a blind, I see several sandhill cranes and Canada geese floating on the two bodies of water. It hits me that this is Richard's "what Wisconsin is supposed to be."

Just before I swing the car around to go back down the road the way I came, I spot two very white birds—almost like ghosts—that are in sharp contrast to the gray and brown forms around them. Raising my camera to look through the telephoto lens, I see the unmistakable red crowns of whooping cranes. I watch this "spirited species" on the water for twenty minutes, until they seem to dissipate into the foliage along the shore.

## HOW TO HAVE A GENUINE
## WHOOPING CRANE ENCOUNTER OF YOUR OWN

Richard King says the best place on the **Necedah National Wildlife Refuge** to look for whooping cranes is from the Observation Tower, which is situated close to the Visitor Center.

When encountering a whooping crane, remain at least one hundred to two hundred yards from the bird so that it will not become accustomed to humans. If possible, stay concealed in a vehicle. It is especially important to avoid disturbing cranes on a nest or during evening roosting.

The Wisconsin Society for Ornithology has developed a bird-watcher's Code of Ethics, which can be found at wsobirds.org/?page_id=1929.

Another spot to see whooping cranes (although in captivity) is at the **International Crane Foundation**, located between Baraboo and Wisconsin Dells, just off of Highway 12. Go to www.savingcranes.org for more information.

## HOW TO BECOME INVOLVED WITH
## WHOOPING CRANE CONSERVATION EFFORTS

The Natural Resources Foundation of Wisconsin is a major supporter of the whooping crane project. You may donate to the foundation by going to www.wisconservation.org and clicking on the tabs that read "Donate Now" and "Support Whooping Cranes."

To donate directly to the Necedah National Wildlife Refuge, call (608) 565-2551 or e-mail necedah@fws.gov.

Richard King would also like you to know that part of your federal income tax funds national wildlife refuges. "It's that one time annually," he says, "when you can feel good about paying your taxes." But since budgets fluctuate from year to year, write to or talk with your Congressional representatives about the importance of places such as the Necedah National Wildlife Refuge.

Remember that whooping cranes depend on wetlands for nesting, chick rearing, and avoiding predators. Private citizens own and manage 75 percent of Wisconsin wetlands. Protection of these lands and conservation of water quality increase the cranes' long-term chances for survival.

Report whooping crane sightings using the form at www.fws.gov/midwest /whoopingcrane/sightings/sightingform.cfm. By keeping track of the birds and the areas they use, more is learned about their biology and ecology.

And educate yourself about whooping cranes by visiting the Whooping Crane Eastern Partnership website at www.bringbackthecranes.org. You can also learn about the birds by attending the Whooping Crane Festival. The venue changes from year to year, so visit the Operation Migration website at www.operation migration.org for up-to-date event information.

♋︎

# Sandhill Cranes:
# Going Out for the Night, as They Come In

## Crex Meadows Wildlife Area in Grantsburg

### FALL WILDLIFE FESTIVAL

They stand alongside crows, Canada geese, and pigeons as one of our most familiar avian neighbors. They're big, they're vocal, and they seem to tolerate us well. But of the four, these are the guys we love to spot. They are sandhill cranes.

Steve Hoffman, the wildlife biologist based at Crex Meadows Wildlife Area near Grantsburg, Wisconsin, can attest to the universal appeal sandhill cranes seem to possess.

"Even my wife, who is definitely *not* a birder or an early riser, will come out with me to do sandhill crane counts," he says. "People are just drawn to them for some reason. I can't articulate what that is, but there's something special about them, that's for sure."

Today, sandhill cranes can be found from Mexico to Siberia and from the Pacific to the Atlantic Coasts. I suggest to Steve that since whooping cranes (see chapter 9, "Whooping Cranes: Saving a Spirited Species") are one of the rarest cranes in the world and sandhills are the most numerous—and since Wisconsin has both—perhaps we are drawn to them precisely because of that dichotomy, that they are the quintessential "everyman's crane."

"Maybe that's it," he says, but with a tone that tells me he's not quite convinced that's the whole story. "*Maybe* that's it."

### SIGNING UP FOR SANDHILLS

Probably like almost everyone in Wisconsin, I've seen sandhill cranes near my home, especially in cornfields. I've even seen them in the very small marsh a half mile down the road from my house. But I've rarely seen them in groups of more

Although it's hard to define what it is that draws us to them, sandhill cranes seem to have universal appeal. (Photo: John T. Andrews)

than two or three. I have yet to experience hundreds—or even thousands—of them darkening the evening sky, as they come in to roost for the night.

That's why I'm going to the Fall Wildlife Festival at Crex Meadows this early October Saturday. I've signed up to take one of the sandhill crane tours that starts at 5:00 p.m. We registrants will gather at the Crex Meadows Wildlife Education and Visitor Center, where, along with our guide, we'll board a bus that will take us to the best spots for stopping and watching as—we hope— sandhills numbering in the triple digits will come in from their daytime feeding grounds to their night roosts.

## GOVERNMENT ACTS AND
## PUBLIC APPRECIATION

But such an event as a sandhill crane tour in Wisconsin hasn't always been possible. In fact, sandhill cranes have made a remarkable comeback.

In what has become an all-too-familiar story regarding so many species, as European settlers pushed west across North America in the eighteenth and nineteenth centuries, unregulated hunting and the drainage of wetlands led to a significant reduction in the numbers of sandhill cranes. Unfortunately for the birds, the six- to fourteen-pound cranes made for a delicious meal. In an account published in 1622, Edward Winslow, one of the Plymouth colony's founders, and William Bradford, governor of Plymouth for thirty years and a chronicler of its history, noted that during the Pilgrims' first year in North America, a "fat crane" was a welcome addition to any meal. Some have even suggested that a sandhill crane was likely to have been on the original Thanksgiving dinner table—either in place of or along with a turkey.

At this same time of open hunting, the productive soils of many shallow marshes were drained in preparation for farming, significantly reducing sandhill crane breeding habitat. Luckily, in 1918 the Migratory Bird Treaty Act halted the hunting of migratory birds, such as sandhill cranes, unless "due regard" had been demonstrated as to "the zones of temperature and to the distribution, abundance, economic value, breeding habits, and times of migratory flight." While the act helped the sandhills' numbers by eliminating unregulated harvest, the loss of habitat was still a major hurdle.

In 1929, when a young forest service biologist named Aldo Leopold could find only five pairs of sandhills in the state, he chastised museums and other collectors for continuing to seek out specimens. In February 1936, President Franklin D. Roosevelt called the first North American Wildlife Conference to assess the status of and stimulate conservation for many wildlife species. At this conference, Franklin S. Henika, the Madison-based regional game manager for the Wisconsin Conservation Department (predecessor to the Department of Natural Resources), estimated that there were only about twenty-five nesting sandhill crane pairs here, along with a few small breeding populations in other Great Lakes states.

Says Steve Hoffman, "Even if Franklin S. Henika had underestimated the number of sandhill cranes here, if you read Aldo Leopold, you know that not many of them were around in the 1940s. And just thirty or forty years ago, you still wouldn't have seen a lot of sandhill cranes. Since the time of pristine, presettlement Wisconsin, we've lost half of the wetlands and marshes we had. And sandhill cranes need wetlands to nest.

"When groups come through the Wildlife Education and Visitor Center at Crex," continues Steve, "I talk to them about why we lost the animals we did. I tell them to look at old photos of early cities, villages, and farmsteads; there were no trees—everything was gone. Here at Crex, they even attempted to drain the marshes. They cut ditches with plows to try to get the water out. They burned them and tried to plant crops on them. You can almost immediately rectify overly generous harvest levels by protecting wildlife with laws. But when habitat is gone, it's gone for a long time, and you can't replace it easily."

Gradually, thanks to conservationists such as Aldo Leopold, appreciation for the value of wetlands grew and habitat important to wetland species received some protections, setting the stage for the recovery of the sandhill crane.

It's difficult to get an accurate count of the number of sandhill cranes in the state today. But on the basis of estimates by volunteer crane counters for the International Crane Foundation's Annual Midwest Crane Count in April—the one that Steve Hoffman and his wife participate in—and fall fly-out counts requested by the U.S. Fish and Wildlife Service at various sites, it is believed that Wisconsin may have as many as twenty thousand greater sandhill cranes.

That number prompts some to say that a fall hunting season should be instituted in order to protect farm crops from undue damage caused by cranes, to keep the sandhill crane population from exploding, and to afford the state's sportsmen with another hunting opportunity. Others say that the present number of sandhill cranes is not increasing, except in a few counties. Therefore, hunting is not necessary for population control. They would argue that crop damage is only minor; besides, a fall hunting season would not solve the problem of crop damage in the spring. The International Crane Foundation is currently helping to develop a new technique that it hopes will treat corn seeds with a "crane deterrent."

## OF MOOSE AND MEN

The ditches dug with plows to drain the marshes for farms that Steve Hoffman spoke of are just part of the heavy tapestry of human history that must be examined to understand the present fabric of one of the largest state-owned wildlife areas in Wisconsin.

Located in Burnett County, Crex encompasses thirty thousand acres of wetlands, prairies, and forests. Its acreage is part of the Northwest Sands (see chapter 3, "Sharp-Tailed Grouse: Liking the Land Between"), one of sixteen distinct, ecological landscapes recognized by the Wisconsin Department of Natural Resources (DNR). This large, sandy plain was left when the glacier retreated about ten thousand years ago. The sands extend from northern Polk County up to southern Bayfield County—an area that covers 1.2 million acres. The southern portion of the Northwest Sands, where Crex is located, contains huge marshes—leftovers from an ancient lake called Glacial Lake Grantsburg.

When European settlers first arrived, they found the sandy soil of what is now Crex covered with scattered red and jack pines, brush, and a variety of prairie grasses and flowers. Naturally occurring wildfires had maintained these plant communities. After settlement, however, when wildfires were routinely extinguished, the landscape grew into an oak and jack pine forest.

"Settlers tried to farm Crex, but they soon gave up," says Steve. "People pretty much starved on the upland farms because the sandy soil was so poor. They tried planting wheat, but that didn't work well. The same thing happened with potatoes. You can raise potatoes a couple of years, and then things go downhill."

In 1912, an eastern corporation purchased twenty-three thousand acres of what is now Crex Meadows for the site of the Crex Carpet Company, a producer of grass rugs and wicker-type furniture. The name Crex is derived from the genus name of sedges: Carex. The company set up three carpet "camps" on the edges of the marshes, on what is now both Crex Meadows property and the Fish Lake Wildlife Area, just six miles south of Crex.

Explains Steve, "The crews in the camps would cut the sedge grasses, and then they would be shipped to Minneapolis–Saint Paul, where the grass furnishings would be made. At that point in time, grass carpets were the best floor covering you could have. And that's how they advertised them: 'The finest carpets ever made. Don't be fooled by cheap imitations!'

"Then, two things happened," Steve reports, "the invention of linoleum for floor covering and the stock market crash of 1929. By 1933, the Crex Carpet Company was pretty much out of business. Linoleum was better wearing. And a lot of the people that were here and just hanging on found that they couldn't make it through the Great Depression and the drought years; by 1940, nearly two-thirds of the land here had become tax delinquent. So, in 1946, the DNR purchased twelve thousand acres of this tax delinquent land to start the Crex Meadows Wildlife Area."

Since that time, managing Crex has focused on restoring the wetlands and prairies that historically had been here. "A fellow by the name of Norman Stone was our first wildlife biologist," says Steve. "He was really the Father of Crex Meadows; he had a lot of vision and plenty of drive for acquiring land and building flowages. Working in conjunction with the county highway department, he got a lot of those flowages built in the 1950s and 1960s. It took a huge amount of effort to get what we have here now. If it weren't for Norm Stone, this would be a totally different-looking place."

In fact, since its purchase by the state in 1946, twenty-nine flowages have been built and seven thousand acres have been restored. Says Steve, "We now have again a whole host of species on our wetlands and upland, brush-prairie types of habitats: probably more than 270 species of birds, including Canada geese, sharp-tailed grouse, upland plovers, yellow rails, and sharp-tailed sparrows. We've also got white-tailed deer, black bears, wolves, coyotes, foxes, fishers, badgers, voles, and meadow jumping mice. We've even had a moose wandering through! For three or four years now, we've seen the moose at the same time of year—the first week in September to almost the middle of the month. It's a bull, and he seems to be getting bigger every year. You have to wonder, What's on his mind? Does he just take a little walkabout at this time of year or what?," Steve jokingly asks.

## A LINK TO THE ANCIENT PAST

But it is the greater sandhill crane (*Grus canadensis tabida*) that is particularly suited to Crex's mix of wetlands and open landscape.

Says Steve, "Typically, to build a nest, two sandhill cranes will go to a marshy area and pile up a mound of vegetation. They'll form that into a five-foot-diameter bowl and line it with small, fine plant stems and twigs. Then, the female lays two olive-colored eggs, which are spotted with reddish-brown. Both parents incubate the eggs for about a month. The chicks leave the nest soon after hatching and will fly at ten weeks. But they stay with their parents until the following spring.

"In the marsh," continues Steve, "they can take their young out and wander around. When I'm in that sedge marsh, though, and walking through it, I'm sinking in up to my knees in sphagnum and sedge and water. But sandhills stay high. They're light enough and they've got big enough feet so that their weight is displaced over a large area, making it so that they can almost walk on water all over out there," he says in amazement.

The greater sandhill crane stands about four and a half to five feet tall, thanks to its long legs. The adult has gray plumage with a bushy tuft of feathers over its rump and a red patch on its head. Its cheeks are white.

During nesting season, sandhill cranes will sometimes preen ferrous mud into their back and chest feathers, making them appear to be a rusty-brown color that blends into the brown grasses and sedges of their nesting areas. The juvenile is grayish with tawny mottling and lacks the red head patch. Sandhill cranes fly with their necks and heads outstretched like other cranes.

Distinguishing a sandhill crane from a whooping crane is easy, if you keep in mind two features. Explains Steve, "I've had calls where a person will say to me, 'I think I see a whooping crane out there.' So I drive over to take a look, and usually it's a sandhill. You'll see some very light-colored ones at times, but they're not white. And whooping cranes have black wing tips. That's the key; if

The plumage of sandhill cranes is typically gray. But in spring, the birds will camouflage themselves by preening ferrous mud into their feathers. This new, rusty-brown color helps them blend into the grasses and sedges of their nesting areas. (Photo: John T. Andrews)

you've got a question in your mind at all, the black wing tips and a very white color should determine it.

"Sandhills are also one of the few birds out there that are sometimes confused with a white-tailed deer—especially when they're bent over and feeding—because their coloration is the same as a deer's summer coat," he adds.

And according to Steve, sandhill cranes are not particular about what they are bent over, feeding upon. "They eat not only seeds," he reports, "but just about everything that moves out there: grasshoppers, insects, squirrels, small mammals, and frogs. Frogs are common food, especially in the fall when a lot of leopard frogs go up into the fields. Sandhills will eat anything up to the size of a thirteen-lined ground squirrel, if they get the chance."

It is thought that sandhill cranes not only *resemble* an ancient bird species (see chapter 6, "Loons: Counting on the Croix"), they *are* the oldest living bird species on earth. While a 10-million-year-old crane fossil from Nebraska could be the direct ancestor of the sandhill crane, the oldest unequivocal sandhill crane fossil is 2.5 million years old—still more than one and a half times older than the earliest remains of most living species of birds, which date from about 1.8 million years ago.

It's no wonder, then, that coming close to losing this particular ancient bird is what inspired Aldo Leopold to become an impassioned advocate of conservation.

## SNOWBIRDS

Today, from their population lows, the sandhill crane has recovered to more than six hundred thousand birds worldwide. The most abundant cranes on the planet, sandhills nest in the north in Canada, the northern Soviet Union, and the northern United States; in smaller numbers, they nest in the south in Florida, Mississippi, and Cuba. Only the sandhills that nest in the north migrate. They winter mostly in Texas, New Mexico, and Mexico.

According to the International Crane Foundation, based in Baraboo, Wisconsin, six subspecies of sandhill cranes are recognized:

+ *Grus canadensis canadensis* (lesser sandhill)
+ *Grus canadensis tabida* (greater sandhill)
+ *Grus canadensis rowani* (Canadian sandhill)
+ *Grus canadensis pratensis* (Florida sandhill)
+ *Grus canadensis pulla* (Mississippi sandhill)
+ *Grus canadensis nesiotes* (Cuban sandhill)

Within the three migratory subspecies (*Grus canadensis canadensis, Grus canadensis tabida,* and *Grus canadensis rowani*), the U.S. Fish and Wildlife Service defines six populations, on the basis of geographic ranges and migration routes: the Pacific Flyway (of lesser sandhill cranes), the Central Valley, the Lower Colorado River Valley, the Rocky Mountain, the Eastern (of greater sandhill cranes), and the Mid-Continent (of lesser, greater, and Canadian sandhill cranes). The largest population of sandhill cranes is the Mid-Continent, estimated at 450,000 to 500,000 individuals. Wisconsin is a core part of the Eastern Population (the largest population of *greater* sandhills), which numbers nearly 60,000.

The majority of the Eastern Population breeds across the Great Lakes region (Wisconsin, Michigan, Ontario) and winters in southern Georgia and in Florida. In late summer and early fall, these cranes leave the breeding grounds and congregate (or *stage*) in large flocks with as many as 100,000 birds.

Eastern Population cranes stage for several weeks before beginning their southeast migration through their primary corridor, which passes through Illinois, Indiana, Ohio, Kentucky, Tennessee, and Alabama, en route to Georgia and Florida. And one of the places they stage is at Crex Meadows, which makes it one of the best places in the fall to see large numbers of sandhill cranes and makes Crex's sandhill crane tours popular.

Says Steve, "Including both the Crex Meadows Wildlife Area and the Fish Lake Wildlife Area, ten thousand to twelve thousand birds is probably a good estimate of what we'll have staging here before the fall migration. Sandhill cranes leave as soon as the weather changes. Usually by the time the marshes freeze up, they're gone. That used to be by the first of November. But now, more and more with our changing weather patterns, we still have cranes here until the middle of deer season, which starts the Saturday before Thanksgiving. To begin that long, arduous, migratory trip, there has to be a reason for it. For the cranes, that reason is snow on the ground and frozen marshes. That's what drives them out."

After the sandhill cranes take off from Wisconsin, the Jasper-Pulaski Fish and Wildlife Area in southern Indiana is typically the next stop. Because of our recent mild winters, however, some sandhills don't feel the need to go all the way to Florida. They may overwinter in Tennessee, Kentucky, Indiana, or even in southern Ontario on Lake Erie.

"It's always amazing to me how quickly they come back north again," says Steve. "They leave here in November, and quite often there are sandhill cranes back in southern Wisconsin by the end of February or by mid-March, for sure—even up in Crex. I think in spring, they get restless and want to get to their breeding grounds as soon as possible."

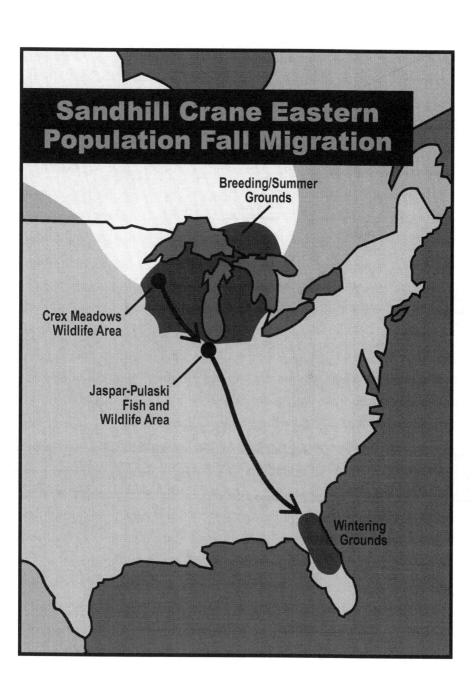

Sandhill Crane Eastern Population Fall Migration

Breeding/Summer Grounds

Crex Meadows Wildlife Area

Jaspar-Pulaski Fish and Wildlife Area

Wintering Grounds

Some of those cranes will stay to breed on Crex Meadows, while others will continue going north. "In spring, the cranes will usually come in numbering in the hundreds versus the groups of thousands that they leave in during the fall," says Steve. "If they've got their mates with them, they're anxious to start working on establishing territories and making preparations so they're ready to go with breeding as soon as conditions allow."

Like whooping cranes, sandhill cranes are territorial breeders. A pair will claim an exclusive area of twenty to two hundred acres for nesting and brood rearing. Courtship includes unison calling and an elaborate "dance," involving quick steps, half-spread wings, and leaps into the air.

Of the two eggs sandhills lay, only one young (called a *colt*) typically makes it to fledge. Within twenty-four hours after hatching, colts are able to leave the nest by walking or swimming.

Parents feed the growing colts at first, then lead them to food. Sandhill cranes are "teenagers" from two to seven years old, when they *may* pair up and nest. Many at this age, however, do not successfully raise a colt to independence. As they grow older, they become more experienced at bringing young into the world.

Nonbreeding cranes sometimes form small flocks in summer consisting of young birds, failed breeders, and adults without territories. Sandhills are long lived, often surviving more than twenty years. The oldest-known wild sandhill crane lived to be thirty-five years old.

### Coming in for the Night

After having spent the afternoon driving the self-guided, twenty-four-mile-long auto tour of this vast area, I manage to get to the Crex Meadows Wildlife Education and Visitor Center before 5:00 p.m., the departure time for my sandhill crane tour. Before I board the bus, I decide to take a quick walk on the short nature trail behind the center. A boardwalk lets me travel easily over a pond and a sedge marsh. All is quiet and serene.

Beyond the water, I step off the boardwalk into woods. Not far in, I climb an observation platform to get an overview of this southern portion of the vast Crex property. I look across Hay Creek Flowage, which is ringed by trees. A bald eagle suddenly glides down out of the pines on my right and drifts across my view into a dense stand of trunks on my left. Before I'm even sure I saw him, he has disappeared.

Back at the education center, I meet my fifteen fellow tour-takers and our guide. He tells us that we'll go to the south end of the Refuge Extension Flowage this evening, since the sandhills are roosting on the far end of the "refuge" (which is the marsh just beyond the flowage).

From the bus window, I watch as we travel past Phantom Lake and its flat expanses. Today, this "lake" is the largest body of water on Crex. In the early twentieth century, the shallow marsh that was here originally was drained for farming. In 1954, a 2.6-mile-long dike was constructed to create a large wetland habitat for waterfowl and other aquatic wildlife. The entire northern half of this two-thousand-acre flowage now contains a vast stand of wild rice—perhaps the largest in Wisconsin. Trumpeter swans, Canada geese, ducks, blackbirds, rails, coots, red-necked grebes, yellow-headed blackbirds, marsh wrens, and the occasional least bittern are just a few of those who drop in for a meal or a respite.

Before my tour, Steve had told me "one of the best things about Crex is its big, open spaces. It's cool to stand in some of these areas on Crex, look out, and take in the large, unbroken vistas. There are not many places in the state where you can have thirty thousand acres of wild land to look out at and roam around in." I now know exactly what he means.

Soon, we turn onto Main Dike Road, which takes us to the Refuge Extension Flowage. As the sun starts to get low in the October sky and the bus is parked, we begin to get out and set ourselves up to witness the flocks of sandhills that we hope will fly right over our heads.

"Sandhill cranes are a favorite target for a lot of photographers who come up here," says Steve. "It's definitely a good opportunity to take shots of birds in flight. And as the crane numbers have increased over the years, so have the numbers of people wanting to come out and watch them.

"It's just wild to see the cars parked along the roads near the refuge during the month of October," Steve goes on. "People bring their lawn chairs so they can sit outside on a nice fall evening and watch these birds fly overhead. Sometimes, they even set up tables with wine and cheese. I was told when I first started working here that that's what would happen. I didn't believe it then, but I sure do now!"

In the fading light tinged with gold that Wisconsin falls are famous for, faint "rattles" are starting to be heard. Soon, groups of these noisemakers begin to fly in: first, three or four sandhill cranes at a time, then twenty or thirty. Then, hundreds come winging in from the southwest, passing through the airspace just above us. They easily breeze by and then angle down to settle back in the marshes of the refuge. Bird after bird, the sound of their calls is deafening. Most of our heads seem to be permanently tilted upwards; but every once in a while,

I drop mine to look around and try to temporarily catch the eye of a fellow crane-gazer. When that happens, we smile at one another, each knowing how fortunate we are to be under this beating, bleating, breathing umbrella for these few minutes.

It's clear to me now why the sandhills guarantee a sold-out crowd almost every October evening on Crex. As Steve had told me, "It's an indescribable feeling watching those birds go through the air and land. It's something that's been going on forever, and I think people realize that. Here, in real life before you, are these big, prehistoric-looking and prehistoric-sounding birds, and that strikes a chord in all of us. Everything about them speaks of wild places."

In his now famous essay titled "Marshland Elegy," which appeared in *A Sand County Almanac* (1949), Aldo Leopold wrote that "the last crane will trumpet his farewell and spiral skyward from the great marsh." Fortunately in Wisconsin, it has not.

Sandhill cranes are favorite subjects for photographers. Adults have expressive faces with unfeathered, reddish- to dark-pink-colored skin on their foreheads. (Photo: John T. Andrews)

Such a successful recovery, of course, means that humans and sandhill cranes will have increasing interactions. But as we work to live together again, let's hope that this time we remember that sandhill cranes have been trumpeting their songs through the centuries long before we made our first grunt.

After reflecting upon it, I think I need to revise my theory on why we are drawn to this "everyman's crane." It's not because it is so numerous and accessible. It's because it holds that thing that we can't afford to again almost let go of forever, that thing that Steve alluded to and that Aldo Leopold once named "wildness incarnate."

## HOW TO HAVE A GENUINE
## SANDHILL CRANE ENCOUNTER OF YOUR OWN

Crex Meadows features a twenty-four-mile, self-guided **auto tour.** You can pick up the tour booklet, along with bird lists and other pamphlets, at the Wildlife Education and Visitor Center, located on Highways D and F.

Says Steve, "Many of the roads in the Crex Meadows Wildlife Area run across the tops of the dikes. This increases your opportunity to have encounters with wildlife in their natural habitats—right from your car."

But Steve also encourages exiting the car once in a while. "There are some **hiking trails** on Crex. But remember that you may **walk anywhere here except in the refuge.** In the brush-prairie, you never know what cool stuff you're going to find," he says.

To specifically view sandhill cranes, Steve recommends going to the **south end of the Refuge Extension Flowage,** just north of Main Dike Road. Since the sandhill cranes roost in the refuge, you can usually see them flying in at night or leaving in the morning from Main Dike Road.

Another good place to watch for sandhill cranes is on the **big marsh north of the North Fork Flowage.**

The **Fall Wildlife Festival** is held at the Crex Meadows Wildlife Area every October. Go to www.crexmeadows.org to learn more. **Sandhill crane tours** are typically held from 5:00 p.m. until dark on most Saturdays in October.

## HOW TO BECOME INVOLVED WITH
## SANDHILL CRANE CONSERVATION EFFORTS

To support Crex Meadows Wildlife Area and sandhill cranes, consider the following options:

- Donate to Crex Meadows Wildlife Area. If you are a wildlife-watcher, you are part of the 70 to 80 percent of the 120,000 visitors who go to Crex each year solely to view wildlife. Yet it is the other 20 to 30 percent—who are hunters or trappers—who provide nearly all of the funds for land acquisition and for wildlife management. The monies come from the sale of hunting and trapping licenses, duck stamps, and from a federal tax on guns and ammunition. So, if you are a wildlife-watcher, do your part to support Crex by going to www.crexmeadows.org/Donations.html.
- Become a member of the Friends of Crex. Doing so will keep you up-to-date on the wildlife area's news and activities. Go to www.crexmeadows.org/FOC.html.
- Purchase a federal duck stamp. To learn more about duck stamps and how to buy them, visit www.fws.gov/duckstamps. If you want to support wetland projects in the state of Wisconsin, purchase wildlife collector stamps at any DNR Service Center or by going to dnr.wi.gov/topic/wildlifehabitat/stamps.html.
- Encourage young people to get outside. Says Steve, "Our mission at the Crex Meadows Wildlife Area is to connect people with nature. In the spring, it's especially great to see families driving around on the dikes. That's the time when the goslings are out, and the kids invariably have their noses pressed up against the windows, watching those little geese running down to the water. The sooner young people develop an interest in and begin to care about nature, the better stewards of wildlife and wild areas they will be as adults."
- Become a member of or donate to the International Crane Foundation. Go to www.savingcranes.org to learn more.

# 11

# Saw-Whet Owls:
# Touching What's Wild

*Woodland Dunes Nature Center and*
*Preserve in Two Rivers*

OWLFEST

He threw the black glove, and it just stopped in midair—mystically suspended at eye level. We had all expected it to rapidly arc downward to the ground, as if it were one of the fall leaves spiraling around us, riding a whirlpool wind to the earth.

It was an attention-getting trick. The "reveal" was that the glove was being held in place by an all-but-invisible net, the kind used to catch saw-whet owls. Bernie Brouchoud had tossed his glove smack into the center of it, knowing his sorcery would delight the dozens of children watching him. This is just the kind of magic they were hoping for.

I'm standing on the grounds of the Woodland Dunes Nature Center and Preserve in Two Rivers, Wisconsin. It's a picture-perfect October Saturday, the kind when red and gold leaves make every deciduous tree a wonder, and the sun shining off the surface of Lake Michigan fabricates stars on the water. Only the silhouette of a big tanker far out from the shore breaks the endless line where sky meets water.

Today is the annual Owlfest at the preserve, and scores of children and adults from across the state and beyond have come, hoping to get up close with Wisconsin's tiniest owl.

And the star attraction is just about to appear. Bernie gathers the children—many of whose faces are colored in blues, yellows, and oranges by way of a face-painting station set up in a tepee—in front of the nature center building's deck. He brings forward a dark box. That amazing glove, now placed back on Bernie's hand, reaches inside. He slowly pulls out a diminutive owl: child-size, you could say. But this owl is no baby. It is a full-grown northern saw-whet.

Bernie hands the owl to a volunteer and brings out two more. Gently placing the birds' legs between their fingers, Bernie and other Owlfest staff walk the birds around the crowd, so all have a chance to see the little feathered ones just inches from their faces. The fingers of the adults in the crowd madly click camera shutter buttons, while the children's reach out from everywhere, anxious to touch what's wild.

### Owlfest: Banding and Bonding

Owlfest, a literal "hands-on" event, is something the Woodland Dunes Nature Center and Preserve has been doing well since the late 1970s. And according to Bernie, who is now the preserve's environmental education director, including the public in the work and learning that goes on here was in the plan from the very beginning.

"The policy at most banding stations is to *not* let the general public in," says Bernie. "As a bird bander, I know that when I'm measuring and weighing birds, if someone is watching and asking me a lot of questions, I'll tend to get

Saw-whets don't seem to mind being shown to groups of people, such as those at Owlfest. Attention grabbers, the tiny birds are the perfect ambassadors of the wild. (Photo: John T. Andrews)

my numbers goofed up. So, that's one of the reasons that banding stations are just simply not open. But we decided early on that we wanted to share this experience with people."

In fact, being a bird banding station is how Woodland Dunes got its start—and the starter was Bernie himself. "I actually began banding birds here in 1965," he says. "Because of the large number and variety of birds we banders were catching, several of us thought that this area should be preserved. Our official establishment date is 1974, when we started a quarterly newsletter, bought our first land, and set up a board of directors. Then, by the late 1970s, we began putting on an event we called NatureFest—the precursor of Owlfest—which included banding demonstrations and the showing of saw-whet owls."

For more than thirty years, then, a festival at Woodland Dunes has been forging a bond between people and a tiny emissary from the wild, natural world.

## Hiding in Plain Sight

Owlfest takes place on the third Saturday of October, in the midst of the saw-whet owl migration. The birds make their way to the Woodland Dunes vicinity from the Lake Superior region and points north. In the fall, when the north-west winds begin to blow, many saw-whets take flight toward Green Bay. When the birds get to the edge of Lake Michigan, their flight path shifts directly south, along or within a mile or two of the lakeshore. That's when they typically reach Woodland Dunes in Two Rivers. Some saw-whets will continue flying south, to places such as Illinois, Indiana, and Ohio. At least one that was banded in Wisconsin was recovered in North Carolina.

States Bernie, "The saw-whets fly southeast through the state—from Green Bay toward Woodland Dunes and then toward Cedar Grove. A lot of birds use 'sight lines' for their migration routes, such as a shoreline. The large Lake Michigan provides a great one. While many birds avoid flying over big bodies of water, they will follow a shoreline as a guide. And the south end of Woodland Dunes is only about a quarter of a mile from Lake Michigan."

While banding stations such as the ones at Green Bay, Woodland Dunes, and Cedar Grove are providing more and more knowledge about where some of the saw-whets are going in the winter, no one, specific wintering ground has yet been found.

"A lot of people are doing research on saw-whet owls, especially on the East Coast," Bernie reports, "and many books say that they are found in evergreens and conifers. But I have a feeling that the reason they can't find a *specific* wintering ground for saw-whet owls is that a lot of people are looking up in the mountains, in the southern Appalachians where there are spruces. In Wisconsin, we find that they're in deciduous shrubs. Farther south, you'll find evergreen shrubs, such as rhododendrons. But those shrubs are below; not high up in the mountains. I don't think that in the wintertime the saw-whet owls are in the dense evergreens, as the books say they are. Because what we find here is that when they migrate through, if we put our nets in real brushy areas—shrubby stuff—*that's* where we catch them."

The brush of Woodland Dunes makes saw-whet owls quite common here in the fall, although people rarely see them. Says Bernie, "Saw-whet owls don't fly before dark because they're food for the bigger owls. So they stay totally concealed. Big owls can't fly through the brush, but little ones can. So the brushy areas—not the forested ones—are the saw-whets' hiding place."

The nets at Woodland Dunes are set up the last week of September and remain up and open until the week before Thanksgiving. On almost every night in October, if it's not raining or extremely windy, there will be owls in the nets. On average, two hundred to four hundred saw-whets are captured every year.

"The nets aren't very high," says Bernie, "only about four or five feet tall. When we first started banding, we had nets that were twice as high. We'd leave them open, day and night, during the spring and fall migrations. When we left our nets open in the spring at night, we'd catch a lot of woodcocks and whip-poor-wills, among other birds. In the fall, though, we'd catch a lot of saw-whet owls. The Wisconsin Society for Ornithology used to have a little asterisk by the name *saw-whet owl* in their bird checklist. That meant that that particular bird had been seen and reported less than five times a year in Wisconsin. However, I have a picture of me holding thirteen at one time!"

Since 1965, when Bernie began banding birds at the Woodland Dunes site, the record number of owls caught in one night was seventy-two. And that night happened within the last ten years. "People come from all over the state to see the saw-whets at Owlfest," states Bernie. "But when we first began putting up nets, we tried setting them up in backyards that were maybe a block away from the lake, and then two blocks away from the lake, and then a mile away from the lake. In the fall, in every place where we had put up a net, we were catching saw-whets. But still, even a lot of the local people have a hard time believing that these birds can be found in their own backyards."

## A PLACE OF MUCH SIGNIFICANCE

Although you could say that bird banding and Bernie are the "founder" and "face" of Woodland Dunes, Bernie would add another leading element in the mix that created this preserve: Gordon Bubolz.

"Years ago, I worked as an assistant manager at an A&P grocery store in Green Bay," says Bernie. "I got acquainted with conservationist Gordon Bubolz, who, at the time, was an attorney, a realtor, and the president of an insurance company in Appleton. Gordon's personal goal was to have a natural area in every northeastern Wisconsin county. At the beginning of Woodland Dunes, there were thirty-three different landowners in the area. Gordon helped with buying that land. We'd sit down at kitchen tables with people and work out the sales. Our goal for Woodland Dunes was always twelve hundred acres, which we're almost at now," says Bernie proudly.

Gordon Bubolz founded a group called Natural Areas Preservation, Inc. He was also instrumental in creating Hobbs Woods, located three miles south of Fond du Lac and Mosquito Hill Nature Center in New London. A nature center in Appleton bears his name.

"It goes on and on with how many places he started up," says Bernie. "In the case of Woodland Dunes, Gordon originally bought the land and registered it in Outagamie County. That allowed a group of us to have the time to raise enough money to pay Gordon back. We then incorporated, and exactly according to the original plan that we set up, all the land was transferred from the Outagamie County Courthouse to the Manitowoc County Courthouse. And that's how it went. Although hundreds of people were involved in this project, we could never have gotten a start on acquiring all of this land without someone like Gordon Bubolz."

In 1992, Woodland Dunes was designated a State Natural Area by the Wisconsin Department of Natural Resources (DNR) for its importance to migratory and breeding birds and its rich biodiversity. More than 400 plant species, 260 resident and migratory bird species, 40 mammal species, 7 species of amphibians, and thousands of species of invertebrates populate the preserve, which contains at least five wetland types.

The DNR also considers Woodland Dunes a place of ecological significance because of its forested dunes (or ridges) and swales (wet troughs), one of only two examples of such a landscape in the region (the other is Point Beach State Forest, a few miles to the north) and of only a few, similar habitats in the world. Says Bernie, "Once, we went down to the University of Wisconsin in Madison and looked at satellite photographs of the whole Great Lakes region. We saw parallel ridge-and-swale areas—such as at Kohler-Andre Park, The Ridges Sanctuary, and Point Beach State Forest—but couldn't find any others that were fan shaped, such as they are at Woodland Dunes."

This rare ridge-and-swale topography was created by Lake Nipissing, a postglacial ancestor of Lake Michigan. More than five thousand years ago, Lake

Nipissing was nearly thirty feet higher than the present water surface of Lake Michigan. Glacial ice once blocked the escape of water from the lake, but as the ice melted and the water level fell, the shoreline of the lake moved south and east. As it did so, breaking waves scooped up and redeposited the sandy bottom, forming a series of parallel, underwater ridges and troughs. As the water surface fell, the ridges became long, low sand dunes, with perennially wet troughs between them. Fourteen such ridges and swales are the geological foundation of the Woodland Dunes preserve.

Over time, a beach-dune plant community populated the bare sand dunes and wet swales, followed by shrub carr, and then a rich forest containing many plant species. Today, about two-thirds of the ridges are timbered with aspen, white birch, and red maple. A mature forest of yellow birch, beech, hemlock, and white pine covers the remaining third. The understory flows with shining clubmosses, spinulose woodferns, starflowers, naked miterworts, and bluebeads. In the swales, ash, elm, and alder thrive, with occasional patches of dogwood, willow, white cedar, and sedges.

The DNR has bestowed a third honor on Woodland Dunes: officially, it is an Important Bird Area. Shorebirds frequent a nearby river marsh and often forage in adjacent farm fields. Warblers, thrushes, and many other songbirds use the forested portions of the dunes during migration. Several southern bird species, such as hooded warblers, blue-gray gnatcatchers, and white-eyed vireos are found here, and during the fall migration, all of Wisconsin's raptors use the lakeshore as a guideline.

## Ranking High on a Cuteness Scale

While it is one of Wisconsin's most majestic and large raptors that receives all the attention on the Wisconsin and Mississippi Rivers in the winter (see chapter 14, "Bald Eagles: Watching a Winter River"), in the fall around Lake Michigan, it is the state's smallest owl that is the headliner.

The northern saw-whet owl (*Aegolius acadicus*), Owlfest's tawny and tiny attraction, is only seven to eight inches high. The bird has a wingspan of fourteen to sixteen inches and weighs just a couple of ounces. Saw-whets have large heads compared with their bodies, which could, arguably, account for their cuteness.

Saw-whets have a large facial disk and vertical, brown streaking on their white breasts and bellies. Their eyes are yellow, and specialized feathers around their eyes direct sound to their amazing ears: one sits higher than the other to help them hear even better. Their bills are dark.

Saw-whets seem to prefer a one-note song, which sounds like a *too-too-too-too* whistle. Occasionally, they may issue a *sch-whet* call, which has been said to be reminiscent of a saw blade being sharpened. That may be the genesis for the owl's name; however, that cry is rarely heard.

While you may hear their calls, you won't hear owls flying. For most birds, flight is noisy. Air rushing over feathered wings produces turbulence that most prey animals can hear as a "swishing" sound. But nocturnal owls are able to make their silent forays for three physiological reasons: First, the primary feathers on the leading edge of an owl's wings are serrated. This design breaks down turbulence into smaller currents, allowing the air to pass through and eliminating sound. Some have suggested that these feathers may also shift sound energy to a higher frequency than prey can hear. Second, the feathers on the back end of an owl's wings are tattered like a scarf's fringe. As the bird flies and air flows over its wings, these trailing, tattered feathers break the sound waves. Third, an owl's legs and the rest of its wings are covered in velvety, down feathers that absorb any remaining noise created in flight.

Owls' ability to fly in silence has captured the attention of aircraft engineers, who are looking at the unique design of owl feathers for potential applications in the aeronautics industry. Since major airports have restrictions on how much

Unlike some other owls, saw-whets do not possess ear tufts. They do, however, have prominent facial disks, which amplify sound. (Photo: John T. Andrews)

noise they can generate per day, what is learned from studying owl feathers could someday help to make planes quieter. Researchers have postulated several ideas, including a retractable, brush-like fringe to mimic an owl's trailing wing feathers and a coating of soft material on aircraft landing gear to simulate downy legs.

Says Bernie, "When we catch the saw-whets in our nets for banding, we also weigh them and measure what's called the *wing chord*, which is a natural curve from the bend in the wing to the tip of the wing. If the flight feathers on the wing are all one color, that means that the owl hatched in that year. If there are two or three different colors in a pattern on the wings, that indicates that the owl is at least one year old; it did not hatch in that year. A lot of the knowledge that we now have regarding saw-whets comes from banding operations."

The three Rs in the world of bird banding are repeats, returns, and recoveries. "The *repeats* are the birds that we band and recatch within three months," explains Bernie. "If a bird we banded ourselves over a year ago is recaptured, that's called a *return*. And if one of ours gets caught by somebody else or we catch somebody else's, that's called a *recovery*. All of that information is sent to the Bird Banding Laboratory in Patuxent, Maryland. They compile the results from all of the banding stations in the nation, and we receive a copy of the final, composite report."

## Night Stalkers and the Night Gang

Reports and tales about owls, in fact, go back to a time when people routinely handed down stories around campfires. Because owls are nocturnal birds, there has always been something mysterious, ominous, or hidden about them. All over the world, the owl has either been a harbinger of doom or, in some cases, a carrier of wisdom.

The ancient Greeks saw the owl as a symbol of darkness and knowledge; the Egyptians associated them with death, night, and coldness; the Hebrews linked them with blindness; and the Japanese and Mexicans believed they were omens of death.

An old Breton myth explains why the owl is nocturnal. Wren, seeing that humankind did not have the gift of fire, decided that she would find some in heaven, and fly it back to earth. On the return trip, as the little bird struggled through the hole between the two worlds, she scorched herself and lost many of her feathers. All the other birds each gave her a feather to help her replace what she had lost—all, that is, except Owl. That is why today the owl appears only at night; he is too ashamed to face the other birds in the daylight.

In a similar Menominee myth, titled "The Origin of Night and Day," Rabbit, on a walk through the forest one day, encounters Owl, sitting on a tree branch. Small bits of light peek through the trees, but it is very hard for Rabbit to see. Rabbit tells Owl about his problem and that he would like to make the forest bright with daylight. Owl says to Rabbit that they should have a contest to see whether the forest should remain dark or be light all the time. Rabbit and Owl call all of the birds and animals together to witness the competition. Some of the animals want Rabbit to win but aren't sure if they want it to be light all of the time. Others, liking the darkness, hope that Owl will prevail.

The contest begins. Rabbit must keep saying, "Light, light," and Owl has to repeat, "Night, night." The trick is not to say the other's phrase. If one of them should state the wrong word, then that animal loses the game.

Rabbit and Owl keep saying their words as the other animals cheer them on. Finally, Owl mistakenly says, "Light." Rabbit is proclaimed the winner, and he makes daylight come to the forest. Yet he decides to let there be night as well for the benefit of all the animals. This makes everyone happy, and thus night and day are born.

Owls' proclivity for the night, of course, persists to this day. And because of that, today Woodland Dunes has a "night gang."

States Bernie, "To be a member of the night gang, you must first attend a couple of mandatory meetings. Then, in the fall for a period of about six weeks, you may sign up for a two-hour shift starting at 10:00 p.m., midnight, or 2:00 a.m. The nets are opened after dark and closed before dawn. There are always two people scheduled per time slot. Our night gang members are educated about the kind of lights to bring with them, how to take the owls out of the nets, and where to put them after they get them out of the nets. Last year, we had thirty people on the night gang. That's another way that we let the public participate in what's going on here at Woodland Dunes."

Bernie does admit, however, that being on the night gang isn't for everyone. Some screening is involved; for instance, children aren't allowed near the nets at night, and the distance you have to travel to get to Two Rivers is taken into consideration.

"We've had people from Green Bay and Milwaukee who have wanted to do this," relates Bernie. "That generally doesn't work. I particularly remember one lady from Milwaukee. One of our rules for night gang members is that they must call our hotline number before they come out. If there's a pending storm or it's very rainy or windy, we close the nets. But the Milwaukee lady had driven all the way here, and when she arrived, the nets were closed. I found her in the parking lot all by herself, sleeping in her car. I don't think she was very happy about it. So, being a night gang member is a little more difficult if you live far away. But if the weather is such that the nets are open, you have to be here at your designated time. If you understand that and you're willing, we'll welcome you in."

## A SHIFT IN TIME

Bernie has taken shifts on the night gang for more than twenty years, and his favorite is the one most people avoid. "A lot of folks who sign up for the night gang tend to shy away from the early morning hours," says Bernie. "It's easier to get people to sign up for the 10:00 p.m. slot than it is for the 2:00 a.m. one. I try to convince people that that's the best time to be out. Traffic is pretty quiet, so there is reduced highway noise. Often, I'll hear packs of coyotes yelping at each other, or I'll discover salamanders. Once, one of the night gang guys saw a gray fox near a net, running along. And that's the best time to see the northern lights. After you do it for a while, you really get to like it. You'll find a lot of stuff going on early in the morning."

## A FEATHER IN THE FOREST

Back on the preserve's grounds in front of the nature center building, Bernie lets go of the saw-whet he's been holding. It flies to one of the nearby trees and perches on a branch, looking down at us. The bird appears calm and just waits, mostly with its large eyes closed. Saw-whets seem to be highly amenable to being shown to groups like this. That ability makes them the perfect species to capture a child's attention and awaken an interest in nature.

By noon, the festival is over and the crowd starts to disperse. I decide to linger a little longer at Woodland Dunes. I take a hike on the Goldenrod Loop of the Willow Trail, just behind the nature center. Ducks swim quietly in Todd's Pond, and I notice that two rubber bats have been affixed to some tree branches. No doubt the preserve is getting ready for another event and an influx of children on Halloween.

Across Highway 310 off of Goodwin Road, on another piece of property that belongs to Woodland Dunes, there are more trails I'd like to explore before heading home. For centuries, early native peoples and animals have walked the backs of the ridges in this area, and I feel as if I'm following in their footsteps. The Yellow Birch Trail makes for an easy, 0.3-mile trek through a forest and a hardwood swamp, all on boardwalks. It leads into the Black Cherry Trail, a 0.8-mile walk that is partly on boardwalk and partly on a yellow- and

After a wild saw-whet is released at Owlfest, it flies to one of the nearby trees and perches on a branch. There, it closes its large eyes and calmly waits. (Photo: John T. Andrews)

red-leaf-covered footpath. Surprisingly, on this perfect, golden Wisconsin October Saturday, I meet no one else here on these ridges and swales, in the shadow of ancient Lake Nipissing. I wonder why that is.

I hear a light rain beginning to fall, but the canopy of trees provides me a raincoat, so that I actually feel no drops. Just steps away, I spot a beautiful, two-tone feather on the trail—a reward for my being the only visitor to this section of Woodland Dunes today. The multicolored feather is likely that of a hawk, I think, as I bend down to examine it. But I instead imagine that it was left behind by a much more petite predator.

### HOW TO HAVE A GENUINE
### SAW-WHET OWL ENCOUNTER OF YOUR OWN

**Owlfest** is held at the Woodland Dunes Nature Center and Preserve on the third Saturday of October. Go to www.woodlanddunes.org to learn more about the preserve and its events.

### HOW TO BECOME INVOLVED WITH
### SAW-WHET OWL CONSERVATION EFFORTS

To help support the Woodland Dunes Nature Center and Preserve and aid in the purchase of owl nets, you can "adopt" a saw-whet owl. Your twenty-five-dollar adoption packet will include your adoption certificate, a band number from the owl you're adopting, a logbook, and a photo of a saw-whet owl (a different owl is chosen to "model" every year). If your owl is then captured as a repeat, return, or recovery, you will be notified so that you can record your owl's travels in your logbook.

Says Bernie, "Once, a couple adopted an owl for their teenage son. The following year, we caught his adopted owl again. Later, it was captured a third time, and that's when things really got exciting—for us and the adopter!"

Call the Woodland Dunes Nature Center and Preserve at (920) 793-4007 to get your packet.

# 12

# Canada Geese:
# Dealing with Dueling Attitudes

*Horicon National Wildlife Refuge and*
*Horicon Marsh Wildlife Area in Southeast Wisconsin*

FALL MIGRATION

If you live in Wisconsin and someone mentions the word *marsh* to you, you can't help but conjure up the image of a wetland in fall at sunset, with a V-shaped line of Canada geese flying across a golden sky. Blame it on Aldo Leopold or the calendar photos our state inspires, but *marsh-in-fall-with-geese* is almost inseparable into its three component parts in Midwest psyches.

So it's the geese we see in our mind's eye over the marsh, with their black eye masks, their elegant hoods, and their sunlit throats. As much as the wolf is the feral denizen of our forests (see chapter 15, "Gray Wolves: Tracking and Howling"), the Canada goose represents the wild citizen of our skies.

But now, picture a Canada goose not flying over a marsh but walking in your neighborhood park or golf course. How quickly that image of the large bird changes. The word *overabundant* comes to mind, or even *nuisance*. It appears we are fickle in our estimations of *Branta canadensis*.

My goal today is to confront this dueling, double attitude we seem to have about Canada geese in our state. I'm traveling to the Horicon Marsh Wildlife Area and the adjacent Horicon National Wildlife Refuge on this October 24. I want to see the phenomenon of the Canada goose fall migration and to hear from the experts who deal with the flocks of geese—and the people who flock to see them.

Perhaps no other species today commands more observers in the wild yet still causes regular op-ed articles regarding the need to get rid of them from our backyards. As the Montana-based, contemporary nature writer and conservation advocate Rick Bass writes:

On the Horicon National Wildlife Refuge, a floating boardwalk on the north end of the great marsh provides passage over what is often called the Everglades of the North. (Photo: John T. Andrews)

*"Sometimes I think the geese are just resting—both from the exhaustion of the long trip here, and in preparation for the one that lies ahead, only five or six months away. I try to drink in the beauty, the grace, of the mere and miraculous sight of them—as if they are a thing that is here only for the moment—only this moment—and that if I do not see it now, drink it all in and feel it now, it will be gone, taken away."*

Here in Wisconsin—for certain Canada geese, anyway—that moment almost was.

## LESSON ONE:
### DIFFERENT CANADA GEESE, DIFFERENT TRADITIONS

The first thing that I learn about Canada geese when I arrive on the premises of the International Education Center on the southern, state wildlife area portion of Horicon Marsh is that the Canada geese that reside here most of the year and the migratory Canada geese that people come to the marsh to see in the fall are not the same type of goose.

Bill Volkert, a wildlife educator and naturalist for the Wisconsin DNR for twenty-seven years, will be giving a talk at the center on this Saturday afternoon titled "The Geese of Horicon." I plan to attend the presentation and then use it as my introduction to this vast wetland and its geese before I go out to watch them fly over for the first time this evening.

After greeting those of us who have gathered for the talk in the lobby of the education center, Bill takes us downstairs to a meeting room where we find seats at long tables that stretch from windows to door. Some of the tables are littered with books and papers, and feathers and skins; a group of Boy Scouts had been working on achieving their Nature merit badges earlier in the week. It's a good feeling to see the room in this messy flurry of recent activity; we can still sense the excitement of budding environmentalists here, and it fuels our own curiosity.

"Basically, there are three populations of Canada geese on Horicon," begins Bill. "The giant Canada goose [*Branta canadensis maxima*] is our local nesting bird. We also have what's called the *interior subspecies* [*Branta canadensis interior*], or what we refer to somewhat generically as *migrant geese*—even though the giants do migrate a bit. The more specific term for the migrants is the Mississippi Valley Population or MVP. These birds nest south of Hudson Bay and west of James Bay."

The third variety of Canada goose that frequents the marsh is the group known as *cacklers* (*Branta hutchinsii*). Says Bill, "Cacklers look like Canada geese but they are somewhat different. They are what used to be called the *lesser Canada goose* or the *Richardson's race of the Canada goose*. This group of geese has now actually been split off from Canada geese and has been reclassified as a distinct species. These geese are the real little guys, the pint-sized geese that are a little bigger than a mallard duck. The reason they're called *cackling geese* or *cacklers* is that, because they are so small, they can't produce the deep honk that the giants or migratory geese do.

"The cacklers are a high Arctic breeder," continues Bill. "They go northwest of Hudson Bay to nest. So there is a progression: the largest of the geese, the giants, nest in Wisconsin and the Upper Midwest. The midsize goose, the interior or MVP, nests around Hudson Bay, and the smaller ones, the cacklers, go even farther north to lay their eggs."

However, those geographic distinctions get muddled during fall's southern migration.

"The cackling geese tend to migrate down through the prairie states west of the Mississippi River," Bill tells us. "Although their main flyway is just a little west of us, that population does mix in with the interior population, or the MVP, and some do come through Horicon. A number of times on the marsh, I've overheard people who see a mixed flock going by say, 'Oh, look. They've got their babies with them.' But if you think about it, goslings are full grown by fall. Those 'babies' are a distinct species."

Learning that we could be seeing three different types of geese on the marsh this evening has already been an eye-opener for most of us. But it turns out that among Canada geese experts, the breakdown is even more extensive than that.

While Bill would say there are a dozen subspecies of Canada goose, there are some who claim that there are many more.

"A waterfowl biologist from Illinois named Harold Hanson thinks he can sort out as many as two hundred variations of Canada geese in North America," reports Bill. "But the classic studies—such as the one outlined in the 1976 book *Ducks, Geese, and Swans of North America* by Frank Bellrose—lists eleven sub-species of Canada geese. For management purposes, however, we might divide it a little differently."

When I later query Kent Van Horn, the migratory game bird ecologist for the DNR's Bureau of Wildlife Management, he has an alternate perspective. "Technically, they're not all *subspecies* but *populations*," he tells me. "Because Canada geese migrate and because they're governed by international treaty, ulti-mately the management and protection of them is a federal issue. So the U.S. Fish and Wildlife Service is the official agency responsible for Canada geese in this country. And the service defines eighteen populations."

Back at the education center, one of the talk's participants raises his hand. He asks Bill about how much interaction takes place among the three different variations of Canada goose found at Horicon.

"These primary populations, or subspecies, don't interbreed," answers Bill. "They can't, of course, if one group, the giants, are breeding in Wisconsin; another, the interior geese, are breeding near Hudson Bay; and the third, the cacklers, are breeding in the high Arctic. That's why we have such distinctive traditions among these populations of geese: They return to the same breeding grounds, select a mate from that population, inbreed separate genetic charac-teristics, and learn somewhat separate migration routes. But these birds *will* mix together when they're going south, so that's why every once in a while, you may see some little cacklers joining in with the MVP. Or, once the geese are on the marsh, you may see them flock together as they fly in and out on daily feed-ing flights. There's safety in numbers. But what's really going on in the overall migration is that these birds have their own traditions."

Those daily feeding flights are another facet of Canada goose behavior that is often confusing. "Every couple of years," says Bill, "I'll get a question from someone along the lines of: 'What's wrong with the geese? It's the fall migration;

they should all be going south. I just saw thousands of geese, and they're all flying north. What's going on?'

"The answer," says Bill, "is that what those people are seeing is *not* migration. They're watching a feeding flight. The geese have *already* flown south to come here. During the month and a half or two that they hang out at Horicon, they may fly out east, west, north, or south, depending on where the food is located from the marsh. When they do that, they'll join whoever is around—a cackler or a giant. That's when they mix up."

Lesson One: It appears that one Canada goose isn't just like another.

## LESSON TWO:
### LOSING THE GIANTS AMONG US—AND GETTING THEM BACK

What might be even more astonishing is that the giant Canada geese—the ones we find in our city parks and on our golf courses, the ones a lot of people complain about—almost went extinct.

Around the turn of the nineteenth century, the giant Canada goose population was decimated by pioneers coming into the state, both through hunting and egg collection. By 1906, giant Canada geese south of central Iowa had just about been wiped out. They began to disappear farther and farther north. They became rare in northern Wisconsin by the early 1930s. By the early 1950s, biologists believed that we had exterminated them.

Then, in the late 1950s and early 1960s, a few, small, remnant giant Canada goose populations were discovered—including one in Rochester, Minnesota, and one in Janesville, Wisconsin. People were maintaining some of these small flocks, so a restoration program was begun.

"The very first place in Wisconsin where a captive breeding program for giant Canada geese was ever tried was right here at Horicon Marsh," says Bill. "And that's the funny thing that a lot of people don't understand. Here's a bird that we were so afraid was going to go extinct in the 1960s, and by the 1990s, it was a nuisance problem! They had come back *so well*."

I ask Bill whether the population of giant Canada geese exploded because of the captive breeding program or because the early practice of rampant harvest and egg collecting was reined by stricter hunting regulations.

"If you take a look at the growth of any population," says Bill, "it follows the same growth curve of an individual, whether that's a puppy or a child or a goose. That entity will start out growing very slowly, and then it will go through a growth spurt, followed by a tapering off and a plateau. That progression is illustrated by the classical 'Gompertz curve' or an 'S curve.' In other words, if you were to graph age and height for a child, the growth in the first couple of years would be slow. All of a sudden, as that child gets into adolescence, he would begin to really shoot off. Within a couple of years, he would gain a lot of height. As the child gets close to adulthood, however, the curve would flatten out.

"The same thing happens with a wildlife population," Bill goes on. "If you had only two geese left, and subsequent generations produced only two geese, then you'd have four, then eight, and then sixteen—the growth is slow. But all of a sudden, you get to five hundred. Within the next generation, that five hundred becomes one thousand. Five thousand soon becomes ten thousand, and so on. Now, you've got exponential growth. And then, usually, those populations start to stabilize when they reach the saturation point for the environment."

With Canada geese, however, humans made reaching that saturation point an ever-moving target.

"We're totally responsible for the second part to this story," explains Bill. "At the same time that the Canada goose population was rapidly growing in the 1990s, Americans were developing suburbs. What's a suburb? It's not only residences but big, green spaces, such as golf courses and parks. We also created 'industrial parks,' which consist of buildings, little ponds, and mowed acreage. Anywhere you have water *and* grass is perfect goose habitat.

"So it was both the natural growth rate of the population plus our incidentally managing *for* them that the giant Canada goose population exploded," says Bill. "In addition to ideal goose habitat in our suburbs, we also created refuges. Today, most people see giant Canada geese as a nuisance and a conflict, and I always have to remind them that this was a population of birds that was nearly extinct fifty years ago. When I say that to group after group, the typical response is 'Really?' 'Well,' I say, 'ask your grandpa if he remembers seeing geese when he was a kid.'"

## Lesson Three:
### Becoming an Identity for Horicon Marsh

Grandpa may not have seen many Canada geese around, but those growing up in the 1970s certainly did.

Bill informs us that Horicon was originally established for ducks, not geese. But when it was realized by the late 1950s that Canada geese were in serious trouble, Horicon biologists stepped in and ended up becoming critical for turning their numbers around.

"When the Canada goose populations started to build up again in the 1960s and 1970s," says Bill, "wildlife managers established food plots for them off of

Highway 49 in the northern part of the national wildlife refuge section. Farmers had started to complain about crop damage, so the idea was to keep them out of the farm fields by feeding them on the marsh.

"Unfortunately," Bill continues with a smile, "this resulted in a concentration of geese adjacent to a major state highway, and it caused traffic jams! One historic photo taken on a Sunday afternoon on Highway 49 shows state troopers standing in the middle of the road, trying to route traffic. One of the old stories that I've often heard is that people who had to drive across the refuge to get to their homes in Waupun would get stuck in the fall traffic on Highway 49. It would take them two to two and a half hours to get across that five-mile stretch that runs across the north end of the marsh. Once you got in, there was no getting out because both shoulders of the road would be parked full.

"So, they unwittingly created this huge spectacle of two hundred thousand Canada geese right off the state highway," reiterates Bill. "Soon, of course, that became the identity for the marsh. In the 1970s, in fact, a local photographer named Edgar Mueller took a photo that became famous. The entire picture is nothing but solid geese as far as you can see."

The Canada geese in the Mueller photo were probably a mix of both giants and interior geese because during this same time period, wildlife managers were also concentrating on attracting migrant geese to the marsh. Early accounts indicate that the MVP did not stop at Horicon in large numbers; their main flyway followed the Mississippi River to their wintering grounds in the South. During the 1940s, only a few thousand Canada geese were counted on Horicon Marsh during fall migration. By the 1970s, that number had risen to two hundred fifty thousand.

Today, the largest migratory flock of Canada geese in the world comes through Horicon.

LESSON FOUR:
FROM MARSH TO LAKE—AND BACK TO MARSH AGAIN

Together both sides of what is commonly referred to as just Horicon Marsh—the Horicon National Wildlife Refuge, managed by the U.S. Fish and Wildlife Service, and the Horicon Marsh Wildlife Area, managed by the DNR—encompass thirty-three thousand acres. It is thirteen and a half miles long and three to five miles wide, making it the largest wetland in the Upper Midwest.

The maker of the marsh was the Green Bay Lobe of the Wisconsin Glacial Episode, the last major advance of continental glaciers in North America. As the glacier retreated ten thousand years ago, it carved out a shallow basin, which now forms the bottom of the great marsh. On the east side of the marsh is a ledge that forms part of the Niagara Escarpment, a ridge that runs from Wisconsin eastward through Michigan, Ontario, and New York State and is the cliff over which the Niagara River plunges to become Niagara Falls.

It is claimed that almost every major prehistoric Indian culture known to the Upper Midwest has used Horicon Marsh over the past ten thousand to twelve thousand years. Bill takes over the narration from the entrance of the first European settlers in the state.

"In the 1840s, early settlers built a dam in the town of Horicon to power a sawmill. At that time, the marsh became the largest manmade lake in the country; 'Lake Horicon' even had steamboats on it! But because the high water began to cause conflicts with nearby farmers, the dam was removed by court order in 1869. As it returned to a marsh, tremendous numbers of ducks came to the area, and the wetlands were used primarily for hunting from 1870 to the early twentieth century. There were shooting clubs all around the marsh, and market hunting was big. As a result, the waterfowl here were devastated," he relates.

By the early twentieth century, with the ducks all but gone from the "duck marsh," it was thought that the land could best be put to use for crops. So, the marsh was ditched and drained. Diane Kitchen, the assistant manager for the Horicon National Wildlife Refuge since 1992, explains. "The main ditch ran north and south, up and down the marsh, and lateral ditches branched off its sides," she says. "Digging the ditches was a huge effort; it took years. Those ditches are still out there today, although we're working on getting rid of them."

However, the settlers weren't happy with the crops the former marshland produced. Their potatoes tasted like peat. "So, they then tried to burn the land," continues Diane. "Those fires got into the peat—which goes down very deep— and they burned for almost twelve years. The entire ecosystem was destroyed. That's when a local public campaign, led by hunters and conservation groups such as the Izaak Walton League, got started to restore the marsh. And because funds were needed, the interested parties urged the State of Wisconsin to get involved."

In 1927, the Horicon Marsh Wildlife Refuge Bill was passed, providing monies to buy small parcels of land on the marsh every year for ten years. At the end of the ten-year period, however, only one third of the marshland had been acquired. In 1941, the federal government stepped in to finish up the purchasing job.

Today, although it is most commonly thought of as one big marsh, the two sides are managed slightly differently. On the *Horicon Marsh Wildlife Area*, people may hike, hunt, fish, trap, go birding, engage in wildlife photography, canoe, and kayak. On the *Horicon National Wildlife Refuge*, however, different rules apply. Says Diane, "The National Wildlife Refuge System Improvement Act of 1997 identified six priority uses of national wildlife refuges: wildlife observation, wildlife photography, hunting, fishing, environmental education, and nature interpretation. However, the public uses on a given refuge must be compatible with that particular refuge's stated wildlife-related purpose. In the case of Horicon Marsh, our purpose is the 'protection and preservation of migratory birds.' So on the Horicon National Wildlife Refuge, no waterfowl hunting, no boating, and no canoeing—among other restrictions—are allowed."

## LESSON FIVE:
### A BIRD IN THE HAND CAN BE DANGEROUS

The "wildlife observation" priority use that Diane spoke of is relatively easy for Canada goose watchers—even for neophyte birders—because the geese are such very large birds.

Giant Canada geese have wingspans of up to six feet, making them the largest waterfowl—with the exception of swans. They range from thirty to forty-three inches in length, and they may weigh from seven to twenty pounds. These large-bodied birds have long necks; large, webbed feet; and wide, flat bills. They have black heads with white cheeks and chinstraps, black necks, light tan to cream breasts, and brown backs. Although at least one wild Canada goose was known to have lived for thirty years and four months, they seldom survive more than five years in the wild.

In spring and summer, Canada geese concentrate their feeding on grasses and sedges, including skunk cabbage leaves and eelgrass. During fall and winter, they rely more on berries and seeds, including agricultural grains from farm fields. They're very efficient at removing kernels from dry, waste corncobs and seem especially fond of blueberries.

During much of the year, Canada geese will associate in large flocks, with many of these birds being related to one another. They mate for life with very low "divorce" rates, and pairs remain together throughout the year. Geese mate *assortatively*, which means that larger birds will choose larger mates and smaller ones will pick smaller mates. In a pair, the male is usually the larger of the two.

While interior Canada geese do not breed until they are three to five years of age, giants typically nest at two to three years of age. Clutches for interior Canada geese usually number one to seven eggs (typically four), while giants lay one to eight eggs (five is average). The creamy white eggs are incubated for twenty-five to twenty-eight days.

Hatchlings are covered with yellowish down and their eyes are open. They leave the nest when they are only one to two days old, depending on the weather. They can walk, swim, feed, and even dive.

Says Kent Van Horn, "Canada geese tend to go through a short, 'teenage' period. During spring migration, they'll fly north with Mom and Dad, and then go hang out somewhere else with the other teenagers for a while. They'll often end up nesting in an area very close to where they were hatched.

"Typically," Kent goes on, "three or four will survive to fly south for the winter with the family group. They'll probably head back north together, too. One of the interesting things about Canada geese is that they tend to stay together in their family groups and learn habits from their parents, uncles, and aunts. I believe that's one of the reasons that biologically they've developed these 'populations' that have certain habits and traditions where they all migrate to the same places."

But distinguishing those populations—telling an interior Canada goose from a giant Canada goose—in the wild can be difficult. Says Bill, "Sometimes, when seeing them fly overhead, you'll be able to pick out a large, giant Canada goose from a midsize interior Canada goose, especially if they're flying side by side. But there is overlap in size and weight. The real distinction is apparent if you measure the length of the bill, the length of the wing, and part of the leg—the upper foot portion. If you do all those measurements and total body length, the giant Canada goose on average is larger than one from the interior population. But from a distance, if a goose is by itself or with birds of all one kind, it's hard to tell whether you're seeing a big bird flying a little higher or a smaller bird flying a little lower.

"Another way to tell them apart, of course," states Bill, "is that any goose you see between May 1 and September 15 is a giant because all the others have left. But once we get past the middle of September, it gets harder and harder unless you actually have them in the hand."

But having them in hand is not always the best idea, as Kent Van Horn can attest. "In the mid-1980s," begins Kent, "I was a wildlife intern in northern Illinois, and we were rounding up Canada geese to band them. I was selected to be the person who got put in the pen. My job was to catch the geese and hand them out to the people who would put the bands on. So, I grabbed one bird and lifted it over the top of the cage, which was about six feet tall. I was handing it to my supervisor at the time—well, the Canada goose decided to let loose just as I swung it over the top! And big blobs of goose poop landed right on my supervisor's eyeglasses!"

And, just *how* do you grab Canada geese? I ask Kent. "You grab them around the body and try to carry them like footballs," he replies. "You really have to secure their wings and then make sure you angle the feet away from you. The feet are what can really do damage; they can scratch you up pretty good. They have claws at the end of their webs—on every toe. And then they can whack you with their wings, of course, and they're fairly strong birds. It's not so much the bill but the wings and the feet that can really hurt you."

When geese use those big wings to fly, it's in the iconic V formation. Although we've often heard that the "point man" is the leader or wisest of the geese, Bill debunks that myth. "The V is simply an effort to reduce wind resistance," he explains. "There is no leader. Multiple family groups fly together, and the only ones who don't know where they're going are the young who are on their first migration.

"Here's the analogy I use," Bill goes on, to explain further. "Imagine you're standing on a freeway bridge and you're watching cars go by. Did you ever notice they come in little packs? There will be little groups of five or ten cars, then one or two, a gap between, and then another little pack. Is the guy in front leading everybody? He's not *leading* them, because they all know where they're going, too. It's just that somebody has to be in front because you only have two lanes. If you're flying in a V, somebody gets stuck out front, and somebody has to be behind him.

"The legend of the oldest and strongest bird leading everybody on to find Horicon Marsh—that sounds good, but that's just anthropomorphizing. Geese have a more egalitarian social structure than we do," he states.

One young man in our group raises his hand and asks Bill why sometimes you may see a single line of geese in the sky. "That's still a V," answers Bill, "but it's just a half of a V. That's because by staggering themselves at about a thirty- to forty-five-degree angle, they're riding the winds that are coming off their wingtips. If they were right behind each other, it would be like following a semi in a little car. The wind whips you around. The geese are actually drafting. It's more efficient. Quite honestly, when you really understand Canada geese, I think the facts are more fascinating than the myths."

## LESSON SIX:
### THE MIGRATION "TRIGGER" IS NOT THE COLD

And one of the most captivating facts about Canada geese—the interior or MVP flock, anyway—is their migration. It's *the* reason people come to watch them at Horicon Marsh.

However, even the giants go through a mini-migration. No geese stay on Horicon Marsh all year long. Says Kent, "Because these Canada geese are so large, they can survive winter just fine as long as they have food and they can find water somewhere. In this day and age with all of the power plants and effluent flowing out into lakes, there's always someplace they can find water. So, in Wisconsin, if we have a mild winter, these birds will end up wintering in southern Wisconsin and northern Illinois. If the winter is harsher, then the birds will tend to move farther south into central and southern Illinois."

The same trend is being seen with the MVP. They are split roughly into three migratory traditions: the southeast James Bay group goes through Michigan, Ohio, Indiana, Kentucky, and Tennessee. The western Hudson Bay group goes down through Minnesota, Iowa, Missouri, and Arkansas, toward Texas. The birds that travel through Horicon Marsh come from south of Hudson Bay through Wisconsin and winter in Illinois, western Kentucky, and Tennessee. However, with the available agricultural crops and somewhat milder winters, the interior geese often aren't going to Kentucky and Tennessee anymore. They're going only as far south as central Illinois.

Says Bill, "The migration is stimulated by what we call the *photoperiod*, or the duration of time an organism is exposed to light in a twenty-four-hour span. In summer, as you get farther north, the days get longer. And high up in the Arctic Circle, the sun will stay up not for just one day but for days and weeks on end. And if you go far enough north, the sun stays up for as much as three and a half months. In the wintertime, the opposite is true: The days get very short. In fact, in the dead of winter, you get one day when the sun never comes up.

"So what does that mean for geese going to the far north?" asks Bill. "First of all, they get the benefit of really long days, so they can feed around the clock. That's how they can raise their young so quickly up there. But it also means the days begin to shorten as we get into late summer and early fall. It's that shortening of day length that signals to the Canada geese that it's getting near the time to migrate. And that's why these birds move like clockwork. The first migrants always arrive on roughly the same day. I can just about guarantee that our first geese from the MVP flock will be at Horicon Marsh sometime between the fifteenth and twentieth of September. They will always depart in spring between the seventeenth and twenty-first of April. The *actual* day they go on depends on the weather conditions. They are very sensitive to barometric pressure changes; they can tell when fronts are coming through.

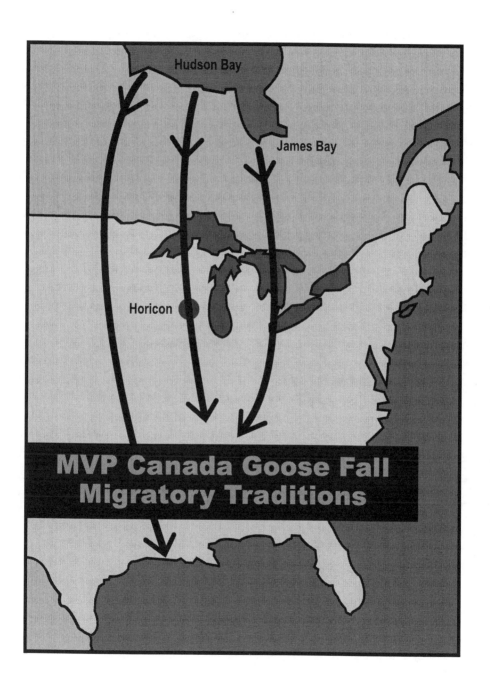

Hudson Bay

James Bay

Horicon

**MVP Canada Goose Fall Migratory Traditions**

"The geese will always take advantage of the winds," continues Bill. "In fall, if we have a north wind following a cold front, they're going to fly south. In springtime, it's just the opposite. They need a warm front with a south wind to push them north. And those birds will fly as far as the winds are going with them. They may depart the breeding ground and come down to, say, the north shore of Lake Superior and linger. Then they might fly over Lake Superior and stop in northern Wisconsin and the UP for a while, before finally reaching Horicon Marsh. Or, if we have a really big weather system, they'll make a nonstop flight from Hudson Bay all the way down here."

Horicon Marsh reaches its peak of migrant Canada geese in late October or early November. Incremental build-ups of the birds occur every time a cold front passes. So from mid-September when the first migrants arrive, it could take six weeks to reach the peak number, which is about two hundred thousand Canada geese on the marsh.

"They will remain at Horicon until, again, the weather catches up with them," says Bill. "Once the ice forms out on the marsh, the first batch will leave to go south again. So we get a pretty good thinning of the birds—more than half of them—once the ice forms. But there's always a few that will stick it out, right to the very last. The birds that do that *might* overwinter in Wisconsin, *if* they can find access to food.

"The big misunderstanding regarding bird migration, though," Bill informs us, "is that the birds start going south from here because it's getting cold. Canada geese are well insulated. I've seen them standing out in twenty-degrees-below-zero weather. But the cold does bring frost, snow, and ice, and that wipes out food."

## LESSON SEVEN: HUNTING IS ESSENTIAL

So all the while the migrating, interior Canada geese are inspiring our awe, it is the giants that incur our wrath. With about 1.6 million giant Canada geese nesting in the Mississippi Flyway today, they are a success story that played out a little too well.

"Geese primarily graze on low vegetation, just like a cow," says Kent Van Horn. "And just like a cow, they create a lot of excrement. And that's where the problem comes in. If you have an urban park with a small beach and a bunch of grass, geese will walk from the water to the grass and eat it, and walk back and leave droppings all over. Then no one wants to use the beach.

"Here in Wisconsin, if you look at our history, the amazing migration and staging of hundreds of thousands of Canada geese on Horicon Marsh was an event of international significance. People from all over the country would come to see it. But then in the 1980s, the *local* population began to really increase. In 1986, we counted about 11,000 breeding Canada geese in Wisconsin. This year, we counted 176,000. And so, as it shifted from a species that was very localized on a neat place like Horicon Marsh to something where it was overflowing in our neighborhoods, the public attitude toward the bird changed.

Canada geese have claws on the ends of every toe of their webbed feet. These birds can scratch if you get too close. Adult geese with goslings or eggs in a nest are particularly defensive—they might even chase people. (Photo: John T. Andrews)

"And because they are so strong," Kent affirms, "in parks where they get naturalized to people, they can be pretty rough. I saw a security-camera video taken from outside an office building in Milwaukee. A goose had a nest nearby. The video shows a person exiting the building, and the goose comes out hissing and with wings flapping! It chases the person down the sidewalk!"

Bill agrees with Kent that the giants have become a problem for some city-scapes. "I think people would like to go to a park and see half a dozen geese there and let the kids have a little contact—not to feed them, but to just witness a wild bird. But you don't want to go to a park and see so many there that you can't get out of the car because the ground is covered in droppings and you're afraid the kids will get into the mess."

The problem for wildlife biologists then becomes how to manage such an abundant population. On Horicon Marsh, part of that solution is hunting.

"For a hunted, managed population of animals or for an endangered one, for the most part, it's about numbers," says Bill. "There are three things you can do with a managed population. One, increase it, especially if the species is endangered; two, if it's incredibly successful and overabundant, such as Canada geese or white-tailed deer, bring numbers down; three, if it's doing all right, then keep it the same. Don't harvest more than what that species can reproduce.

"For the Mississippi Valley Population of Canada geese," Bill goes on, "we want to keep that population's numbers the same. So, we adjust our regular tagged, goose-hunting season (after the migrants have arrived) according to good or bad nesting seasons."

The regular, tagged hunting season for Canada geese typically starts after mid-September and goes to early December. There are two hunting zones in Wisconsin for Canada geese: the Horicon zone and the rest of the state.

"A percentage of the total tags in Wisconsin are given to what we call the *exterior zone* or what is the rest of the state," says Bill. "In the exterior zone, when you shoot Canada geese, you must call an 800 number to report the harvest. Normally, the number of hunters who shoot in the exterior, the number of days they spend out there, and their average hunting success within the fall season that we allow doesn't go over the quota. But if we see that the hunters are hav-ing a really exceptional year by what they're telephoning in, we do have the authority to shut down the season under emergency order. So in the end, we don't shoot any more birds than what they raise, as far as our proportion of that total hunt. There's science behind our hunting regulations and very intensive mathematics. It would blow people away, how much survey work we do."

Horicon Marsh is one of the most popular sites for goose hunting simply because of the large numbers of geese found there. The odds of success for a hunter on Horicon are pretty good. Bill explains how the marsh's hunting harvest goal is set: "When the birds reach their nesting grounds on Hudson Bay, the Canadian Wildlife Service and the Ontario Ministry of Natural Resources conduct breeding-ground surveys. First, they fly over the Hudson Bay coast to estimate the number of nesting pairs per mile to ascertain density. Roughly about half the population is old enough to nest. Once the geese have laid eggs, ground crews will check nests to get the average number of eggs laid per pair. Together, the density of nesting pairs and the average number of eggs per pair comprises what we call *nesting efforts*.

"The last big variable," says Bill, "is: from those nesting efforts, how many young are actually, successfully hatched out and raised, increasing the population? So, as we get into August, we're just starting to get that data regarding how large that population has grown. That becomes the hunting quota.

"Now, of that quota," Bill continues, "some of those hunting opportunities will go to Ontario, and other percentages will go to Wisconsin, Illinois, western Kentucky, Tennessee, and Michigan. Wisconsin and Illinois both get 26 percent each of the total quota. Out of that, we allocate a large proportion to Horicon. If you want to hunt Horicon geese, you have to have an application in by the first of August. So now we know the total number of hunters and how many geese to split them up between. This year for instance, the hunters are getting six tags, but they can only shoot two a day."

From survey work, it's known that about 85 to 90 percent of the people who apply for tags (and get them) actually go hunting. About 90 percent of those will shoot a goose. Far fewer will manage to shoot two. And according to Bill, only a few people are good enough to ever shoot six.

"So," he says, "you have this declining success, or what's called a *regression curve*. Basically, we can give a lot more tags out than there are birds to shoot. For giant Canada geese, we could actually make that quota fifty a day, since hardly anyone will ever shoot that many in twenty-four hours. But we want a safe and thoughtful hunt, where people aren't shooting every which way or where there are injured geese out there. We don't want that image of a hunter. If you're going to shoot something, you want to make sure you effectively dispatch it."

But even this hunting system, which carefully takes into account Canada goose population numbers weighed against hunter success, has its further nuances. Says Bill, "I have a number of hunters who think the main objective is to just shoot enough geese to hold the population down. They'll often say to me, 'I could have done you and the DNR a favor. I could have shot all six in one day. Now, I've got to come back.' Well, that's the idea. It's not the *number* of geese you shoot; that's only part of controlling the population. The biggest control is the fact that you're out there hunting and shooting *at* them. A farmer may have 2,000 geese in his field. If you shoot 2 of them, that's all you got. But what do you think the other 1,998 of them did when you shot? They took off, and they're not coming back.

"It's the constant disturbance that's important," Bill points out. "Because of that, they only nibbled a bit in this farmer's field, before they really got accustomed to showing up day after day, cleaning him out. Now, they'll move around a bit. So hunting is *critical* to managing geese today, because if we didn't have it, first of all, this population would continue to grow because of the endless food supply. We've farmed everything. And secondly, the farmers would never be able to make a living. I always tell people there's two ways to manage geese: hunting or not hunting. If you don't like hunting, I've got a simple solution for you: Stop all farming and stop mowing all grass. If you do that, the food supply is going to rapidly diminish for geese. Of course, *we'll* all die of starvation."

Along with requiring hunting tags, a two-geese-per-day limit, and an early or late hunting period, there is another regulation that helps us all live with geese. "Every hunting license we sell in Wisconsin has a one-dollar surcharge on it," states Bill. "That dollar goes into a special account to pay back farmers for crop losses that are excessive. Most people think that money for reimbursements comes from taxes. It does *not*. If you didn't buy a hunting license, you didn't pay a penny toward crop damage compensation. So hunters are the mechanism we use to control the Canada goose population, and we do it within the framework of hunting traditions."

To specifically manage the giant Canada goose population, extra measures are being taken. "For the first fifteen days of September," says Bill, "before the migrants arrive, we have an 'early season' on Canada geese. Hunters may shoot five a day. Unfortunately, the first fifteen days of September are a little early for hunting for a lot of people. Labor Day weekend falls during that time, and in early September we've had days where it's been in the eighties or pushing ninety degrees—not exactly prime hunting weather. No matter how liberal we make the season, it's often a challenge to get sufficient participation from hunters that early in the year. But, lately, we've been doing better."

In addition, some towns and municipalities are issued permits to do a roundup to remove some of the birds. "In midsummer," says Bill, "the Canada geese go through a complete molt—where the adults can't fly—at the same time that the young ones aren't old enough to take flight. With a team of people, you can round them up like cattle. The geese are then either banded—so we can follow them and use the resultant data to look at distribution and to set hunting harvests—or loaded onto a truck and taken to a poultry factory."

One out of every ten geese is tested to make sure it meets USDA food standards. The goose meat is then ground up and given to food kitchens. "You won't see them in the supermarkets," explains Bill, "because federal law does not allow you to actually sell goose meat. That ban was put into effect after the market hunting days. We wanted to take out all financial incentives for shooting wildlife. The problem with market hunting is the more you shoot, the more money you make and that was what was leading to the near extinction of a lot of species. Geese, like white-tailed deer, are a public resource. Those deer and those geese belong to you, me, and to everyone else. Why should I be able to make money on what is really already your property? How can I sell it to you when you already own it? So, under federal law, Canada geese have to be given away; they can't be sold."

## The Wild Outside in the Inner City

But despite all we hear about the Canada goose being a "nuisance," there is much to admire about the bird.

"Canada geese can survive under a lot of conditions," says Kent Van Horn. "It's not uncommon for the MVP birds to fly to their nesting grounds in May, set up a nest, lay eggs, sit on them, and then get snowed on. And then, they just stay there on their nests, dutifully, with snow covering them and only their little heads sticking out!

"The most interesting part of their story, however, is how they've been able to adapt to people over the hundreds of years that European settlers have expanded across the continent," continues Kent. "Before modern agriculture, geese fed primarily on seeds, tubers, and leaves of wetland plants. But as the landscape has changed to agricultural grains, they've taken advantage of that. They primarily eat in croplands after harvest. But they will come through in spring and eat new shoots coming up. Some of the farmers have problems with that, of course. Canada geese got knocked back, but now they found a way to survive and excel in the world we've created."

Bill agrees that their adaptability is something to be admired. "They can live as well in the suburbs of Chicago and Milwaukee as they do in the Arctic and out in the wild lands and farmlands of Wisconsin," he says. "They're a big enough bird that they can fend off a good number of predators, so they're fairly successful at rearing young. They're fairly long lived, and they tend to mate for life.

"But here's what else Canada geese can do for us," Bill goes on to say. "A large proportion of our population that lives in inner cities has very limited contact with the outdoors and nature. They have to take a trip to even get to what you and I might think of as 'the outdoors.' It's always been a challenge to get people who are somewhat removed from nature to become aware of environmental issues. Why should someone in New York City care about pandas? 'I'll never see one except in a zoo' is the typical response. Well, is it important to humankind overall and to the planet? Minimal contact has always been a bit of a barrier for overcoming that attitude. So, now you actually have a bird that is so adaptable that it can live in a city. Lucky you! You can see some wildlife in an urban environment. You can watch them fly over the neighborhood."

## LIVING WITH WILD THINGS

The lecture is over. I get ready for my evening on the marsh. It's a brisk, late afternoon, around forty degrees. Most of the talk attendees are leaving, having arrived earlier in the day than I did. I take the short walk from the education center out to the marsh. This will be my first experience with watching what could be "Wisconsin's greatest bird migration."

When I later phone Bill to get a few more questions about Canada geese answered, he tells me about his first experience seeing the migration. "Oh, gosh, I still remember it from when I was a kid!" he says excitedly. "It was in the late 1960s, and it was a fall weekend. I was one of those millions of people who came to watch the geese off of Highway 49. We had heard about the migration—probably read about it in the *Milwaukee Journal*. It was only about an hour's drive away, so my dad, my brothers, and I jumped in the car, and we went to see the Canada geese. It was a really raw, cold day and we couldn't stand outside the car very long. I was dressed a little bit light. But wherever I looked, there were geese. It was quite a phenomenon."

Whether I see giants, interiors, or cacklers this evening, it really doesn't matter to me. I just want to witness that music of the marsh that Aldo Leopold wrote so eloquently about when he penned:

*"There are some of us who can live without wild things, and some who cannot. For us of the minority, the opportunity to see geese or wild flowers is a right as inalienable as free speech."*

I choose a spot on the marsh's edge and stop to gaze at the auburn sky. As if the geese had been cued, I soon start to hear their honks. As the sky deepens from golden brown to violet and then a beautiful burnt orange, the geese increase. The crescendo of honks gets louder. And then the silhouettes of long, dark, outstretched necks crossed by wings begin to dot the pinkish clouds. It's not long before the sky is filled with geese, and the marsh ripples up with their every landing.

Bill had mentioned to me on the phone that this never gets old, and I can see why. After twenty-seven years on the marsh, day in and day out, he had said, he still looks up when the geese are overhead. "I've seen our biologists actually stop and cock their heads whenever a flock goes by," says Bill. "And after almost thirty years here, I look up almost every time. Gosh, we've all seen millions of them fly by. But it's just something that's become so quintessential to Horicon Marsh. It wouldn't be fall without Canada geese flying over *this* marsh.

"And this is a *new* phenomenon," Bill reminds me. "The geese weren't coming here in these kinds of numbers a hundred years ago—before the restoration of the marsh and so much agriculture. But this *is* Horicon Marsh today. As much as people say 'Canada geese are a problem in my neighborhood' or 'I've got this many geese at home,' there's something different about seeing them at Horicon. You do not have two hundred thousand Canada geese at home. And

By Horicon standards, two hundred to three hundred Canada geese in a flock are not a lot. Although giant Canada geese came close to becoming extinct, they have now found a way to survive and excel in the world we've created. (Photo: John T. Andrews)

you don't have a chance of seeing a flock of five thousand at a time flying in at the end of the day. That doesn't happen in your city park. Even two hundred to three hundred in a flock are not a lot by Horicon standards."

The cocked heads of the Canada goose watchers that still tickle Bill would have done the same for Aldo Leopold. He once shared his concern for the future of his children in his renowned essay "Goose Music," which first appeared in *A Sand County Almanac*:

*"I hope to leave them good health, an education, and possibly even a competence. But what are they going to do with these things if there be no more deer in the hills, and no more quail in the coverts? No more snipe whistling in the meadow, no more piping of widgeons and chattering of teal as darkness covers the marsh; no more whistling of swift wings when the morning star pales in the east? And when the dawn-wind stirs through the ancient cottonwoods, and the gray light steals down from the hills over the old river sliding softly past its wide brown sandbars—what if there be no more goose music?"*

That may be the best Canada goose lesson of all.

### HOW TO HAVE A GENUINE
### CANADA GOOSE ENCOUNTER OF YOUR OWN

For people who want to watch the birds, here are a few recommendations from Bill Volkert:

+ **Time of year:** "Beginning in October, Canada goose numbers start to build up. If there is a mild fall, however, peak numbers of Canada geese may not occur until early to mid-November. But people don't come to see just maximum numbers of geese—they come for a total fall experience. So if you come November 1, you'll see a lot of geese, but you'll also see a landscape that is pretty drab. All the leaves will be down, the majority of the other birds will be gone, and the weather can start to get a little cold. People usually come to the marsh to watch the Canada geese in **mid to late October,** before we actually reach the peak of the population. That's when you'll catch the colors and the beauty of fall, which the Canada goose symbolizes for Horicon. We may not have two hundred thousand geese; we may have only a hundred thousand or a hundred fifty thousand, but that's still a lot."

+ **Place:** "You may want to get up near the **north end of the marsh** because the big, open water is on the **national wildlife refuge,** and the geese will concentrate there. There is a public viewing area just off of Highway 49 with a parking lot for about a hundred cars on the northeast corner. We do, however, get a nice flight on the **state wildlife area, near the education center.** There are also some good spots on some of the **high grounds.** Off of County Z, there are a few viewing sites with small parking lots. There is another nice observation area off of Rockvale Road."

+ **Time of day:** "Avoid this mistake: People commonly get here on the weekend at around nine or ten in the morning. They'll drive around, hike, or have a lunch. By three o'clock, they start heading back so they can get home before dark. However, the geese fly out to feed in the first two hours as the sun is coming up, and they fly back in during the last two hours of daylight. It's spectacular to watch the morning flight go out, but it's often hard for people to get here at the crack of dawn. So, I suggest that you **stick with the afternoon, and arrange to drive home in the dark.** A good plan is to spend some time at the national wildlife refuge. Then come down to the southern portion of Horicon Marsh, the state wildlife area. Visit the education center and hike the trails. Then, after our offices close, have a snack and watch the return flight of Canada geese. Remember, though, that no two days are the same. I can't guarantee that every day you'll see a spectacular flight. If there is a very clear sky and it's bright, the geese may feed out in the fields until dark. And if there's a full moon, they may stay out in the field all night, especially if they've just flown a thousand miles to get here and they're hungry."

To learn more about activities on the Horicon National Wildlife Refuge, visit www.fws.gov/midwest/horicon. For information on the Horicon Marsh Wildlife Area, go to dnr.wi.gov/topic/lands/wildlifeareas/horicon.

## HOW TO BECOME INVOLVED WITH CANADA GOOSE CONSERVATION EFFORTS

While Canada geese are presently abundant, here are three things that will aid conservation efforts for geese and for all wildlife:

+ Buy a duck stamp: Diane Kitchen says that most people assume duck stamps are only for hunters, since they are required to buy them. In truth, anyone may purchase a duck stamp. Your fifteen dollars will go toward protecting wildlife habitats and buying more public lands. Duck stamps make great gifts for nature enthusiasts.

• You can buy federal duck stamps at post offices or online at store.usps .com or www.duckstamp.com. Duck stamps can also be purchased at most major sporting goods stores that sell hunting and fishing licenses.

• Join the Friends of Horicon National Wildlife Refuge: The mission of the friends group is to "to promote conservation, awareness, and appreciation of the Horicon National Wildlife Refuge." Go to www .horiconnwrfriends.org for more information.

• Learn about Canada geese: Advises Bill Volkert: "Whether you consider Canada geese a nuisance or just a curiosity in a local park, try to learn about the different flocks of geese you see at various times of the year. That way, your enjoyment while watching them will increase. You may come to the marsh, see thousands of geese fly overhead, and say 'wow' like you would at a fireworks show. But then, you'll begin to have questions. Where are the Canada geese coming from? Have they always been part of the marsh? Why are they flying in Vs? How long do they stay at the marsh? Why is hunting them allowed? How is the hunt managed? Where do these geese nest? There are different sizes of them; does that mean anything?

"One of the biggest rewards I ever had was overhearing a couple who had brought some friends to the marsh who had never been here before. I heard the couple say to their friends, 'Now watch as these birds fly in. See, they're flying pretty low; they were just feeding. And watch now, as the V will break up, and they'll start tumbling and rolling on their sides. And those are family groups there.' What was neat about it was, it wasn't just 'That's a lot of geese.' They understood what the birds were doing; it was making sense to them."

## 13

# Tundra Swans:
# Losing and Looking to the Future

*Upper Mississippi River National Wildlife and Fish Refuge
in Alma, Wisconsin, and Brownsville, Minnesota*

FALL MIGRATION STAGING

Alma is one of those great little river towns, the kind with one main street. In this case, it happens to front the mighty Mississippi, while steep, five-hundred-foot, limestone bluffs buffer the roadway's back. In between river and rock, there's a lot of nineteenth-century charm still hanging on to the town's buildings.

There's the requisite coffee store and bakery, of course, and between the old-timey structures are twelve sets of concrete stairways. They all will lead you up to Buena Vista Park, which overlooks Alma, the great river, a set of train tracks, and eagles' nests in the foliage against the cliffs just below you. It's a glorious view.

Lampposts line the main drag, and this fall Saturday, they fly small banners waving images of elegant swans. In fact, that's why I'm here in Alma on this gray November day. I've heard that the observation platform at the city's Riecks Lake Park is *the* place to view tundra swans during their fall migration.

When I pull into the Riecks Lake parking lot at about 7:30 a.m., however, I'm surprised to discover that I'm the only one here. Already, I can see twelve incredibly white swans on the lake. I park the car and walk to the platform to get a closer look at the birds from the mounted spotting scope. I watch as they sleep, occasionally squawk, and wash and dip their heads underwater. One goes under with such vigor that its butt turns end up, and big, webbed feet are left waving in the air. They stretch out their lovely, long wings and tubular necks, and then gracefully tuck them in again. Canada geese fly in Vs overhead, and a great egret wades nearby.

A couple more cars begin to turn into the parking lot. A few people get out and take their time setting up tripods, waiting for the sky to clear just a bit for a more dramatic shot.

Twelve swans on Riecks Lake hardly measures up to the stories I've heard—about how, in November, you would be able to see thousands of tundra swans off the park's platform.

So, the question is, where are all the tundra swans?

## RIECKS LAKE RUNWAY

Riecks Lake in Alma is just one small part of the Upper Mississippi River National Wildlife and Fish Refuge, which extends for 261 miles along the Upper Mississippi River, from Wabasha, Minnesota, to Rock Island, Illinois. This 240,000-acre refuge was established in 1924. Consisting of the Mississippi and its tributaries, the refuge serves as a migration corridor for large numbers of waterfowl and shorebirds from the Midwest, Canada, and Alaska.

*Midwest Living* magazine says that the refuge draws more visitors each year (3.7 million) than Yellowstone National Park (3.6 million). And Chicagoan Will Dilg, founder of the Izaak Walton League—an environmental organization that promotes natural resource protection and outdoor recreation—and the driving force behind the creation of the refuge in the early 1920s, said, "It is an area so beautiful that it is beyond the power of the human mind to describe, an area that represents to the upper half of the Mississippi Valley the last stand of wild life."

Riecks Lake itself is located at the confluence of the Buffalo and Mississippi Rivers. The Buffalo River empties into Riecks Lake, and Riecks Lake empties into the Buffalo Slough, part of Pool 4 of the Mississippi River. Riecks Lake is where the Alma Tundra Swan Watch began in 1992, when a retired naturalist named Harry Buck volunteered to be at the lake during the fall migration to talk to visitors about the swans. Having overheard some observers misidentifying the swans as great egrets, he saw the tundra swan migration as an opportunity to provide some apparently much-needed public education. That first year, seven hundred people showed up. In the following years, towns all up and down the river, such as Alma, benefited from an extended tourist season of about six weeks.

In the 1990s, tundra swans were literally falling from the sky onto Riecks Lake; some say it used to look as if the surface was covered with popcorn. During those years, according to the U.S. Fish and Wildlife Service, six thousand swans a day could be counted on Riecks Lake.

In the 1990s, tundra swans were quite abundant on Riecks Lake. But over the years, silt and vegetation filled in the lake. Now, most of the tundra swans bypass Riecks and keep flying down the river. (Photo: Bob Leggett)

But the tundra-swan-watching experience is much different today, some twenty years later. Typically, you may see from four to twenty swans on Riecks Lake. The reason is that the lake is filling in with silt and vegetation, partly accelerated by floods in 1993 and 1997. Swans require large areas of *open* water because of the long runways they need to achieve flight. When taking off, swans face the wind, flap their wings, and "run" along the surface of the water—for fifteen to twenty feet. They beat the water with their feet alternately until they have gained enough headway to launch into the air.

Sue Fletcher, a naturalist who works for the U.S. Fish and Wildlife Service and an enthusiastic tundra swan watcher, explains in detail what happened to Riecks Lake. "When the silt came in," she says, "bur-reeds and cattails got a foothold. Cattails can be very aggressive, and bur-reeds choke out other types of vegetation. Swans don't eat cattails and bur-reeds; they eat tubers, such as arrowhead, wild celery, and pondweed. And if the cattails are so thick that the tubers can't grow, there's nothing for the swans to eat, so they're not going to come.

"It's sad, because Riecks Lake was such a great viewing area," continues Sue. "You would feel like you could practically reach out and touch the swans. They weren't skittish; they were used to people being there. There are still some swans in Alma, though. I usually make a run up there at least one day during the migration season just to see how close in they may be."

Scott Mehus, the education and eagle research director for the National Eagle Center in Minnesota and the current Alma Tundra Swan Watch coordinator, says that habitat changes on the Buffalo River watershed and farming have also taken their toll. "In 2005, we received a federal National Scenic Byways grant of about $1 million to do some dredging on Riecks Lake," he says. "It increased the number of tundra swans stopping at the lake a little bit. But we would have to do millions more worth of dredging to restore the aquatic habitat that the tundra swans need for food and for taking off. There are still some tubers out there, but being able to take off in that limited runway space is now difficult."

Scott agrees with Sue that the loss of great numbers of tundra swans at Riecks Lake since the 1990s is disappointing. "I was active in the Alma Tundra Swan Watch when we had six thousand to eight thousand swans on Riecks Lake at once," says Scott. "You could hear them all the way down into the city of Alma. It was quite an experience! Unfortunately, those days are gone. The last couple of years at the observation platform, I'd see the swans fly over in their family groups. They'd circle down like they were going to come in, then it was almost like you could see them thinking, 'No, we can't land here; there's not enough room.' Then they'd start gaining elevation and keep on going down the river."

### MIGRATION DIRECTIONS: STRAIGHT SOUTH AND TURN LEFT

In the fall, by the time the swans are looking for a place to land on the Upper Mississippi, they've already come a long way. Tundra swans (*Cygnus columbianus*) breed and nest in sheltered marshes near the Arctic Circle from northwestern Alaska to the Hudson Bay in Canada. The most common and widespread swan species in North America, tundra swans are divided into two distinct populations: the Eastern and the Western.

The tundra swans that migrate through the Upper Mississippi River belong to the Eastern Population, which today numbers about one hundred thousand individuals. In the fall, they begin to head for the East Coast—for the shallow ponds, lakes, and estuaries near Chesapeake Bay in Maryland and the marshes

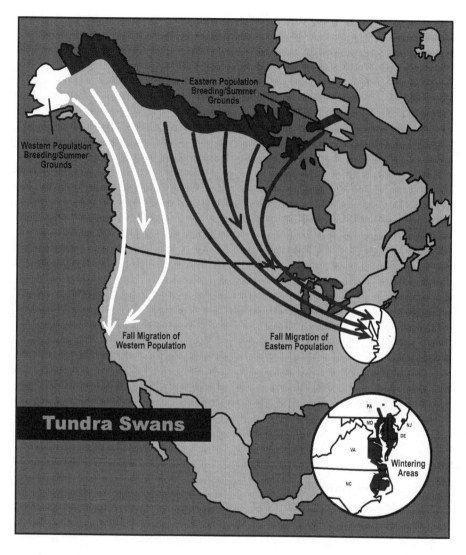

of Virginia and North Carolina. The Western Population travels from the Arctic to California's San Joaquin and Sacramento Valleys.

When ponds in Saskatchewan in southern Canada and North Dakota start to ice over in October and a cold wind from the northwest blows, about a quarter of the Eastern Population of tundra swans will hop on board and ride it to the Mississippi Flyway. They journey south through the prairie provinces of Canada, the Dakotas, and Minnesota to reach the river by mid to late October. There, they stop to feast on tubers in the sloughs before continuing east.

While the 2005 dredging of Riecks Lake in Alma did provide better grow-ing conditions for tubers, they're not yet established. So some swans are now feeding in sloughs farther up on the Buffalo River and others farther down on the Mississippi, near Brownsville, Minnesota. In fact, so many tundra swans began going to Brownsville that a new observation overlook and highway pull-off were built in 2008. Says Sue about Brownsville: "I've seen tundra swans here as early as the first week in October if the weather is really bad, but usually they arrive at the end of October or beginning of November. From here, they may fly nonstop to the Chesapeake Bay area. Tundra swans fly about fifty miles per hour and at heights as much as twenty thousand feet. They usually don't fly quite that high, but they may catch a tailwind and just *go*.

"From the tundra," continues Sue, "the swans fly south to about La Crosse, Wisconsin, and then basically just hang a left and go east. The Mississippi Fly-way is like the interstate: it's a fairly straight route, and it has many stopover points with food. Brownsville is a popular one for them now, not only because it's about the halfway point, but because the habitat is excellent. They can rest, sleep, and fatten up for the second half of the journey."

The last tundra swans usually depart the Upper Mississippi River with freeze-up, typically in mid to late December. Three to four months later, they'll be flying back through. Says Sue, "At the end of March or the beginning of April, we'll get groups of a couple of hundred at a time here. If they stay for a week, that's great. But they don't linger for two reasons: One, they've got the urge to breed, and the breeding season is short on the Arctic tundra. Two, there's not as much food for them here in the spring as there is in the fall. After the winter, everything has been picked over, and new plants aren't growing yet. So they want to get up north as soon as they can."

Believed to mate for life—which in the wild may be up to twenty years—tundra swans pair up for nearly an entire year before breeding at age two or three. Though on their winter grounds they gather in huge flocks, in the spring and summer they breed as solitary couples spread out across the tundra. Each couple defends a territory of about three-fourths of a square mile.

On the Arctic coastline, the swans will pile up grasses, mosses, and sedges within a hundred yards of water. The resulting nests measure about a foot high and six feet across. Tundra swans lay an average of six pale-yellow or creamy-white eggs over six to ten days. Females will incubate them for thirty to thirty-two days, while the males stand guard nearby. The young, called *cygnets*, hatch in late June. The brown-and-gray cygnets have pink bills and enter the water soon after hatching. They fully develop within sixty to seventy days.

"The summer season is short on the tundra, so they have to get going quickly," says Sue. "And then they make the big trip down here. They scatter themselves from near Wabasha, Minnesota, and Nelson, Wisconsin, south to about Lansing, Iowa. But the biggest concentration of them is on what's called Pool 8, which is the area from La Crosse south to Lansing."

In all, tundra swans fly about four thousand miles round-trip between their two distant habitats, and they do it twice each year. If they manage to catch a good tailwind, as Sue mentioned, they may be able to ramp up their speed and travel as fast as one hundred miles per hour.

At least one banded tundra swan is known to have taken off from Wisconsin and arrived in Chesapeake Bay within a day.

### Whistle While You Work

In fact, because of the powerful beating of a tundra swan's wings in flight, it was once known as the *whistling swan*. Those strong wings may span from six to seven feet.

Tundras vary in size from four to four and a half feet long, including a four-inch bill and an eight-and-a-half-inch tail. They stand about three feet high. Males (called *cobs*) weigh fifteen to twenty pounds. Females (*pens*) are slightly smaller.

The rhythmic flapping of a tundra swan's wings produces a tone that once earned the bird the name *whistling swan*. Spanning six to seven feet, those great wings provide the power for a daunting journey of almost four thousand miles—made twice each year. (Photo: Bob Leggett)

In the all-white adult, black facial skin tapers to a point in front of the eye and has a rounded border across the forehead. Many adult tundra swans have a yellow spot in front of the eye, at the base of their slightly concave, black bills. They have round heads and carry their necks erect when on the water.

Tundra swans are often confused with trumpeter swans, the only other native swan found routinely in North America (mute swans are a Eurasian species that has been introduced and now breeds in the wild in some areas). While the two are difficult to distinguish, a few characteristics set them apart. A trumpeter swan has a resonant, loud, low-pitched, bugle-like call. Tundras emit a high-pitched, often quavering *who-who* sound. Trumpeter swans have black bills with, typically, a red border on the lower mandible. They do not have the yellow spot in front of the eye. While trumpeter swans frequently bob their heads and necks up and down, tundra swans do not. And, just at the moment that trumpeter swans become airborne, they will briefly pull their necks into a shallow S-curve. Tundra swans hold their necks straight out for the entire time of takeoff and initial flight.

The swans' long necks equip them to reach the bulbous roots that they dislodge with their large, webbed feet from the bottom of shallow ponds. An adult swan consumes about six pounds of those tubers per day on the Upper Mississippi River. Says Sue, "Tundra swans use their big feet to tread water and kick up the muddy bottom—which is called *pedaling*. That pedaling churns up the vegetation, and then they tip over and reach down with the aid of their lengthy necks and feed on whatever they've loosened up.

"It's pretty smart," she adds. "But even smarter are the mallard ducks that hang around them. They don't do any of the work, but they stay near the swans and grab whatever floats up. So you'll often see this little tugboat of a mallard next to this big, elegant, white swan, feeding as happy as can be—until the swan nips it!"

While wintering on the East Coast, tundra swans may also feed on mollusks and crustaceans—and, occasionally, farm crops.

Tundra swan populations are stable; the birds are not endangered. However, their entire breeding season is subject to the yearly whims of Arctic weather. An early freeze or a late spring could make a significant change in their status at any time.

## Minnesota: Going over to the Other Side

Although I've enjoyed the early morning quiet and relative solitude of watching the swans on Riecks Lake in Alma, I decide I need to see them in greater numbers, if only to understand the phenomenon of the tundra swan migration and experience what Riecks Lake was once like. I get in the car and head south for Brownsville, Minnesota.

From my first sight of the overlook off of Minnesota Highway 26, I can already see that Brownsville has jumped into the tundra-swan-watching tourism business in a big way. Over the past several years, a multistate (Minnesota, Wisconsin, and Iowa) and multiagency (U.S. Army Corps of Engineers, U.S. Fish and Wildlife Service, U.S. Geological Survey, Minnesota Department of Natural Resources, Minnesota Pollution Control Agency, and Wisconsin DNR) habitat restoration project has been going on at Brownsville: dredging out the silted-in areas, using the dredged sand to re-create islands that were washed away when a lock-and-dam system was constructed, and replanting native vegetation. As a result, more and more waterfowl are passing up places like Alma for the better pickings at Brownsville.

"We now have the starchy bulbs and tubers that tundra swans need," says Sue. "Plus, large portions of the Mississippi River are closed to hunters, fishermen, and boaters during the migration season, specifically so the swans can rest. So there's minimal disturbance here."

It certainly has improved the tundra swan turnout. Thousands of them now routinely appear at Brownsville in the fall. Sue tells me about her first experience at the site. "I was driving up from Iowa on the Minnesota side of the Mississippi River when I came around the corner at Brownsville. I nearly drove off the road when I saw all the swans! I thought, *Oh my gosh! Look at all those birds!* It was swans as far as the eye could see.

"Of course, as an avid bird-watcher," Sue continues, "I pulled over and got out my binoculars. But what struck me most as I stepped out of the car was the noise. The sound that these birds make is a beautiful, treble, kind of whistling sound. I really can't say now what caught me more by surprise at that moment: that many swans, the sound of them, or the play of light—the blue water with the white swans on it was absolutely enchanting."

As I pull into the Brownsville Overlook parking lot for the first time, I believe I'm having a Sue-like moment. Already the thousands of swans I see astound me, before I even put the shift into Park. The Brownsville Overlook is slightly raised up over the river, so you can gaze out across the top of the Mississippi from a bird's-eye perspective, so to speak, on the panorama of swans, islands, and water.

Stepping out of the car, I hear a loud commotion out and off to the left. Wings flap furiously, and necks pump energetically. Things soon settle down, and then another feud begins and quickly ends nearby. Raucous squawks, high whistles, and honks fill the air around me.

Several swans come in for a landing, skidding on the water until they come to a full float. While they had been described as "popcorn on the water" at Riecks, here, dropping down from the Brownsville sky, they seem like giant snowflakes, the kind that fall in March in Wisconsin, on a warm winter day.

They fly in and fly out. They swim in little family groups. When another family bunch comes in, there is much noise and flapping of wings. I stand and watch them. When I finally pause to check the time, I'm amazed that two hours have passed since I first got out of the car.

### Hope, with Feathers on Top

While it's clear from the vast numbers of tundra swans at Brownsville that Riecks Lake has lost a lot of its tundra swan magnetism, the future isn't all dire for Alma. Many of those who fondly remember Riecks Lake Park's tundra swan heyday believe the birds could come back someday and that it still provides a tundra swan experience that you can't get anyplace else.

Says Sue, "At the Brownsville Overlook, you can get a really good view of fifteen thousand tundra swans at one time, and you can watch a lot of swan behavior. But the encounter is not quite as intimate as it is at Riecks Lake. The observation platform there puts you in close proximity to the birds; you're almost at eye level with them."

Scott Mehus speaks highly of Alma, too, and offers even something more: hope.

"When Riecks Lake filled in, the younger tundra swans were then trained to go farther south on the river to stop. But as we increase better habitat on this upper part of the Mississippi once more, those swans and their family groups will attempt to rest here again. The swans are flying from the north to the south, and since we're north of Brownsville, obviously they'll be traveling right overhead," he points out.

Scott has faith that the tundra swans will return to Alma again in larger and larger numbers because, perhaps, he's seen faithfulness in the swans themselves. "We had one swan that came back year after year," Scott tells me. "She was originally banded in 1992 in North Carolina, and her band number was K744. She is thought to have flown more than a hundred thousand miles in her lifetime. Ever since 1996, we would see her stop almost every fall on Riecks Lake—even through the really rough conditions. She was still stopping by in 2010, and it was always kind of fun to see her."

Nineteenth-century poet Emily Dickinson once wrote, "Hope is the thing with feathers." It's a favorite quotation with bird-watchers everywhere. However, the lesser-known first line in the second stanza of that same poem reads: "And sweetest in the gale is heard."

It was written, I'm sure, for tundra swans—those like K744.

## HOW TO HAVE A GENUINE
## TUNDRA SWAN ENCOUNTER OF YOUR OWN

Tundra swans rest on the **Upper Mississippi River** during the fall migration, from about **late October to mid-December.**

Although small in number, tundra swans can still be found at **Riecks Lake Park** (located three miles northwest of Alma—an hour upriver from La Crosse—on Highway 35, the Great River Road) or at **Tell Lake and the Buffalo River** (just north of Alma, turn right at Highway 37).

**Other places in Wisconsin to watch tundra swans include:**

+ Big Lake: Big Lake is just south of Nelson. Over the last few years, tundra swan numbers have been increasing here to about five thousand to seven thousand, especially since the area has become a no-hunting zone.
+ Goose Island County Park: The park is located at the intersection of County K and Highway 35. Follow the Beirs Lake Trail loop. On a backwater pond, you can usually find several tundra swans. There is a small observation deck.
+ Along Highway 35 (the Great River Road), between Stoddard and La Crosse: Look for three pull-offs (for fishermen) off Highway 35. Two are less than five miles north of Stoddard; and one, called the Shady Maple Overlook, is about 1.2 miles south of County K.
+ Trempealeau National Wildlife Refuge: There are usually several hundred swans at the refuge, which you may view from the observation deck. You can also walk the Dike Road (by the canoe landing) and look for tundra swans from there.

**In Minnesota:**

+ **Brownsville Overlook:** Brownsville is located fifteen minutes south of La Crescent, Minnesota, not far from the Iowa border. From Wisconsin, cross the bridge in La Crosse to La Crescent, and then go south to Brownsville. The overlook is three miles south of Brownsville off Highway 26.

Personnel from the U.S. Fish and Wildlife Service and volunteers staff the Brownsville Overlook from 10:00 a.m. to 4:00 p.m. every

Saturday and Sunday in November. **Tundra swan numbers peak here between the first and second weeks of November.**

While the tundra swans are there all day, most of the activity is in the early morning and late afternoon. Earlier in the morning, the tundra swans tend to be closer to the overlook. As the day progresses and more and more people exit their vehicles, the swans typically move farther out on the river. Remember, if the swans are close to the road, stay in your vehicle. Your car is your best blind.

The birds tend to come back in toward shore during the evening, around 5:00 p.m. However, Sue Fletcher suggests getting to Brownsville before 3:30 p.m., when the sun is usually hidden behind a hill. "One of my favorite places is afternoon on the Brownsville Overlook," she says. "On a sunny day, the light is beautiful, the water is blue, the swans are hanging out—it's absolutely stunning."

• **Bus tour:** The Upper Mississippi River National Wildlife and Fish Refuge offers a bus tour out of Winona, Minnesota, the second Saturday in November for Waterfowl Observation Day. Onboard interpreters answer questions and provide binoculars and spotting scopes. There is a fee. Reserve a seat on the tour by calling (507) 452-4232. For tundra swan viewing updates, check the "Fall Flights" on the refuge website at www.fws.gov/refuge/upper_mississippi_river.

## HOW TO BECOME INVOLVED WITH TUNDRA SWAN CONSERVATION EFFORTS

Says Sue Fletcher, "The number one thing that swans and waterfowl need is appropriate habitat, so get involved in protection efforts. For example, if you live along a river, participate in a cleanup campaign. If there's an organized event to pull invasive species, such as purple loosestrife, volunteer to help. And please don't plant invasive species in your own yard."

Respect for the birds and the long journeys they undertake are also of utmost importance. "When the birds are here on the Mississippi," says Sue, "they need to rest. One of the worst offenses I see is when people get out of their cars and walk closer to the birds in order to take a better photograph. As a photographer, I understand wanting to achieve a good picture. But when you advance toward the birds, they get disturbed and fly off, burning up much needed energy. It's good to keep that in mind."

# WINTER

(Photo: Candice Gaukel Andrews)

# 14

# Bald Eagles: Watching a Winter River

*Wisconsin River in Prairie du Sac*

BALD EAGLE WATCHING DAYS

It was like a big, brown shadow that just suddenly materialized in front of me, hovered for a moment, and then silently floated off over my head. It was only after it was gone that it came to me that I had just seen a bald eagle.

That was the first time I had witnessed our national emblem in the flesh in Wisconsin. I clearly remember that it was on December 31, and I was standing on an overlook in Wyalusing State Park near Prairie du Chien. As I gazed out over the place where the mighty Mississippi and Wisconsin Rivers meet, that feathery ghost rose—with absolutely no warning. The bird had lifted up from somewhere down below me, like a weightless balloon. It paused for a few seconds in midair, then drifted away and up into the gray winter sky, somewhere out there, over the rivers.

That's how it is with eagles. They seem either to soar over your head like a suggestion or to elevate from somewhere down below you. But always, *always*, they do it without a sound. Such grace seems counterintuitive for such a big, substantial, strong bird of prey. It's no wonder our country chose the bald eagle as its symbol of freedom and power.

Despite their large size, bald eagles are, indeed, agile fliers. While they are capable of bursts of speed and rolls when pursuing prey or interacting with each other, they can also glide for long distances by holding their wings out stiffly. Such abilities are an eagle requirement. Most of their prey is wary—quick to react to danger by diving under cover or by speeding away. Many are camouflaged. Some prey that live in groups—such as grouse, geese, and rabbits—even post a lookout for any threat while others feed. Therefore, a hunting eagle must see his potential prey before it sees him, he must plan his approach to maximize the element of surprise, and, finally, he must execute a quick, clean kill. A bald eagle must be a smart strategist and an efficient worker. There's no squawking or screeching. As an eagle, you just endeavor to make a good living—quietly— in Wisconsin.

And while the bald eagles are watching for prey, we Wisconsinites are watching for them. Since the ban of DDT in the early 1970s, bald eagle spotting has been growing as a winter sport here.

One of the easiest places to see them is along the Wisconsin River near Prairie du Sac.

## A PERFECT PLACE FOR EAGLES

It's another gray winter day, like that one years ago in Wyalusing State Park. Only this time, the month is January, and instead of being surprised by an eagle, I hope to spot one first. It's 7:00 a.m., and I'm standing in the parking lot off of Water Street in Prairie du Sac, where the Ferry Bluff Eagle Council has built a viewing platform on the shore of the Wisconsin River. The spit of land in the middle of the river, known as Eagle Island, looks empty. I glance over to my left toward the dam, but it's shrouded in fog. I doubt whether I'll see much of anything today.

Then, I detect movement, and my eyes register two expansive wings, as a lone bald eagle tracks over a stretch of the river. It's a good omen, because this is the start of Bald Eagle Watching Days, a two-day annual festival celebrating the great raptor. For the past two decades, at the spot where Sauk City and Prairie du Sac share a ribbon of the Wisconsin River, there has been a winter weekend gathering of birds and people.

Kay Roherty, a Ferry Bluff Eagle Council member since 1998 and a cochair for Bald Eagle Watching Days since 2003, says Sauk Prairie (as the two towns are jointly known) has four features that provide the perfect habitat for wintering eagles: (1) the dam, which provides open water in the winter, where eagles can hunt for fish; (2) an undeveloped shoreline on the east side of the river, where the birds can rest during the day; (3) forested bluffs with valleys that give the eagles places to get out of the wind when they are roosting at night; and (4) nearby agricultural fields where they can find carrion—mostly dead deer.

Another factor drawing the eagles here in winter could be one that also attracts people: tradition. According to an article in USA Today, the results of an impact study conducted in 2005 revealed that "during the six weeks of peak eagle season, fifty thousand tourists bring $1.2 million into the towns" of Sauk City and Prairie du Sac. For a community of about five thousand residents, this is eco-tourism in a big way.

I'm about to add to that $1.2 million. With an hour to go before the official start of the festival, I'm going to catch breakfast at the Eagle Inn on Water Street. Still decked out in strings of tiny, bright-white Christmas lights and festooned in green boughs with red ribbons, the small, hometown eatery looks just too comfy and warm to resist on this chilly, thirty-degree, January early morning.

## A Spotting Scope and a Pickup Truck

After breakfast, I head over to the Sauk Prairie High School, where many of the Bald Eagle Watching Days events are being held. Even if I didn't know about that impact study, I would be able to tell that this is a community that revolves around its wintering eagles. Affixed to the outside wall of the high school is a huge cutout of the school's mascot—an eagle—with a sign that reads Welcome to Eagle Country.

Every year, twelve hundred to fifteen hundred people show up for the organized programs that are part of the weekend. Live bird shows, exhibits, lectures, and children's activities all take place in the high school. I check over the long list of events posted at a table inside the doors and make my plans for the day. I choose to go to a presentation from a local wildlife photographer; hear a talk titled "Eagles in Wisconsin and Local Conservation Efforts," by Pat Manthey of the Wisconsin DNR's Bureau of Endangered Resources; and watch the "Birds of Prey" show, put on by the Raptor Center of the University of Minnesota.

In addition to the programs at the high school, during the festival and on most of the other Saturdays in January and February, volunteers from the Ferry Bluff Eagle Council conduct one-hour, rotating bus tours. The buses stop where eagles are most often seen: at the dam, the VFW Memorial Park, and the Ferry Bluff Eagle Council Overlook in the municipal parking lot, where I had stopped this morning.

According to its "official" history, the Ferry Bluff Eagle Council (FBEC) got its start in March of 1988, when a small group of interested people met to discuss the future of the wintering eagles that were using the Ferry Bluff State Natural Area as a night roost. Just two years before, in 1986, a DNR Bald Eagle Recovery Plan was approved by the state Natural Resources Board. The plan's objective was to increase Wisconsin's self-sustaining population of bald eagles—whose numbers had been decimated—to 360 breeding pairs by the year 2000.

There are probably several reasons why bald eagle numbers had declined in the state and across the country. But the main culprit was the pesticide DDT, which was banned by Wisconsin in 1970 and by the federal government in

1972. In that year, Wisconsin had just eighty-two pairs of bald eagles. They were placed on the Wisconsin Endangered Species List in 1972 and on the federal List of Endangered and Threatened Species in 1973.

By July of 1988, just four months after the group of eagle enthusiasts in Sauk Prairie had met, the Ferry Bluff Eagle Sanctuary was incorporated. Its purpose, said Rae Onstine, one of the founding members, was "to help manage the local roosts and feeding areas; to provide viewing areas for the public where [eagles] can be observed and photographed without being disturbed; and to study the habits of the wintering birds as an aid to future management."

By January 1990, the FBEC had begun assisting the DNR's Bureau of Endangered Resources in staging Bald Eagle Watching Days. Three years later, a permanent telescope was installed at the downtown Prairie du Sac parking lot.

By 1991, twenty-one years after the ban of DDT, Wisconsin exceeded its bald eagle recovery goal when 414 active pairs were located. That winter in Prairie du Sac, nine roosts for wintering eagles were also found.

Although this "official" history tells us much about the Sauk Prairie community and its love of bald eagles, Kay Roherty tells me a story of how Bald Eagle Watching Days began that has become local folklore. And like all good creation myths, the tale centers on the passions of one individual.

"Bald Eagle Watching Days were started, you could say, by Randy Jurewicz," says Kay. "He worked for the DNR Bureau of Endangered Resources. Randy was on the eagle project in 1988 when the DDT ban was just beginning to bring the eagles back to us, when the birds were starting to recover. Randy would drive to the Prairie du Sac parking lot in his pickup truck and set up a spotting scope in the back of it. He would then just invite people to come on over and take a look," she explains. "And Randy's still with us; he's a volunteer at the annual festival."

## AN UNCOMMON CLOSENESS

What may have motivated Randy to pick Prairie du Sac as the place to set up his scope—and the reason for my choosing this area along the Wisconsin River from among many winter eagle watching spots in Wisconsin—is the fact that this is one of the closest encounters you may ever have with a bald eagle in the wild. On this narrow part of the Wisconsin River, the raptors become concentrated. It's not quite as easy to see the birds on the wider Mississippi.

In December, when the rivers farther north begin to freeze over, bald eagles from northern Wisconsin, the Upper Peninsula of Michigan, and northeastern Minnesota fly to places such as Prairie du Sac. A recent satellite study showed that an eagle that nests in Manitoba, Canada, has even wintered here. The seasonal travels of these "sea eagles" are mostly influenced by the availability of open water. And here, in this little community in south central Wisconsin, the birds find the Prairie du Sac hydroelectric-generating dam quite accommodating for two reasons: The dam's turbulence keeps the water open in the winter, and fish tend to get injured while going through the dam. The opportunistic bald eagles find plentiful food.

The best time to watch bald eagles fish is in the first few hours of the morning and in midafternoon. While they like a wide variety of seafood, eagle favorites are muskies, bullheads, northerns, and suckers. Live fish are captured with the bird's strong, sharp, curved talons; dead ones may be scavenged near the dam or along the riverbank. Skilled hunters with keen eyesight, eagles will also take other frequenters of the shores: waterfowl, muskrats, and turtles. An eagle consumes and digests all of its prey; only the biggest bones will remain.

Winter is the one time of the year when bald eagles will tolerate being in close proximity with one another. In other seasons, they will fight to the death to defend a territory. By the end of February, most of the wintering eagles will

For such a big, powerful bird, the bald eagle emits a surprisingly high-pitched, sharp, short call. The long, drawn-out screech you often hear in movies when a soaring eagle is depicted is actually dubbed in: it's the voice of a red-tailed hawk. (Photo: Bob Leggett)

have left Prairie du Sac. As spring approaches and the days begin to lengthen, they tend to want to get back home as soon as possible. For then, it's time to start building nests and raising families.

## CONCERNING BALD EAGLES

Although bald eagle watching is purely a winter phenomenon in Wisconsin, evidence of nesting eagles on the lower Wisconsin River has been mounting with each year. In the summer of 1993, the Wisconsin DNR reported six active eagle nests on the Lower Wisconsin Riverway. In 1995, the FBEC group's members were monitoring a successful eagle nest visible from Highway 60 near Highway C, probably the first such nest in Sauk County for forty years. And in the summer of 2003, two FBEC members discovered a new nest about eight miles below the Prairie du Sac Dam, which is probably the first one to be situated there in fifty years. The pair successfully fledged two young, despite a storm that blew the nest down in early July.

Bald eagles (*Haliaeetus leucocephalus*) build their nests, called *eyries*, in the tops of tall trees—up to 150 feet above the ground—that are near water. While some eagles may have five or six nests in a territory that they will defend, they tend to use the same eyrie every year, especially if that nest has proven successful for rearing young. A territory could include a small lake, several lakes, or a bay. Each year, an eyrie will be renovated and added to, increasing in size—at times reaching up to one thousand pounds—until either its own weight or a winter storm brings it down. Wisconsin ranks third highest in bald eagle nesting states (Alaska is number one and Minnesota is number two).

Bald eagles lay one to three off-white eggs, which are incubated by both parents for up to thirty-five days. For one or two months after hatching, the eaglets will remain dependent on their parents. At nine or ten weeks of age, they strive to leave the nest. Young that walk sideways on a branch or balance on the edge of the nest to experiment are called *branchers*.

It takes five to six years for a bald eagle to look like a *bald* eagle. When the eaglets leave the nest, they are still very dark. Immature bald eagles are mottled brown and white until they reach sexual maturity, at four or five years of age. Only then do they acquire the distinctive white feathering on their heads.

The increasing number of golden eagles in the state makes distinguishing an immature bald eagle from an immature golden eagle difficult—unless you see it in flight. A juvenile golden eagle will have white patches on the undersides of its wings and a broad, white tail with a dark band. The tail and wings of an immature bald eagle are mottled brown and white on the underside. The most notable mark at any age is on the legs: a presence of feathers that go all the way down to the toes means the bird is a golden eagle, while the bald eagle has a considerable amount of exposed leg showing.

Bald eagles grow to an impressive size: thirty-one to thirty-seven inches in length, with a wingspan measuring from seventy-nine to ninety inches. Females are usually bigger than the males and can weigh between nine and eleven pounds. We've all heard of "eagle-eyed" people, and the phrase is well deserved. All eagles have very large eyes, which are sometimes brown, but more often they are colored red, orange, or yellow. Such bright eyes give the bird a fierce and piercing expression. Not only are those eyes cosmetically striking but they are far more efficient than ours. An eagle can spot a rabbit feeding in a field two or three times as far away as we can.

In captivity, bald eagles have lived up to fifty years. In the wild, it was long thought that they typically lived to be twelve to twenty years of age. However, on May 16, 2008, the carcass of a thirty-one-year-old, female bald eagle was found on the shore of Razorback Lake in Vilas County. The bird wore a leg band that DNR biologist Ron Eckstein was able to trace back to 1977. She is believed to be the oldest eagle to have lived in the wild in the Midwest. She had hatched in Michigan's Ottawa National Forest. Her long-ago nest, which had sat in a large white pine, is still active.

Unfortunately, the mortality rate for most bald eagles—the young, especially—is high. Fishers and raccoons occasionally get into nests. And when first learning to hunt, young eagles often make deadly mistakes. While scavenging dead deer on the roads, bald eagles are often hit by cars. They may swallow poisonous lead from bullets lodged in deer carcasses, and sometimes they fly into power lines.

Although removed from Wisconsin's Endangered Species List in 1997 and the federal list in 2007, bald eagles still have some national protection under the Migratory Bird Treaty Act of 1918 and the Bald and Golden Eagle Protection Act of 1940. Further, there is an "eagle feather law" (Title 50, Part 22, of the United States Code of Federal Regulations) that states that only individuals of certifiable Native American ancestry enrolled in a federally recognized tribe are legally authorized to obtain eagle feathers. The U.S. Fish and Wildlife Service maintains a National Eagle Repository at the Rocky Mountain Arsenal National Wildlife Refuge in Denver to provide Native Americans with bald or golden eagle feathers to use in ceremonies. An eagle feather already in possession, however, may be handed down to family members from generation to generation, or from one Native American to another for religious purposes.

While bald eagles are no longer considered endangered, they are still officially a species of "special concern" in Wisconsin.

## A Famous Opinion on the
## Bald Eagle's Moral Character

And "concern" is exactly what Benjamin Franklin felt after the bald eagle was designated as the national emblem for the United States in 1782. On January 26, 1784, Franklin wrote a letter to his daughter saying that he wished the bald eagle had not been chosen as a "representative of our country" because it is a "Bird of bad moral Character." In his opinion, "Like those among Men who live

Benjamin Franklin once wrote that the bald eagle was a "Bird of bad moral Character." His choice to symbolize the essence of our country would have been a turkey. However, one bald eagle in Wisconsin would later prove him wrong. (Photo: Bob Leggett)

by Sharping and Robbing, he is generally poor, and often very lousy." His choice to symbolize the essence of our country would have been a turkey.

Almost a hundred years later, however, one bald eagle in Wisconsin would prove Franklin wrong when it came to principles of conduct.

In the summer of 1861, on one of the Flambeau River's North Fork rapids in northern Wisconsin, a twenty-five-year-old Ojibwe by the name of A-ge-mah-we-go-zhig (Chief of the Sky) captured an eaglet. He sold this young eagle a few weeks later to a man named Daniel McCann for a bushel of corn. According to an article published on the Wisconsin Historical Society website, McCann, in turn, offered his eagle's services as a mascot to the Eighth Regiment Wisconsin Volunteer Infantry Company C, feeling that "someone from the family ought to serve."

Company C named the eagle Old Abe in honor of President Abraham Lincoln. The soldiers placed red and blue ribbons around the bird's neck, hung a rosette on his breast, and swore him into the United States Army. They designed a special perch for Old Abe and proudly carried him into forty-two battles and skirmishes during the Civil War.

It's reported that Old Abe conducted himself with extreme valor during warfare. A contemporary wrote: "At the sound of the regimental bugle, which he had learned to recognize, he would start suddenly, dart up his head, and then bend it gracefully, anticipating the coming shock. When the battle commenced, he would spring up, spread his wings uttering his startling scream, heard, and felt and gloried in by all the soldiers. The fiercer and louder the Storm, the fiercer, louder and wilder were his screams." Confederate troops starting calling Old Abe the Yankee buzzard. They tried to capture and kill him several times but never succeeded.

At the end of the Civil War, Company C presented Old Abe to the State of Wisconsin. He was awarded a home in the basement of the capitol in Madison. Old Abe continued his duties by making public appearances all over the United States, including the 1876 Centennial Exposition in Philadelphia and the 1880 National Encampment of the Grand Army of the Republic in Milwaukee.

On a cold evening in the winter of 1881, however, a fire started in a stash of paints and oils stored in the capitol's basement, near Old Abe's cage. He screeched, calling watchmen and attendants. When they opened the door of his perch-room, Abe swept out and away from the flames. The blaze was put out, but it had created an enormous volume of black smoke.

After his ordeal with the fire, Old Abe never really seemed to recover. He remained in a half-comatose condition for a few days. Then, on March 26, 1881, with a slight shake of his body and a few, weak flaps of his wings, he died in the arms of his keeper, George Gillies. According to the 1885 book *Old Abe, the Eighth Wisconsin War Eagle: A Full Account of His Capture and Enlistment, Exploits in War and Honorable as well as Useful Career in Peace*, by Frank Abial Flower, "George said that Abe seemed to know he was about to die, for when he asked solicitously, 'must we lose you, Abe?' the old bird raised up his head and looked wistfully into his keeper's face and then sunk back into his arms and passed away. Around him were numbers of one-legged and one-armed veterans whose sad faces showed that they had lost a beloved comrade."

At first, it was thought that the eagle, who had lived for at least twenty years, should be buried in Forest Hills Cemetery in Boston, Massachusetts, where several hundred Union and Confederate dead rest. In the end, however, he was turned over to a taxidermist who, after stuffing the warrior-bird, affixed him to a perch in the Civil War Museum in the Wisconsin capitol. Unfortunately, his body was destroyed when a second capitol building burned in 1904.

## WISCONSIN PRIDE

The majestic bald eagle is not only an emblem for our nation but a special icon for Wisconsinites. The bird's return is proof of an environmental victory.

The DNR estimates that today the state is home to 1,273 nesting pairs of bald eagles, or about 11 percent of the 9,789 pairs believed to be breeding in the lower forty-eight states by the U.S. Fish and Wildlife Service. In fact, since 1975, Wisconsin has sent 215 eaglets to ten other states to help increase the national eagle population. Wisconsin eagles have even been released near the U.S. Capitol in Washington and in a Hudson River Valley park in New York City.

## THE COMEBACK TOUR

My eagle learning and looking in Prairie du Sac are coming to an end on this January day, but there's one more group activity I want to experience. I board a bus for one of the bald eagle watching tours.

Kay Roherty is traveling along in my bus, and during our third stop, which is at the Ferry Bluff Eagle Council Overlook in the parking lot—where I had started my day hours earlier and where Bald Eagle Watching Days began so long ago—I ask her what it is that keeps her wanting to return here year after year and volunteer her time. "I do it for the joy," she says without hesitation. "Bald Eagle Watching Days are truly a family event, and we see lots of children. At the lookout spotting scope, we have a stepstool all set up, so even small children can get the chance to see an eagle in the wild. One time, one very small child said to me after looking through the scope, 'I saw the eagle eye!' He was so thrilled. Then he added, 'That eagle winked at me!' And that's the reward," Kay tells me, smiling. "That's the reward."

At the end of the bus tour, our guide tells us that he heard a rumor that some bald eagles were roosting in the hills behind the Wollersheim Winery, which is located nearby, on a hillside overlooking the Wisconsin River. A national historic site, the winery and its location seem fitting for a national, historic bird.

After my bus tour, I decide to drive to the winery before going home. Although I spot no bald eagles there, I do pick up a bottle of Eagle White wine. The Wollersheim Winery produces an "eagle wine" every year, and donates a portion of the sales to preserving local habitat for bald eagles.

I know that after a glass or two, I'll sleep well tonight and dream of silent eagles, rising up from below.

## HOW TO HAVE A GENUINE
## BALD EAGLE ENCOUNTER OF YOUR OWN

In Wisconsin, December, January, and February are the best months to search for bald eagles. When lakes and rivers freeze over, dams and power plants provide areas of open water in which the eagles can fish. Bald eagles especially like places that have open water and a protected place to roost nearby, such as a broad valley with big, mature trees.

The best time to watch for bald eagles is in the first few hours of the morning, just after daybreak, and in midafternoon, when they'll make a return fishing trip to stock up for the night.

Remember that eagles are sensitive to disturbance by humans. In winter, the birds try to conserve energy, and any added disturbances can cause stress. In Prairie du Sac, visitors are advised to stay in their vehicles for viewing, except at the designated Ferry Bluff Eagle Council Overlook in the downtown parking lot.

Bald eagle watching festivals in Wisconsin include:

+ Bald Eagle Watching Days at Sauk City–Prairie du Sac (Sauk Prairie), www.ferrybluffeaglecouncil.org/eagledays
+ Cassville Bald Eagle Days, www.cassville.org
+ Bald Eagle Appreciation Day in Prairie du Chien, www.prairieduchien .org/visitors/eagles.htm

## HOW TO BECOME INVOLVED WITH
## BALD EAGLE CONSERVATION EFFORTS

The Wisconsin DNR maintains an Adopt-an-Eagle-Nest Program. Your donations will be used to protect nests and rescue and rehabilitate sick, injured, and orphaned eagles. Go to dnr.wi.gov/topic/endangeredresources/adopt.html to learn more.

# 15

# Gray Wolves: Tracking and Howling

*Treehaven in Tomahawk*

WOLF ECOLOGY WORKSHOP

The human body was badly decayed, but still you could see that its hand was definitely holding *something*. For twelve thousand years, the bones in those once lithe fingers had clutched that thing close, treasuring it. Archeologists determined that it was a pup, but whether it was the offspring of a dog or a wolf, no one could be sure. The human remains—and companion animal—had been placed there long ago by hunter-gatherers in what today is the country of Israel.

What is certain is that this is one of the earliest pieces of evidence we have regarding the dog's domestication, which was underway by about fourteen thousand years ago. While researchers still don't know whether humans adopted wolf pups and then natural selection favored those that were less aggressive and better at begging for food, or whether dogs domesticated themselves by adapting to the new niche of human refuse dumps, dogs undeniably became our best friends.

Since that ancient time in Israel, nothing much has changed at the molecular level. The DNA of wolves and dogs remains almost identical. And that may be why we are all fascinated by wolves, the wild "cousins" of our most beloved pets.

## MAKING TRACKS FOR TOMAHAWK

Of all of our state's and nation's greatest animal icons—the wolf, the bear, the eagle—it's the wolf that I've most wanted to hear or see in the wild. More so than a bruin growl or an avian whistle, I've wanted to catch carried on Wisconsin winds the wildest of all calls: the howl of a wolf. And while our state is home to more than eight hundred gray wolves, I have never managed to hear or see one on any of my excursions into the Northwoods. Perhaps I made too much noise. Maybe there's too much forest to hide in. Or it could be that, after all we've done to eradicate wolves in the state—and throughout the country—they know we're still not ready to fully accept their presence.

While I have had the great fortune to see wolves in Yellowstone National Park's wide open, panoramic Lamar Valley, seeking to have an encounter with a wolf in Wisconsin's woods is a difficult challenge to undertake. In fact, it's more likely that you may *hear* a wolf than *see* one. That's why I'm heading out this morning to a wolf ecology workshop at the Treehaven natural resources education facility in Tomahawk in north central Wisconsin. Along with lectures about wolf monitoring, management, and history in the state, there will be an afternoon tracking excursion and a nighttime "howling" walk. The purpose of the "howl" is to hear a wolf or wolves howl back.

The workshop is a two-day event put on by TWIN, the Timber Wolf Information Network, whose stated purpose is "to increase public awareness and acceptance of the wolf in its native habitat and its ecological role in the environment." That's a tall order to fill, given people's intense emotions regarding wolves. Perhaps more so than any other animal, wolves provoke strong feelings in us, whether pro or con, and stir our passions—and have for thousands of years, as that old, unearthed body in Israel attests.

It's ten degrees below zero on this dark Saturday morning in late January. To catch the workshop's first lecture, I need to be in Tomahawk by 9:00 a.m. I live in southern Wisconsin, so when my shivering fingers insert the key into the car's ignition, the dashboard clock flickers 5:15 a.m.

Tomahawk is currently the home of four known wolf packs: the Averill Creek–North Pack, the Averill Creek–South Pack, the Ranger Island Pack, and the Harrison Hills Pack. However, packs are fluid entities, with members trotting in and out—and new groups being formed and dissolved—constantly. Trying to get a bead on exactly what packs are where at any one point in time is almost impossible. An estimation is about all you can hope for.

The sun slowly cracks open the January dark while I drive a northward beeline on Highway 51. Three hours later, as I make the turn onto Pickerel Creek Road, it seems as if this is the border where the constant buzz of high-speed travel is no longer allowed. The chirps of birds and the creaks of snow-covered conifers standing like sentinels on both sides of the road take over the soundscape with a suddenness I didn't expect. I crack open the driver's side window and listen to the soft, monotonous murmur of my tires as they roll on top of the thick snow down the long, narrow road. Just before I reach the Treehaven compound, four deer leap across the skinny route ahead of me.

Because there are big dogs and small wolves, telling the two tracks apart can be difficult. But since this paw print appeared in Yellowstone National Park's Lamar Valley, it is that of a wolf. (Photo: John T. Andrews)

Treehaven is a residential education center that is owned and operated by the University of Wisconsin–Stevens Point, College of Natural Resources. Its lodges, classroom, dormitories, cottages, and trails sit on a glacial ridge overlooking fourteen hundred acres of forest and wetlands. Pickerel Creek Road is, in fact, a long-used deer trail, a significant factor in the mix that makes the Tomahawk area an excellent habitat for wolves.

I check in with only five minutes to spare and find a seat at one of the classroom's tables. Our workshop leaders today are Dick Thiel (see chapter 5, "White-Tailed Deer: Ferreting Out a Phantom"), former director at Sandhill Outdoor Skills Center in Babcock and cofounder of TWIN; Ron Vander Velden, also a cofounder of TWIN and a coordinator of wolf trackers in the northeastern part of the state; and Dick Stoelb, a TWIN associate. They ask us to start the morning session with brief introductions. My twenty or so fellow workshop participants describe themselves mostly as "interested folks." They include two retirees from Rhinelander, a zookeeper from outside the state, and a young man who is considering making the study of wolves his lifework.

### WHEN PEOPLE WERE WOLVES

The first part of our workshop weekend is devoted to learning about the history of wolves in our state. It seems wolves and Wisconsin have been part of each other since the retreat of the third glacial maxima of the Wisconsin Glacial Episode ten thousand years ago. The bison, caribou, moose, elk, and deer that roamed our forests, rivers, wetlands, and grasslands were all potential prey for our wolves, as many as three thousand to five thousand of them. Native peoples, such as the Ho-Chunk and Menominee, developed Wolf Clans honoring what they saw as their animal brothers' great skills.

One Ho-Chunk origin myth tells of a Wolf Clan people who came from the water. When they reached shore, these "wolves" transformed themselves into human beings. Because of where they came from, water was very sacred to Wolf Clansmen. They were often called upon to calm the wind when parties of Indians had to travel across large rivers or lakes.

The Wisconsin Menominee had five principal clans. The Bear Clan assumed the duties of civil administration throughout the tribe, while the Eagle Clan were fire carriers, camp laborers, war strategists, and warriors (although all male Menominee adults served as warriors, as well). Crane Clan members were builders, and the Moose Clan oversaw the wild rice beds, supervised rice harvest and distribution, and took care of camp security. It was the Wolf Clan (or *Mahwaew*), however, whose primary responsibility was hunting.

## Giving Wisconsin a Second Chance

At this point in the presentation, Dick Thiel reminds us that while we usually lump the European immigrants and settlers that came to Wisconsin into one big wave, there were actually several. The French arrived here mostly between the years of 1660 to 1760, followed by the British between 1780 and about 1820. From the 1820s on, the new "immigrants" to the Wisconsin territory were now properly called Americans.

And most of those Americans engaged in mining, farming, or logging. From the 1840s to the 1920s, the forests of Wisconsin, Michigan, and Minnesota were used to provide the wood that was building the United States. It was the farmers in particular, however, who had a distinct difference of opinion from the Ho-Chunk, Menominee, and other native peoples when it came to wolves: they were convinced that the animals were destroying large numbers of livestock and therefore were a menace to be gotten rid of. At the same time, subsistence hunters were condemning the state's wolves for killing too many deer, when in reality, thousands were being harvested by humans for food in the logging camps.

It is believed by most historians that the first bounty ever offered in what is now the state of Wisconsin was passed by the territorial government in 1839: three dollars for every wolf killed. Trapping killed most of our wolves, although strychnine poisoning was sometimes allowed. By 1950, the only wolves in the contiguous United States were in the upper Great Lakes region. On June 6, 1957, Wisconsin permanently repealed its wolf bounty.

The last confirmed wolf in Wisconsin managed to outlive the bounty era by about seven months. He was an animal known as Old Two Toes, and he lived in northern Bayfield County. A loner since at least 1954, he was hit by a car on a snowy night in early January 1958. When he refused to die from that impact, he was then bludgeoned with a tire iron and finally succumbed by having his throat slit open with a knife. Dick reports that the hide and skeleton of Old Two Toes now repose in the mammal collection of the University of Wisconsin Zoological Museum.

In 1973, protection for our country's wolves got a boost from the federal Endangered Species Act, when the gray wolf was given endangered species status in the lower forty-eight states. Two years later, the gray wolf was placed on Wisconsin's Endangered Species List.

At just about this time, a wolf pack was detected on the Minnesota-Wisconsin border. "These animals are smart," says Ron Vander Velden. "The wolves knew when it was safe to sneak back over into Wisconsin."

By 1979, two wolf packs were known to be living and breeding in Douglas County. The animals soon spread out, and by 1980, there was confirmation that a pack of wolves had returned to our central forests in Lincoln County, near Tomahawk. It seems that after all we had thrown at them, they decided to take a chance on living in Wisconsin again.

## SCENTS AND SENSIBILITIES

The gray wolf (*Canis lupus*), also known as a *timber wolf*, is the largest of the North American wild dogs. The average male wolf in Wisconsin weighs approximately seventy-five pounds; a female is usually about sixty-five pounds. Wolves have excellent hearing, night vision, and a superb sense of smell. In fact, according to Dick Thiel, in one experiment, a wolf was able to smell one drop of urine diluted in five hundred drops of water just from a small amount of that solution placed on a bush.

Wolves run the gamut of colors from completely black to white. Typically, however, the animals are grizzled, with black interspersed. Their snouts are elongated for pulling down prey on the run.

Our relationship with wolves is complicated. Once extirpated from the state, they have now made a successful comeback. It seems that after all we've thrown at them, gray wolves decided to take a chance on living in Wisconsin again. (This wolf pup is in captivity at the MacKenzie Environmental Education Center in Poynette.) (Photo: Candice Gaukel Andrews)

A *pack* is defined as at least two animals, but most wolves live, travel, and hunt in packs of four to seven members. Packs include a breeding pair, called *alphas*, their pups, and several other subordinate or young wolves. The alpha female and male are the pack's leaders, who will track and hunt prey, choose the den sites, and establish territory. Pack dynamics and numbers may change from one season to the next—even month by month. Even more intriguing is that a wolf will rarely join an adjacent pack; it will attempt to travel across long distances through "open channels." One wolf was found, shot, five hundred miles from home.

Wolves develop close relationships and strong social bonds. They demonstrate deep affection for their families, and there are documented cases where wolves have even sacrificed themselves to protect their family units.

Contrary to popular belief, the alpha wolves aren't always the largest, strongest, or fastest wolves in the pack. In the wild, a subservient wolf will disperse from the natal pack when it is about two years old. If this loner finds a mate and breeds, it will become an alpha wolf over its offspring. Too, if one member of the pack passes away, or another wolf joins the pack, the dominance hierarchy can change. During the mating season, wolf pack rank may shift again.

Wolves den only for the purpose of having pups. Females are in heat from mid-January through February (unlike dogs, who go into heat twice a year). After a sixty-three-day gestation period—similar to that in a dog—the pups are born in April to mid-May.

The average litter size is four to seven pups. Young are born blind and defenseless. Between ten and thirteen days, they will open their eyes. At three weeks, the pups can hear. After reaching about five to six pounds in four weeks, they will leave the den. This is the time when they will begin to howl and eat meat. Adult wolves have the ability to shut down their digestion processes after ingestion, in order to bring food back to the pups by regurgitation.

At two months, the pups are weaned. From mid-May to mid-September, they are moved around to a series of "rendezvous sites," meeting places where the wolves gather to sleep, play, and just hang out. At three months, the pups begin to follow the adults on hunting trips. They can actively hunt on their own at six to eight months of age.

A wolf can run up to forty miles per hour and walks at a speed of about five miles per hour. Wolves traveling together will walk in a straight line, one wolf breaking the trail through snow. Trackers often have to follow tracks a long way until they fan out to know for certain how many wolves they are actually tracing.

Tracking coordinator Ron Vander Velden knows firsthand how patient and persistent a tracker needs to be in order to get the whole story that a set of wolf tracks is trying to tell. Says Ron, "Before every wolf ecology workshop that TWIN holds, I arrive at the location the day before and spend it looking for wolf tracks so we can take participants right to the spots where there has been some fresh wolf activity. Before one particular workshop a few weeks ago, I spent five hours outside looking, and I never found a track. Just as I was about to give up, I came around a corner and saw a flock of ravens and two eagles in a tree. I knew immediately that I was coming upon a wolf kill-site.

"It turned out that three wolves had taken down a big buck," Ron continues. "The snow was more than knee-deep; I measured it at twenty-two inches. I saw melting snow where the buck had slept, so I knew the wolves had come in—in single file—when he was bedded down. And then all of sudden, from the tracks in the snow, I could see that one wolf had taken off on one side and a pair of wolves had gone around to the other. There was eleven and a half feet between their bounds—through that deep snow! They nailed that buck six feet away from his bed.

Wolf pups love to play, and they use the activity as practice for their first real hunt with the adult members of the pack. Pups have been observed stalking each other and "killing" bones, feathers, and the skins of dead animals over and over again. (This wolf pup is in captivity at the MacKenzie Environmental Education Center in Poynette.) (Photo: John T. Andrews)

"The wolves were very efficient," Ron relates. "The buck's neck vertebra was snapped. That's how wolves kill their prey; one bite on the neck and it's pretty well taken care of. They ate all the organs and major muscle masses. I brought our workshop participants to the site the next day, and we did a sort of *CSI* TV-show-type autopsy. We chopped open a leg bone. Normally, marrow is cream-colored. But when fat resources are depleted, the marrow turns red and jelly-like. The interior of this leg bone was definitely like the latter. Next, we examined the stomach contents and found balsam fir needles. A deer feeding on balsam fir is akin to us eating cardboard. There is no nutritional value. So this buck, which I estimated to be more than ten years old by an examination of teeth in the lower jaw, was starving to death. This was a textbook kill," concludes Ron. "Wolves, indeed, usually take the old and the weak."

Whether it's because their large paws act like snowshoes while traveling over powdery landscapes or for some other reason, it's said that wolves "come alive" when it's cold.

It turns out that those hoping to see them in the wild do, too.

## COMING INTO WOLF COUNTRY

Nestled in the Northwoods where four rivers converge—the Somo, the Spirit, the Tomahawk, and the Wisconsin—sits the small town of Tomahawk (population 3,666) in the northern part of Lincoln County. Prior to 1886, this area, like much of the rest of Wisconsin, was a wilderness. In that year, however, the Tomahawk Land and Boom Company began its operations, and by the spring of 1887, the company had laid out the site for the city. The first lots were offered for sale on June 25, 1887. By September of that same year, wolves weren't the only ones making lines of tracks in Tomahawk. The Chicago, Milwaukee & St. Paul Railroad had come to town.

Sawmills and other industries began to spring up. In the 1890 census, just three years after the city was laid out, Tomahawk's population had reached 1,816.

Still today, though, because of the predominance of undeveloped, county lands around Tomahawk—plus some logging—this remains a good place for wolves. Explains Ron, "We have wolves in Tomahawk because we have a food supply for them—in this case, deer. We have deer because we have logging. The wolf kill-site that I found for my workshop participants a few weeks ago was on property where there was active logging going on. Downed treetops are a valuable source of sustenance for deer in the wintertime; it's what's saving a lot of them. Obviously, it wasn't helping that old buck that I found, but for the wolves, it's a no-brainer. You just follow where the deer go. So logging plays a significant role in the North Country for wolves."

A wolf *territory* is defined as "a space defended against others." Gray wolf territories in the lower forty-eight states may be less than 100 square miles, while territories in Alaska and Canada can range from about 300 to 1,000 square miles or more. In the Great Lakes region, wolves normally occupy territories that cover 20 to 120 square miles. Territory size depends on a number of factors at specific times, such as prey abundance, the nature of the terrain, weather and climate changes, and the presence of other predators, including other wolf packs. When other canids, coyotes or dogs, for example, are killed in a wolf's territory, they are being killed not for food but for protection of space. According to Dick Thiel, "Wolves are consummate territorialists—if you trespass, you *are* dead. The territory is a complete system; it is the hunting universe."

Our workshop leaders inform us that our own foray into a wolf pack territory will begin after lunch at the Treehaven lodge. We're given an hour and a half to eat and get bundled up in our parkas, snow pants, and heavy boots. We'll be going in a school bus—to lessen the environmental impact of our traveling individually in separate cars—into Wisconsin's historic Averill Creek Wolf Pack territory.

During the bus ride, I watch out the front windshield as three deer leap across the road—in almost the same spot where I had seen them fly across my field of vision that morning. It feels like good foreshadowing; the wolves *have* to be here, just beyond our knowing.

Off of Whiskey Bill Road, our three-hour efforts to find wildlife stories written in the snow are rewarded: We find the paw prints of trotting coyotes, the distinctive "slide" marks of otters, the footsteps of fishers, the hoof imprints of deer walking down the sides and middle of a plowed path, and what Ron guesses is the signature gait of a bobcat. We also detect the tracks of two or three wolves.

I can't wait for this evening, when we'll try to get even closer to their presence with a "howl."

## WOLFSONG

In the Northwoods, January nights are dark, crisp, and starry. Under Orion's Belt, the Big and Little Dippers, and a full moon, our group gathers to follow Dick, Ron, and Dick on a wolf howl.

Our workshop leaders are quick to emphasize, however, that people should *not* go out to howl where there are wolf packs present just to hear the wolves howl back. Human howling can disrupt wolf communications within and between packs, perhaps even causing a pack harm. So the howl walks that TWIN conducts as part of its workshops are in conjunction with howling surveys. The organization takes great care to ensure that surveyors don't howl too much to the same packs. Dick Thiel will be our designated "howler" tonight.

Howling by wolves serves several functions: to form social bonds, to locate members of their own packs by voice recognition, to establish territorial positions, and to discover dominance rankings. If after a human howl, wolves do come in to investigate, they will do so silently. Ron recalls one experience in Canada.

"It was sunset, and I was on a long, narrow lake with a friend of mine," Ron begins. "When I howl, I always do it at sunset. Well, this time, I didn't even finish getting the first set of howls out when I heard a response on the other side of the lake. It was thrilling.

"That night, my friend and I slept under mosquito netting," he goes on. "Just before I fell asleep, I began to hear this *shooo-ooooo, shooo-ooooo, shooo-ooooo* noise. I realized that the wolf that had called back to me was coming around the end of the lake. So I gave a very soft howl. I got an answer from just about fifty feet away! I could actually hear the saliva in the wolf's throat. After he answered me, he just turned around: *shooo-ooooo, shooo-ooooo, shooo-ooooo.* He went back to wherever he had come from."

A wolf's complex communication system ranges from the iconic long howls of our imaginations—and many Hollywood horror movies—to short barks, whines, and growls. But while wolves don't howl at the moon, they do howl more when it's lighter at night, which occurs more often when the moon is full.

"Howling experiences are all so very unique," Ron tells us. "What *are* the wolves saying? I think we're in a brand-new area of science here, about which we can only anthropomorphize. I guess that's the intriguing part of this."

Ron relates one more memorable howling excursion. "When I go out on howling surveys, I try to bring other people along who I think would appreciate the experience. Now, as grandkids have entered my life, I bring the little ones with me. On one survey I did last summer, I brought my four-year-old granddaughter. We drove to a remote forest road. So, there we are, standing in the dark in the dirt, and I'm howling my lungs out trying to get the wolves to sing. I just couldn't raise a peep. My granddaughter says, 'Grandpa, can I howl?' I told her yes. She started her first howl, and oh, golly, some wolf pups answered! They couldn't have been more than two hundred yards away," recalls Ron, laughing.

"It was her tenor voice that triggered it. My voice, being bass like it is, did not get to them like hers did that night.

"My granddaughter's little eyes got as big as grapefruit!" Ron continues, "As they do with most people. Wolves are so under the radar, that their presence is usually just inferred by outward signs. But when you *hear* them, there's hard evidence that they are there, around you—a direct connection."

While Dick stops to howl several times on our night walk on Treehaven's grounds, no wolves reply. We hear no haunting, throaty chorus or long lament of a loner.

But I *had* walked in their footsteps here in Tomahawk, and I did see proof of their existence. I had gotten close to one of most historic packs in Wisconsin since wolves have made their comeback. Given all that we have done to our wolves, perhaps that's as close as they want us to get for now.

I'm not giving up hope, however. Recently, the paper *Wisconsin Outdoor News* reported that wolves might have taken up residence at Horicon Marsh (see chapter 12, "Canada Geese: Dealing with Dueling Attitudes") in southern Wisconsin. Several people have reported fleeting glimpses of them. The refuge's vast spaces with many uplands and a good population of deer make the sightings entirely possible. Wolves can be living in an area for a long time before people actually see them.

Says Ron, "When wolves receive protection, they show up in all kinds of wonderful places. They're capable of surviving in almost any kind of habitat, as long as humans allow it to happen. They *were* a wilderness species, but not so much now. They've adapted to live in all kinds of habitats."

For this ancient ancestor of the domestic dog, it sounds like a familiar—and familial—story.

---

### HOW TO HAVE A GENUINE
### GRAY WOLF ENCOUNTER OF YOUR OWN

**Wolf ecology workshops** are held in January and February at various venues, such as Treehaven in Tomahawk and the Sandhill Outdoor Skills Center in Babcock. Go to the DNR website at dnr.wi.gov/topic/wildlifehabitat/training.html. For information on Treehaven, visit www.uwsp.edu/cnr-ap/treehaven or call (715) 453-4106. To learn more about the Sandhill Outdoor Skills Center workshops, go to dnr.wi.gov/topic/lands/wildlifeareas/sandhill/calendar.html.

You can access the TWIN (Timber Wolf Information Network) website at www.timberwolfinformation.org.

## HOW TO BECOME INVOLVED WITH
## GRAY WOLF CONSERVATION EFFORTS

Since 1995, the DNR has used volunteers to conduct snow-track surveys of wolves in order to determine the number, distribution, breeding status, and territories of gray wolves in Wisconsin.

To become a volunteer wolf tracker for the DNR, you must complete a wolf ecology course first (such as the one described in this chapter) and then a track training course. Learn more at dnr.wi.gov/topic/wildlifehabitat/volunteer.html.

To see an interactive, Wisconsin wolf pack territory map, go to dnr.wi.gov/topic/wildlifehabitat/wolf/maps.html.

# Appendix

*How to Help Wildlife in Wisconsin*

Wisconsin's wildlife and natural areas belong to all of us. If you'd like to do your part to help ensure the continuance of this heritage for your children and future generations, consider supporting the **Endangered Resources Fund** of the Wisconsin Department of Natural Resources (DNR).

Monies from the fund go toward conserving and managing more than two hundred threatened Wisconsin plants and animals and our remaining prairies, forests, and wetlands. More than one-third of the fund comes from contributions from people like you. Past support has helped successfully protect more than six hundred State Natural Areas since 1952.

**There are three ways to make a donation to the fund:**

+ Look for the loon silhouette under the "Donations" area on your Wisconsin income tax form: Fill in the amount of your donation, which will be matched by monies from the state's general purpose fund, making your gift have twice the impact.
+ Opt for an endangered resources license plate: You can apply at the "Endangered resources license plates" page of the Wisconsin Department Transportation's website, www.dot.wisconsin.gov/drivers/vehicles/personal/special/endanger.htm. The fee includes an annual twenty-five-dollar donation to the endangered resources program, and you'll be able to choose a badger or gray wolf plate.
+ Donate directly to the Endangered Resources Fund: You can donate online with a credit card or e-check at dnr.wi.gov/topic/endangered resources/Donate.html, or call (608) 264-6871.

**Here are a few more ways to help wildlife in the state:**

+ Purchase a State Natural Areas guidebook: Titled *Wisconsin, naturally*, the book features 150 natural areas from around the state, complete with driving directions, maps, and site descriptions. Go to dnr.wi.gov/topic/lands/naturalareas to order.

+ Contribute to the Trumpeter Swan Fund: Donations go toward costs of aerial surveys, health checks, monitoring activities, and public education efforts. Visit dnr.wi.gov/topic/endangeredresources/swan.html.

+ Adopt an eagle nest: By adopting an eagle nest, you help to ensure that bald eagles will not disappear from Wisconsin. Go to dnr.wi.gov/topic/endangeredresources/adopt.html to learn more.

+ Collect information on wildlife and other natural resources: More than 150 organizations—such as the Wisconsin Frog and Toad Survey, the Annual Midwest Crane Count, LoonWatch, or Wisconsin NatureMapping—look for and collect information on plants, animals, streams, and more. Go to the citizen-based monitoring network of Wisconsin at wiatri.net/cbm.

+ Watch for invasive species: Keep an eye out for invasive plants that crowd out our native plants and cause our wetlands, forests, prairies, and lakes to change, affecting our wildlife. Learn more at dnr.wi.gov/topic/invasives/report.html.

+ Participate in Wisconsin's Volunteer Carnivore Tracking Program: You can play a part in determining the status of our forest carnivores. Data received from this DNR program is used to supplement DNR surveys. Visit dnr.wi.gov/topic/wildlifehabitat/volunteer.html.

+ Report rare species: Report sightings of rare wildlife and plants on such forms as the Large Mammal Observation Form (for observations of gray wolves, cougars, lynx, moose, and wolverines), the Rare Animal Field Report Form, the Rare Plant Field Report Form, the Trumpeter Swan Observation Report, the Whooping Crane Observation Form, and the Wisconsin Colonial Waterbird Survey (if you are a professional wildlife biologist or experienced volunteer cooperator and conduct colonial waterbird surveys during spring and summer outdoor activities) by going to dnr.wi.gov/topic/endangeredresources/forms.html.

# Index